# The Complete Idiot's Command Reference

## Shortcut Keys

| Key Combination | Result |
| --- | --- |
| Ctrl+N | Create new project |
| Ctrl+O | Open existing project |
| Ctrl+S | Save project |
| Ctrl+P | Print |
| F7 | Spell check |
| Ctrl+X | Cut cell |
| Ctrl+C | Copy cell |
| Ctrl+V | Paste |
| Ctrl+Z | Undo |
| Ctrl+K | Insert hyperlink |
| Ctrl+F2 | Link selected tasks |
| Ctrl+shift+F2 | Unlink selected tasks |
| Shift+F2 | Access task or resource information |
| Alt+F10 | Assign resources |
| Ctrl+/ | Zoom in |
| Ctrl+shift+* | Zoom out |
| Ctrl+shift+F5 | Go to selected task |
| F1 | Microsoft Project Help |

*cut here*

que®

# Formatting Toolbar Buttons

| Button | Description |
|--------|-------------|
| | Opens a new workbook |
| | Opens the Open dialog box |
| | Saves the workbook file |
| | Prints the workbook |
| | Displays the workbook in print preview mode |
| | Starts the spell check tool |
| | Cuts the selected data to the Clipboard |
| | Copies the selected data to the Clipboard |
| | Pastes the cut or copied data from the Clipboard |
| | Starts the Format Painter tool |
| | Undoes your last action |
| | Inserts a hyperlink |
| | Links tasks |
| | Unlinks tasks |
| | Splits tasks |
| | Provides task or resource information |
| | Creates task or resource notes |
| | Assigns resources |
| No Group | Sorts the current view by defined groups |
| | Zooms in on a page |
| | Zooms out of a page |
| | Goes to a selected task |
| | Copies a picture |
| | Opens Microsoft Project Help |
| | Add or remove buttons to toolbar |
| | Outdents tasks |
| | Indents tasks |
| | Show subtasks |
| | Hide subtasks |
| Show ▾ | Show specified level of subtasks |
| Arial | Change font |
| 8 | Change font size |
| B | Bold text |
| I | Italicize text |
| U | Underline text |
| | Left-justify text |
| | Center-justify text |
| | Right-justify text |
| All Tasks | Filter view |
| | Enable Autofilter by column entries |
| | Format with Gantt Chart Wizard |

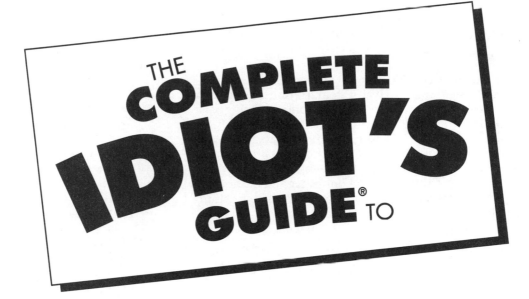

THE
# COMPLETE IDIOT'S GUIDE® TO

# Project Management
# with Microsoft®
# Project 2000

### *by Ron Black*

A Division of Macmillan Computer Publishing
201 W. 103rd Street, Indianapolis, IN 46290

**The Complete Idiot's Guide to Project Management with Microsoft® Project 2000**

**Copyright © 2000 by *Que***

International Standard Book Number: 0-7897-2271-2

Library of Congress Catalog Card Number: 99-067418

*Printed in the United States of America*

First Printing: *March 2000*

02   01   00            4   3   2   1

## Trademarks

## Warning and Disclaimer

**Associate Publisher**
*Greg Wiegand*

**Acquisitions Editor**
*Stephanie McComb*

**Development Editor**
*Gregory Harris*

**Managing Editor**
*Thomas F. Hayes*

**Technical Editor**
*Henry Staples*

**Project Editor**
*Lori A. Lyons*

**Copy Editor**
*Julie McNamee*

**Indexer**
*Sharon Shock*

**Proofreader**
*Harvey Stanbrough*

**Illustrator**
*Judd Winick*

**Team Coordinator**
*Sharry Lee Gregory*

**Interior Designer**
*Nathan Clement*

**Cover Designer**
*Michael Freeland*

**Copywriter**
*Eric Borgert*

**Editorial Assistant**
*Angela Boley*

**Production**
*Liz Johnston*

# Contents at a Glance

# Contents

# About the Author

**Ron Black** is an author, award-winning international speaker, and senior business consultant. He works throughout North America with top managers who want to move their organizations to new levels of performance and entrepreneurs who are launching new products and services. His experience ranges from founder and president of a small mechanical contracting company to a vice president level in the marketing division of a Fortune 500 defense electronics firm. Ron speaks, trains, and consults on project management, team building, business turnarounds, and the launch of new businesses. To contact him, call (503) 618-8703, send email to rblack@thementorgroup.com, or visit his company's Web site at www.thementorgroup.com.

## Dedication

*This book is dedicated to my family—every member! Thanks guys, for all the support, encouragement, and patience. Special honors go to my wife and best friend Janell, who has put up with my projects for almost three decades; to my mother Ruby, for giving me the gift of values and forbearance; and to my deceased father, "Blackie," who taught me how to dream big, work hard, and play like there's no tomorrow.*

## Acknowledgments

*No project is ever successfully completed alone, and this book is no exception. It has been a pleasure to work with so many excellent professionals, all of whom have been essential to this book's success. I am in debt to the stellar Macmillan team who guided, nurtured, and graciously facilitated the process. It's been a delight to work with acquisitions editor* **Stephanie McComb**, *development editor* **Gregory Harris**, *technical editor* **Henry Staples**, *project editor* **Lori Lyons**, *copy editor* **Julie McNamee**, *proofreader* **Harvey Stanbrough**, *and formatter* **Mandie Rowell**. *You've all been terrific! And a special thanks goes to illustrator* **Judd Winick**.

# Tell Us What You Think!

As the reader of this book, *you* are our most important critic and commentator. We value your opinion and want to know what we're doing right, what we could do better, what areas you'd like to see us publish in, and any other words of wisdom you're willing to pass our way.

As an Associate Publisher for Que, I welcome your comments. You can fax, email, or write me directly to let me know what you did or didn't like about this book—as well as what we can do to make our books stronger.

*Please note that I cannot help you with technical problems related to the topic of this book, and that due to the high volume of mail I receive, I might not be able to reply to every message.*

When you write, please be sure to include this book's title and author as well as your name and phone or fax number. I will carefully review your comments and share them with the author and editors who worked on the book.

Fax:     317-581-4666

Email:   consumer@mcp.com

Mail:    Greg Wiegand
         Que
         201 West 103rd Street
         Indianapolis, IN 46290 USA

# Welcome to *The Complete Idiot's Guide to Project Management with Microsoft Project 2000*

This book is about success—yours! It was created to help you overcome the challenges of project management and achieve personal success on every project you undertake.

After all, project management is not for the faint of heart. At best, project management is an exciting and rewarding adventure in building the future. Without project management there would be no new medications, no new schools, no new telecommunications, no new software, and on and on! In a large way, project managers are responsible for turning our best dreams into reality. On the other hand, at it's worst—well let's not even consider the worst. As a project manager, you're here to succeed. And succeed you will! You've decided to use Microsoft's powerful Project software to help you get the job done. That's a good first step!

The project you're currently engaged in may have been thrust upon you. Or perhaps you willingly accepted this project and all its challenges and responsibilities. Or maybe you're planning and implementing your own pet project. In any case, the project's successful completion is not the only thing at risk.

Intertwined with every opportunity is some level of threat. Your team's success may be on the line. In fact, your department or even your company's success may depend on your ability to get this project moving and keep it moving around, over, or through every problem that crops up, all the way to a successful conclusion. And yes, I know it's not nice to shout "fire" in a crowded theater, but you can't forget that your personal satisfaction and possibly even your professional reputation may also be at stake.

I wrote this book for those who have too much to do, too little time, too few resources, or all of the above. So, my goal with this book is not to teach you everything thing there is to know about project management, nor is it my goal to describe every minor feature and function of Microsoft Project 2000. (Why kill all those trees when nobody could lift a book that size, or have enough time to read it anyway!) Rather, the goal of this book is to provide you with the best project management methods, processes, and tools in a format that is easy to learn, fast to implement, and powerful to use.

And so, here it is. The sum total of two and a half decades of professional project management experience (in four industries), combined with the world's best mid-range project management software (Microsoft Project 2000), carefully filtered through hundreds of rookie and seasoned project managers (whom I have personally trained), and all carefully condensed into this book. Voilà—everything you need to make your project a huge success! (Of course you have to supply the project, attitude, and elbow grease.)

# How to Use This Book

You're busy. Probably far too busy to set everything aside and read this book from cover to cover! But don't despair. This book was written to be a desk-side companion. As much as possible, each chapter has been written to stand alone. The options are yours: Begin at the beginning of the book, read to the end, and then plan your project; begin at the beginning, read one chapter, do some planning, read the next chapter, do some more planning, and work your way to the end; or you can jump around anyway you see fit. There are plenty of headings and subheadings to lead the way to the information you need.

If you are new to project management, take the time to read Chapter 1, "Surviving and Thriving with Project Management Skills." This chapter shows you how great project managers look at the world. And it provides you the basis needed to rapidly build your project management skills. This chapter is about you and your success as a project manager. It provides a foundation that will serve you admirably throughout your career.

Both seasoned veterans and rookies will want to spend some time in Chapter 2, "The Project Management Process." This chapter explains in detail the five steps of project management used in this book and how to implement each of them in the real world. You'll get a jump start on initiating a project, gaining buy-in and commitment from stakeholders, making your project's success measurable, and identifying problems before they arise. Veterans appreciate the practical tips and sage advice collected here. Rookies appreciate the easy-to-follow steps and the simple-to-use techniques used to implement the five-step process.

If you are a consistently successful project veteran who just wants to get up and running on Microsoft Project 2000 as quickly as possible, you've got two choices. Begin in Chapter 3, "Getting Started with Microsoft Project 2000," if you have little or no knowledge of computers or the Microsoft Windows operating system. And if you're up to speed with Windows, jump to Chapter 4, "Thinking of Everything, Even If You Don't Know What You're Doing." This chapter explains the work breakdown structure and how the traditional way, your way, and the Microsoft way, can be brought together to build a highway (or anything else for that matter). This is one chapter you will not want to miss.

For the simple project, and when you do not need to schedule or control resources, a visit to Chapter 5, "Estimating Time with Science, Skill, and Fourth Grade Math," Chapter 6, "Sequencing Tasks to Fit Your Needs," and Chapter 13, "Managing Progress," will usually do the trick. You'll be bringing in projects like a pro! (Okay, so a little good luck never hurt.) For more complex projects that require greater control, communication, or creativity, go directly to the chapter that fits your needs. It's all here. (You'll even learn how to create some of your own good luck.)

# Conventions

The information in this book is formatted to help you find what you need as rapidly as possible. A variety of visual elements are used to make you aware of potential hazards, supporting information, project management terminology, software shortcuts, planning tips, and good ideas. At the beginning of each chapter you will find a listing of the major topics to help you locate the information you want. The end of each chapter includes a listing of the concepts covered. You can use these to test your knowledge and select those areas that you may want to learn a little more about.

Communication skills are an important aspect of project management. Wherever possible, I have taken the time to point out how project managers use an otherwise common word or phrase in a special way. In addition, new terms are indicated with an *italic* typeface. And there is a complete glossary, "Speak Like a Geek," with all the project management terminology you could ever want to know, so that you'll be able to act and sound like the consummate, professional project manager.

When entering data into your computer, a **bold** typeface is used to indicate text that you type. A `monospace` typeface indicates onscreen messages or text that appears onscreen.

Pointing and clicking with the mouse is usually the fastest and easiest way to make the program do what you want it to do. So, although there are usually other ways to accomplish the same task in Microsoft Project 2000, I'll focus on those methods that help you get the fastest results.

Along with plentiful screen shots, examples, and annotated figures, you'll notice several other elements I've used to speed your mastery of project management:

### Secrets of Success

You'll find key concepts and special techniques to make your job easier, faster, and more enjoyable. These bits of sage advice and tricks of the trade are the stuff you usually learn only after years of hard knocks! Both rookies and seasoned project managers will find these secrets helpful.

## More Good Stuff

These notes provide additional information, pointers, and good ideas that are important and useful but not absolutely essential. If you want to delve a little deeper into project management or Microsoft Project 2000, watch for these notes and dig in!

## Project Pitfalls

If you hate being blind-sided, watch for these cautionary tips. They're designed to help rookies survive and to help veterans relax. You'll avoid pitfalls and problems, and learn to navigate safely around potential disasters.

## Speak Like a Geek

Learn how to speak the language, understand the shorthand, and cope with the countless conventions that project managers have created over the years. The secret language of project managers is revealed. You'll learn why stakeholders don't hold stakes, why noncritical tasks are essential, and why crashing the project may be the only way to success.

# Part 1

# Focusing on Your Success

*It's that last line item in the job description that gets us into these fixes—"and other duties as assigned."*

*You were caught doing well, and the next thing you know, someone slaps the project of the century down on your desk. Let's face it: Whether you are a project manager by choice or chance, project management responsibilities place you in a high-profile, high-risk position. No matter how poorly conceived, inadequately resourced, or overly optimistic the project may be, it's up to you to make it a success. (Unless, of course, you're really good at telling your boss or customer no.)*

*Part 1 of this book is about two things—project success and personal success—and as you probably realize, the two are inseparable. You'll learn how successful project managers think, what tools they use, and how to build your reputation as a professional. You'll learn what project management software can and can't do, and why Microsoft Project 2000 will help you manage projects successfully. You'll learn the process and the thinking habits required to get and keep you on the road to victory. If it's success you're after, you've come to the right place.*

# Chapter 1

# Surviving and Thriving with Project Management Skills

### In This Chapter

➤ Why project management is one of the most important skill sets you can learn

➤ How project management is different from everything else you do at work

➤ The eight essential roles you'll need to fill on every project

➤ Microsoft Project 2000 is great but it can't do your job

➤ Creating and maintaining a reputation just short of miracle worker

Project management has been described as the ability to create the impossible, with the unwilling, against insurmountable odds, under budget, on time, while singing the Battle Hymn of the Republic and drinking a glass of water. But it's really not that bad. Project managers are rarely asked to sing while drinking. The rest of this description is all too true! Successful project management requires a broad range of skills, the ability to tolerate ambiguity, and a willingness to accept risk.

## The High-Stakes, High-Visibility Job

There are two things you can count on in the world of project management: high stakes and high visibility.

Let's consider the high-stakes project environment for just a moment. Every project that reaches the planning or implementation stage is, by definition, very important. As a rule, organizations don't fritter away scarce resources on projects that are not worthy. (Careful now, I know what you're thinking.) Somewhere along the line somebody spotted a problem, thought of a solution, and decided to implement it (or have it implemented for them). We call this process of implementing solutions a "project." (You can also consider this discussion from an optimistic point of view, by replacing the word *problem* with the word *opportunity*.)

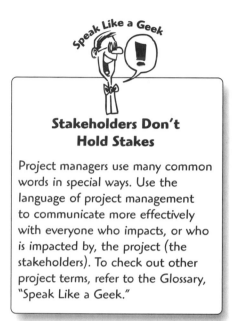

### Stakeholders Don't Hold Stakes

Project managers use many common words in special ways. Use the language of project management to communicate more effectively with everyone who impacts, or who is impacted by, the project (the stakeholders). To check out other project terms, refer to the Glossary, "Speak Like a Geek."

# Why Projects Are Important

Projects are important because they make problems go away. The bigger the problem (or opportunity), the more important the project. The bigger the problem, the more resources the organization is willing to commit to that project.

Projects are always important (at least to somebody). Projects are special because the stakes are high. They get special status, special treatment, and special people. Moreover, high-stakes projects are given to people who can be counted on to get the job done. That's why your project got you!

When you're asked to manage a project, or when you find yourself in that capacity by accident or choice, the project no longer belongs to its originator. The originator steps aside, passing the microphone, the stage, and the bright lights to you. Suddenly, it becomes your show. With all of its problems, all of its ill-conceived ideas, all of its overly optimistic claims, it's now your performance!

# The Originator's Role

At this point, the project originator usually steps out of the project environment, but they don't always leave the theater. This can be good or bad. Sometimes they remain backstage, working with you, offering words of advice or encouragement, helping you set the stage with all the resources you'll need to achieve project success. Isn't that nice! There they are, out of your way and tactfully out of sight, but close by if you need them. You've got to love a project originator like that!

On the other hand, some originators move out front, and with popcorn in one hand and a cellular phone in the other, plop themselves down in a seat right in the middle of the front row. There they remain constantly vigilant, occasionally hurling directives and criticisms at you and your team (that is, when they're not too busy talking on their cellular phones). How good are you at dodging tomatoes?

### Soft Skills are Hard!

Both the technical skills of planning and the people skills of leadership are essential to your success as a project manager. "Hard" technical skills are easier to learn and apply than "soft" people skills. Hard skills don't require the ability to deal with fuzzy logic, ambiguity, mixed messages, or the occasional appendectomy. Moreover, project managers are usually well trained in technology and completely untrained in management. Take the time to develop your soft skills. The results are worth it.

Occasionally, the project originator chooses a seat in the back row, close to a fire exit. These are the ones who like to see and to be seen, but who are ready to dart out at the first sign of fire, smoke, and in some cases, even a little friction.

Once in a while, you'll see one other type (and I do mean once in a while). As soon as the curtain rises, the stage lights come on, and the house lights go down, they're gone! Like some form of exotic butterfly, they flit away to…well that's just it, nobody really knows where these people go or what they do when they get there. They just disappear. (If you don't believe me, try to find one when you really need him.) The next time you're likely to see or hear from this disappearing whiz is at the awards ceremony. He'll be the one dashing across the stage trying to accept your accolades.

### Every Team Member Deserves to Know

When you or your team is "volunteered" for a project, ask (or be prepared to answer) these questions: What will be your role? What is the project environment like? Why were you chosen? What will happen to you when the project is over? What about your old work? Will you learn new skills? How will the project help your career?

When you become the project manager, you become the star of the project. You may have a team of performers, but you're the one at center stage, bathed in limelight for all to see. You're the one making sure everyone else, both on stage and behind the scenes, is performing up to par. Like it or not, you're the focal point. If the program is a success, then by association, you're a success. You'll be looking pretty good if it's a hit. However, what if it's a flop? You'll be the last one on stage, standing there in that excruciatingly bright light!

Professionally speaking, project management is a high-visibility, high-risk game.

## What Is Project Management?

Project management is about getting project results. Formally, it is the application of knowledge, skill, tools, and techniques to satisfy the expectations of the project stakeholders. The knowledge areas included are project planning; definition of scope; estimating and controlling time; estimating and controlling costs; quality assurance; human resource management; the creation, collection, and distribution of information; risk management; and procurement. Whew! That is a lot to know.

Nevertheless, don't be alarmed. You don't have to know everything about project management to make a huge difference in your ability to get the results you want. I've picked the most important items, made them as simple as possible, and put them in this book. With the help of Microsoft Project 2000 and this book, you'll be getting big-time results in no time at all!

### How to Tell the Boss "No"

Sooner or later, you'll likely face the dilemma of having to tell your boss (or customer) "No." To tell your boss no, always start with "Yes, I'd be happy to do that project..." Then add "and, I have a few questions for you." Now take a deep breath, collect your thoughts, and explore every issue you fear. For example, "Yes, I'd like to do that project, and exactly what are we trying to accomplish, and what do you want me to do with the other six projects I'm working on, and what resources will be available for the project that aren't already being used to capacity, and..." Always be positive, upbeat, and brutally honest. Be a professional.

## *A Project by Any Other Name Would Still Smell As Sweet*

Call it anything you want, it's still a project. Many industries have their own pet names for project management. You will hear the terms *product management, construction management, program management, change management,* and others. Regardless of what you call it, a project is a sequence of tasks, with a beginning and an end, intended to create a specific outcome. To some extent, it hasn't been done before.

On the other hand, the work you do every day is not a project. That's normal work all that stuff they originally hired you to do. It's the work you chose as a profession. It's everything you do that's listed in your job description, like engineering, or writing software, or managing a group of workers. It's the ongoing operations, the regular reports, and the daily tasks that must be accomplished.

Projects have greater unknowns, complexity, newness, and risks than do normal work activities. Projects are also more temporary in nature. Various resources are brought together as needed on a project. For example, a team may be created to accomplish a project and dissolved upon its completion.

I hope you like working yourself out of a job. That's what project managers do for a living!

## *Pick a Hat, Any Hat: Facilitator, Planner, Problem Solver, Communicator*

One of the reasons project managers are in demand is that they are capable in many roles. On any given project, some roles are more important than others. Table 1.1 lists roles that are important on almost every project:

### Table 1.1    Key Roles of the Project Manager

| Role | Description |
| --- | --- |
| Visionary | The ability to see into the future, understand what can be, and describe it to others in a convincing manner. |
| Team Builder | Cheerleader, coach, counselor, and teammate who is skilled at helping individuals succeed for the good of the whole. |
| Planner | Identifying needed resources and tasks, scheduling activities, and orchestrating efforts. |
| Estimator | Forecasting with accuracy the time and money requirements of a project. |

*continues*

**Table 1.1    Continued**

| Role | Description |
|------|-------------|
| Meeting Facilitator | The information traffic cop, keeping all people and personalities cooperative, productive, and respected. |
| Collaborator | Creating an environment of trust, respect, and cooperation to produce appropriate decisions that everyone supports. |
| Manager | Administrator of organizational policies, procedures, and controls. |
| Problem Solver | The ability to see what everyone else sees and come up with a better solution. |

Keep in mind that you do not have to personally provide all of these roles. Your job as the project manager is to make sure they all are available on your project. After all, that's what teams are for!

**Outcome Achiever**

The project manager's job is not to manage projects—rather, it is to produce results. Some project managers get so wrapped up in planning, charting, monitoring, meeting, documenting, and the like, that they forget they're supposed to be achieving. Focus on the results you want to achieve and make sure your project team does the same thing.

## For the Professional Who Occasionally Manages a Project

Most people come into project management not as a profession, but rather as a professional who has been given an additional job responsibility—manage a project. Chances are, neither your job title nor your job description says anything about project management (not foregoing that last line in the description: "...and any other duties as hereby directed"). You may see yourself as an engineer, executive, scientist, programmer, secretary, entrepreneur, and so on. And it is obvious, at least to me, that you are pretty good at what you do. (They asked you to manage this project, didn't they?)

When you are given the responsibility to accomplish a project, you become a project manager no matter what your title says. Your professional reputation now hinges on your project management abilities, and possibly on a whole new set of job skills. Ouch! Don't look at me. I didn't say project management was fair.

To focus on your success, and of course the success of the project, learn how to apply the basics expertly. This leverages your time and effort. If you apply Pareto's principle, you can expect 80% of your outcome from 20% of your activity. Because you already have plenty of responsibilities besides this project, be sure to squeeze the right 20% of activities into your workload.

One other common malady affects professionals who assume project management responsibilities: They want to make it perfect. This is especially true for technical professionals. Even though perfection is a good goal in many professions, and the energetic pursuit of that illusive, one best answer, is admirable, this quality can actually cause project failure. In the project management environment, ambiguity is a way of life. There is always more than one way to accomplish goals. Risk can never be completely eliminated.

Project management defies perfection. Foresight is never as good as hindsight. The first time you do anything, it is almost impossible to do it perfectly. After all, a project is the first time something (usually a big and important something) is being done, so don't aim for perfection. Save your energy and focus on success rather than perfection.

## For Aspiring Project Management Professionals

In almost every organization, there is at least one enthusiastic, responsible, capable person who loves the fast lane of project management. Sure, they understand the risks, long hours, and the inevitability that problems will arise. Somehow, they are still drawn like a moth to the flame. Perhaps it is the sense of accomplishment that draws them. For some, it's the challenge, and for others, it's a chance for personal or professional growth. If any of these sounds like you, then your organization is lucky to have you on their team.

Success on difficult projects depends on talented and motivated project managers who are willing to lead the way. People like that are hard to come by, and most organizations know it. That's good news for aspiring project managers. Opportunity abounds for those who bring projects in on time and on budget. Effective project management can put your career on the fast-track.

# Establishing Your Reputation as a Project Pro

Building a reputation is much like building a house out of playing cards. One wrong move, and it all comes tumbling down. It takes much time and effort to pick up the scattered cards and start over again, but it is possible to do. Unlike the house of cards, damage to your reputation can't always be repaired.

### Looking for a Promotion?

No one gets noticed or promoted faster than a successful project manager. If you're seeking added responsibilities and challenges, follow this strategy: Build a successful track record of increasingly robust projects. Manage stakeholder expectations by slightly under-promising and over-delivering. Gain stakeholder support by building their benefit into the project.

To achieve a positive reputation as a project professional, make sure every project you manage has a successful outcome. Consistent success is the only effective strategy. Occasional success will not do. Failure is not an option. One errant move, and your reputation comes crashing down.

Every project is fraught with potential disasters (a.k.a. career limiting experiences). To avoid the disasters and achieve consistent success, project managers must be well versed in priority setting and problem solving.

## Setting Priorities

It has been said that the mark of a great person is not in what he has, but in what he accomplishes with what he has. Nothing could be more true for great project managers.

The prime directive of project management is to accomplish the goals of the project on time and on budget, with available resources. It is the rare project that has unlimited time, money, or resources. More frequently, organizations have unlimited needs and only modest means to achieve them. Within a given project, it falls upon the project manager to set the priorities by which the means will be expended to achieve the intended outcomes.

Project management provides a method of prioritizing the use of resources, thereby maximizing achievement. Simply put, project managers are good at squeezing a dollar's work out of a dime, and figuring out how to hustle every time they are forced to wait.

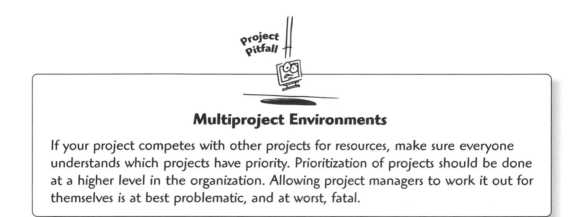

### Multiproject Environments

If your project competes with other projects for resources, make sure everyone understands which projects have priority. Prioritization of projects should be done at a higher level in the organization. Allowing project managers to work it out for themselves is at best problematic, and at worst, fatal.

## Solving Problems

If you don't like problems, you won't like project management! The job is all about problems—problems that could jeopardize the intended outcomes of the project, problems that are just an inconvenience, problems you can see coming, and problems that take you by surprise.

To be successful, you not only have to be able to solve problems, you have to be able to see them coming and judge their importance. There are so many problems in a project that you'll never have time to work on them all. Great project managers focus on the key problems and have the courage and wisdom to ignore the insignificant ones.

## Consistently Creating Successful Outcomes

Establishing your reputation as a project pro requires more than one successful project. Anyone can get lucky occasionally. However, by the time you're on your third or fourth project, you will have had plenty of opportunities to prove your mettle. Those around you and those in power understand this. Naturally, they will be watching. In the corporate world, you win more points for results than for style. Success, no matter how easy it is, carries greater influence, prestige, and reward than the best fought, but unsuccessful battle.

The secret to consistent success is to start out easy and stay there as long as possible! Carefully and gradually, move up the difficulty scale. The last thing you want is for people to think you're a miracle worker. You'll want to stay just short of that lofty title—you don't want only the impossible projects! Eventually these could have a career-limiting effect. (By the way, how good are you at interrogating the boss? You might want to check out the section in Chapter 2 entitled "How to Question the Boss and Remain Happily Employed.")

# What Microsoft Project 2000 Can Do and What It Can't Do

I have learned to love all kinds of software programs over the years, because basically, I'm a lazy guy. If a machine can do it, why not let it? There's no shortage of tasks in my workday and there probably isn't in your workday, either.

Microsoft Project 2000 is one of my favorite programs. Like any good tool, it performs wonderfully in the hands of a knowledgeable artisan. Expecting too much or using it in the wrong situations can be frustrating and counterproductive.

An overview of what Microsoft Project 2000 can and can't do will help you choose what's important for you. First, let's take a look at Figure 1.1 and see how project management software works:

**Figure 1.1**

*Microsoft Project 2000 simplifies the collection, processing, and reporting of project details, allowing you to focus on information evaluation, decision making, and project implementation.*

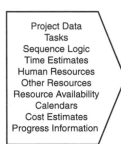

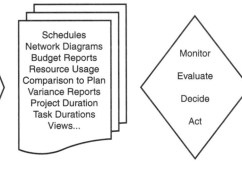

Project Data
Tasks
Sequence Logic
Time Estimates
Human Resources
Other Resources
Resource Availability
Calendars
Cost Estimates
Progress Information

Schedules
Network Diagrams
Budget Reports
Resource Usage
Comparison to Plan
Variance Reports
Project Duration
Task Durations
Views...

Monitor

Evaluate

Decide

Act

## Creating a Perspective for Project Success

"Not being able to see the forest for the trees" is a common problem for anyone who has ever planned a project. Even on simple projects, we are torn between having enough detail to plan and execute, and being buried in so much detail that we lose overall perspective. To overcome this, project managers created several tools. Among others, these include work breakdown structures, task analysis forms, charts of activities, resource tables, and network diagrams. (You will learn more about each of these in later chapters.) Because there is much shared information on each of these tools, even the smallest change or update required a huge amount of effort on the part of the project manager. Consequently, on the old, paper-based system, plans were less flexible, showed less detail, and were almost always out of date!

With Microsoft Project 2000, you are able to gather and control a greater amount of detail, maintain higher levels of perspective, and stay abreast of changes more easily. Microsoft Project 2000 cannot make decisions for you, but it can provide you with the right perspective, at the right time, for your decision making process.

## The Resourceful Use of Resources

Some project managers seem to get a lot more accomplished with their resources than their peers do. There seems to be an almost magical quality to their productivity. Closer examination reveals that although they may not be equipped with a magic wand, they do understand and use the tools of resource planning. In fact, it's likely that they're using Microsoft Project 2000 for resource tables, loading, leveling, allocations, constraints, calendars, workgroups, histograms, and scheduling. When you have all those tools at the touch of a button or two, well that does look pretty magical to the rest of us!

## Counting on Change and Making Change Count

Several years ago, the U.S. Department of Defense adopted the philosophy that it wasn't enough to have the biggest and best military resources. They were intent on creating an implementation methodology that could consistently achieve success in highly unpredictable environments. Victory in any theater of operations, they reasoned, would consistently go to the force that packed the biggest punch, was highly adaptive, and most able to act decisively. (Sounds like something a project manager could use, don't you think?)

They called their new approach "C3" for communications, command, and control. Realizing that quality information was the key to their success, the defense electronics industry jumped into high gear and responded with hundreds of new products, from frequency-hopping secure radios to smart bombs to Global Satellite Positioning Systems. As you are probably aware, the C3 philosophy proved its worth in the deserts of the Middle East.

Some of the most successful project managers use this same philosophy. They understand that to act decisively in unpredictable environments, they need quality information, and they need it now.

Microsoft Project 2000 provides all the electronics you need for a communications, command, and control system. Like the military, Microsoft has taken our ability to communicate beyond the normal bounds of paper charts, graphs, tables, and diagrams. They have incorporated powerful new tools to gather and distribute information to and from any team member, anywhere in the world, who has access to email or the Web. You know, this is much better than the military's systems—they've got frequency-hopping radios, but we've got email!

## Staying On Time and In Tune with Communication Tools

One of the most difficult problems you face as a project manager is keeping your team informed, communicating, and up-to-date. Microsoft Project 2000 includes the workgroup messaging to solve these issues. It works through email, on the World Wide Web, or on your organization's intranet.

17

### To Communicate is Divine

Always choose the best communication tool for the job. Just because you can do it on the computer doesn't make it better. Successful project managers use the communication vehicle that's most effective for the recipient of the message. This could be email, voice mail, U.S. Mail, or a piece of string stretched between two empty tin cans. Use the method that works best for the recipient.

Workgroup messaging's capability goes beyond simple email messaging. Now you can create *workgroups* (a set of resources and their manager) and then distribute task assignments, track progress, make schedule changes, and update the plan, all without having to enter each separate piece of information by hand. Although you do not have to use all these features, after you collect project status and update the plan electronically, you'll never want to do it by hand again! You'll love the ability to send group messages, assignment requests, and status reports with such ease.

You can send reports, charts, graphs, data, or network diagrams to a colleague at a moment's notice. You can send an entire project file to your planning team for review before it is finalized. Using the workgroup messaging capabilities, your information will be on time and in tune with reality.

## Publishing Your Progress to the World

Thousands of pieces of data make up a project plan. However, data is not information until it arrives in the hands of the person who can use it, and in a format they can understand.

Microsoft Project 2000 gives you a multitude of information viewing options and makes it as simple as possible to understand even the most complex project:

➤ At almost every point, you may drill down to greater depths of detail or zoom out for the big picture.

➤ You can use predefined reports about tasks, resources, assignments, schedules, costs, and progress, or create your own custom documents.

➤ You can use filters and autofilters to limit what you see.

➤ You can use sheet, graph, form, and calendar views as well as Gantt and network diagram charts.

➤ If all this weren't enough, you can even split the screen and really give yourself a headache. (Just joking about the headache!)

Every one of the publishing options can be printed on paper, sent electronically, posted on a World Wide Web site, or just stared at in the glow of your monitor and the tranquility of a darkened, after-hours office.

---

### The Least You Need to Know

➤ The true job of a project manager is not to manage a project, its budget, people, or resources but to create desired project outcomes.

➤ Your personal success as a project manager depends on your ability to consistently achieve the goals of the project on time, on budget, and with the available (although not necessarily adequate) resources.

➤ Project managers wear many hats: that of visionary, team builder, planner, estimator, facilitator, collaborator, manager, and perhaps most importantly, problem solver.

➤ Microsoft Project 2000 facilitates the use of project data and helps to keep you up-to-date and in tune with what's going on. Nevertheless, your judgment and skill are still the most important tools on the project.

# Chapter 2

---

# The Project Management Process

Do your projects seem to stall out when they're nearing completion? Does the last 10% of your project take 90% of your effort to complete? If you have trouble completing projects, you're not alone! The final stages of a project are frequently fraught with issues. Every problem that wasn't effectively dealt with earlier in the project comes back as if to make one last desperate derailment effort. In the completion stage, life can be difficult for the project manager. The good news is that it doesn't have to be. With an effective project management process in place, your project won't stall out. Rather, it will actually pick up speed as it approaches completion.

## Don't Proceed in Complete Chaos!

Imagine this. Your boss (or biggest client) walks into your office, sits down, and leans forward with a serious look on his face. After a dramatic pause and with the over-enthusiasm of a high school actor, he exclaims, "I've got a terrific opportunity for you!" Immediately, you get the feeling that this could be a prelude to bad news.

"You did such a great job on that last project," he continues, "I've decided to give you a shot at an even bigger one." His over-indulging praise confirms your suspicions. This is serious.

"You're going to love this project. It will be great for your career!" With his last desperate effort to sell you on the project, the clincher is delivered. Your final hope smashed, you sink back into your chair, trying to resolve yourself to the prospects of the grim, chaotic project lurking just ahead.

Wait! You don't need to panic. You have a new system! After that last nightmare of a project, you decided to find a better way. You got Microsoft Project 2000, loaded it on your computer, and armed yourself with this book. Now you've got a system and no matter how crazy it gets, you can remember it forever with this mnemonic device: Don't Proceed In Complete Chaos. Define, plan, implement, control, and close. Hey, you're ready to rock!

## Define, Plan, Implement, Control, and Close

You are not the only project manager that has ever been threatened with a challenging project. Those who have come before you forged a simple and effective project management process. You can use it as well.

### Some of the Best Ideas Never Change

According to one very successful project manager, "The way to success is first to have a definite, clear, practical ideal—a goal, an objective. Second, have the necessary means to achieve your ends—wisdom, materials, and methods. Third, adjust your means to that end." This man's name was Aristotle.

Before you jump to the conclusion, "It won't work for me," think about what has been done with this approach. It has created buildings, rockets, computers, and artificial organs. The approach has made it possible to talk to anyone, almost anywhere in the world; it has brought us refrigerators, cars, and toaster ovens. The approach has helped us write books, improve schools, and wipe out disease; it has even been used to build parking lots. (My favorite is NASA's Apollo mission—they left a moon buggy in what has become the first lunar parking lot. Do you think they get a long-term parking rate?)

Trust me. This five-step approach is effective. From small projects to large, high-tech to no-tech, science to humanities, this system will get the job done, and it will make you look good.

Let's take a look:

The major processes of project management are organized into five steps. Each step has a primary purpose. The results of the previous step become the input for the next. How much effort is placed into each step varies from project to project and industry to industry, but all steps are used in every project to some extent.

A project manager in the construction industry doesn't spend as much time in the definition process—an architect has already completed most of this with end-user interviews, miniature renderings, building plans, and specifications (the *specs*). On the other hand, a project manager in charge of the next revolutionary software program (the killer app) may spend a considerable amount of time defining the new product, interviewing end users, testing concepts, and creating a set of application specifications.

### Table 2.1 The Five Steps of Project Management

| Steps | Process and Outcomes |
|---|---|
| Define | Goals and objectives defined; statement of scope prepared; project constraints identified; risks estimated; commitment to project made; project initiated. |
| Plan | Activities identified; durations estimated; resources identified; costs estimated; tasks sequenced; schedule prepared; budgets created; risks identified; resources committed; go ahead provided. |
| Implement | Project staffed; procurement executed; communications executed; work activities executed. |
| Control | Progress, quality, and costs monitored; problems identified and resolved; corrective actions applied as needed. |
| Close | Work accepted; contracts closed; staff reassigned; project reviewed and evaluated. |

## Project Management Is an Iterative Process, Iterative Process, Iterative Process...

The project management process is both sequential and iterative. Generally, each step is taken in succession. As our understanding of the project grows, we must sometimes revisit a previous step. A project manager whose project is overly difficult to implement may need to revisit the definition stage to limit the goals, choose alternate implementation strategies, or perhaps, reduce the project's scope.

Project management is a process of learning. Hindsight is always better than foresight. As a project progresses, alternate approaches and unforeseen problems may arise. The project manager becomes evermore the expert as each of the five steps is undertaken (see Figure 2.1).

**Figure 2.1**

*The project management process is both sequential and iterative. Do each step in order and return to previous steps if necessary.*

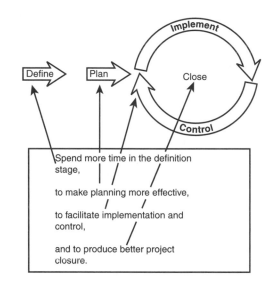

Spend more time in the definition stage,

to make planning more effective,

to facilitate implementation and control,

and to produce better project closure.

## Keeping Your Project Focused

Revisit the project initiation document before starting the planning, implementation, and closing steps. This helps keep your team focused, makes sure the needs addressed by the project still exist, and helps halt the project if it no longer addresses those needs.

# Defining Success with Goals and Objectives

Goals and objectives are used to describe the intended outcome of the project. Although some professionals use these terms interchangeably, project managers are careful to discriminate between the two.

For the project manager, the goal is *what* you will have when the project is completed (the outcome). The objectives are *how* you will make it happen. Project goals are realized when project objectives have been achieved.

## *Both Victor and Vanquished Begin with a Project Definition*

Your success as a project manager depends on your ability to meet or exceed the expectations of the project's originator, its stakeholders, and end users. Your reputation for consistency and success has little to do with the difficulty of the project or the amount actually accomplished. Rather, meeting or exceeding expectations is what makes you

professionally successful. Fall short of stakeholder's expectations, and the victor becomes
the vanquished.

Under-promise and over-deliver is the best
approach. But be careful. Give stakeholders
too much and they'll think you're either a
lucky rookie or a sandbagging veteran.
Experienced project managers are careful to
deliver just slightly more than they promise
on every project.

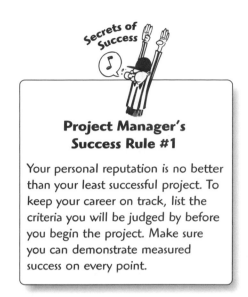

**Project Manager's
Success Rule #1**

Your personal reputation is no better
than your least successful project. To
keep your career on track, list the
criteria you will be judged by before
you begin the project. Make sure
you can demonstrate measured
success on every point.

## How "SMART" Is Your Project Goal?

The single, most important item that must be
accomplished to achieve a successful project
is to develop a good project goal. The project
goal is the threshold for every other project management process. It sets expectations; provides a basis for planning; helps identify all the required resources, activities, and budgets; and becomes the standard by which we measure achievement,
outcomes, and ultimately the project's success. If you are too busy to develop a solid
project goal statement, you are too busy. Don't try to go forward without it.

If you have only 10 minutes to plan a project, spend 8 of them on the goal. Get it
right and everything else will fall into place.

To build a good goal statement, use the "SMART" approach. This acronym will help
you remember that every goal needs to be Specific, Measurable, Agreed-upon,
Realistic, and Time-bound.

### Making Your Goal Specific

To create a "SMART" goal, begin with a specific target in mind. It must be narrow
and precise. Boil the project down to its ultimate essence, a *verb* and an *outcome*. Find
these two most important components and use them to keep both yourself and your
project team focused on the core issues.

Let's return to the scene earlier in this chapter when your boss just landed the big
news on you. "Our profits have been down this quarter," he says. "I want you to
design, build, and deliver a new product that will turn the company around and
return us to our former glory days of high profitability."

What is the precise focus of the project? A project manager could interpret this project to focus on several different key outcomes: design a new product, enter a new
market, manufacture a new product, market a new product, increase company profitability, return organization to glory, and perhaps even save the company. Successful

project managers keep their teams focused on the primary outcomes. This allows them to make the right choices later when problems arise, and they almost always do! (When you're hip-pocket deep in crocodiles, it's hard to remember you were draining the swamp.)

If this were my project, I would choose the verb and outcome "increase profitability." In my judgement (and it is a judgement call), this focus will set the tone and direction of the entire project and make it clear what needs to happen. If I choose "build a new product," the team may be encouraged to ignore all that must b e done (and building an unprofitable new product would add to the company's problems). "Save the company" is too broad to provide direction (and besides scaring half the team away, may incline those left to create a merger, cut expenses, or reduce staff, totally ignoring the new product strategy).

The first two elements of your goal statement, the verb and outcome, funnel your team's attention. Choose them carefully to magnify importance and maintain a narrow, achievable focus.

### Measuring Your Way to Success

Thus far, our goal is not yet complete. Next, make the outcome "measurable." Don't worry about grammar at this stage. If you must, it is okay to create the world's longest run-on sentence. Describe exactly what your project will accomplish. Use as many descriptors and numbers as you can. Leave nothing to the imagination. Describe what will be accomplished and make it as empirical (observable) as possible.

During the closing stage of the project, you'll need proof positive that you've accomplished everything the project was intended to do. It is in this definition stage that you create that proof positive. You create the finish line you will later cross. Make the finish line clear to all stakeholders.

In this example, you can measure "increased profitability" in several ways: a net amount, a percentage of sales, or an amount per unit. Because an increase in overall company profitability is needed to save the company, it is probably wise to use the net amount approach. The better the goal can be measured, the easier it is to determine the project's level of success. Remember, goals that can't be measured can't be achieved.

### Agreeing on the Goal While It's Still Possible

Next, it is important to ensure that all stakeholders agree on what you're trying to accomplish. This includes the project originator, the planning team, the implementation team, and the end users. To avoid problems, all must agree on the goal and how it will be measured. Without early consensus on this key issue, it becomes dramatically more difficult to plan and implement a successful project.

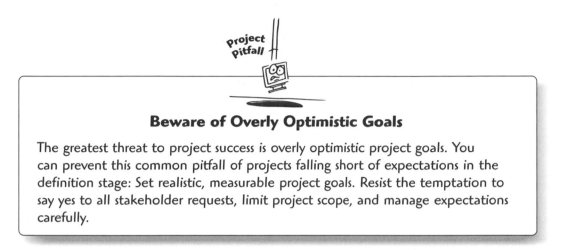

### Beware of Overly Optimistic Goals

The greatest threat to project success is overly optimistic project goals. You can prevent this common pitfall of projects falling short of expectations in the definition stage: Set realistic, measurable project goals. Resist the temptation to say yes to all stakeholder requests, limit project scope, and manage expectations carefully.

## *Time for Action*

Let's skip over the realistic for a moment and consider the timeframe. The timeframe for the overall project is sometimes established in conjunction with making the goal measurable (create an assembly line that can go into production within 90 days). In other situations, the time available for the project is a given constraint, dictated by external factors (amend the software program tax tables before they take effect in the next calendar year). In any case, make sure your goal identifies the time available or deadline of the project. Goals without a timeframe are rarely begun and less frequently completed.

## *Where Are the Realists When You Need Them?*

Refresh your coffee and clear your head. You've come to the biggest decision in the goal setting process: Is this specific, measurable, agreed upon, time-bound goal realistic? Can we make it happen?

Being overly optimistic is one of the most serious errors made by a project team. Sure, if everyone got along, showed up, worked hard, had no accidents, stayed on task, wasn't interrupted, didn't have 10 other important responsibilities, and our friend Murphy never showed up, this project might be a piece of cake. However, it is unlikely that you will have an ideal project environment. (I suppose it's possible. People do win the lottery.) Although this is no time to be a pessimist, it certainly isn't a good time to be an optimist, either. At this stage of planning, try to be ever the realist, and do yourself (and everyone involved on the project) a big favor! Ask yourself and your project team, "In average conditions, can we do this?" If the answer is a resounding yes, you're good to go. (Of course you need to be careful. Situations change rapidly!)

### Judgment or Skill?

Most serious project problems are caused not by a lack of skill but rather by a lack of good judgment. Always be careful when making decision based on judgment. For example, is the goal realistic? Will resources be available? Are the stakeholders committed? Can you trust that vendor? Is the plan workable? Are the time estimates accurate? Will the technology work? In project management, poor judgment calls cause the most grievous problems.

If the answer is less than a resounding yes, join the club. There will almost always be someone who is worried, whining, over-extended, overly cautious, or just plain in over their heads. You may have to proceed anyway. Again, this is a judgement call. And sometimes it's a tough one. When in doubt, scale things back until your confidence rises to an acceptable level. Your reputation is on the line here. Do what you have to do.

# Understanding the Physics of Project Management

As any high school physics student can describe, there are three requirements to start a fire and maintain combustion: fuel, heat, and oxygen. Remove any one of the three and you no longer have a fire. The physics of projects is similar. Every project has three basic components: performance (outcomes), time, and money (resources). All three exist and are interconnected in every project. They are known in project management as the triple constraints.

Okay, quit yawning. Maybe none of this physics trivia surprises you. Just bear with me, I'm trying to make an important point here!

Let me ask you this: Which of the three elements is most important when building a fire? Okay, so you're right again—it takes all three. They are all equally important.

Now, one last question: Which of the triple constraints is most important in project management?

Ha! I think I got you this time. That was a trick question. As the project manager, you don't get to decide which of the triple constraints is most important. (Sorry, I really shouldn't have asked you. I admit that was a dirty trick.) You see, only the project originator can answer the question, "Which of the triple constraints is most important? It's their project, so it's their call. They get to set the physics of project success. And if you are going to be successful (at least from their point of view), you must honor their outlook on the triple constraints.

Let's use an example to further illustrate: You're going to a conference next week and because you'll likely meet some new colleagues, you decide to check your stock of business cards. Alas, only a few shop-worn cards remain, and furthermore, your email address has changed. You decide to visit a printer and order some new cards. Arriving at the printer's counter, you order 500 cards with your new email address and a four-color logo, for delivery as soon as possible, and you want rock bottom pricing. You want to have your cards fast, good, and cheap. Unfortunately, you've ignored the physics of project management. As the old printer's adage says, "You can have it fast. You can have it good. You can have it cheap. Pick any two."

The physics of project management (the triple constraints) restricts choices and decisions. Each one affects the other two. If you want greater performance (the four-color logo), it will cost more and likely take more time. If you want them faster, you may have to spend more and cut out the fancy logo. To spend less, cut out the logo and let the printer fit it into their workload conveniently. And the printer (the project manager) doesn't get to choose. This is your call (the project originator). And it is the job of the project manager to help the project originator understand what is and is not possible.

Good and fast? Fast and cheap? Good and cheap?

## Prioritizing the Triple Constraints

The triple constraints set the tone for every decision you'll make as a project manager. It is therefore important to understand which of the constraints is most flexible and which is least flexible. By definition, the driving constraint (the least flexible) must be achieved or the project is a failure. Successful project managers make sure they identify and achieve the driving constraint on every project.

The weak constraint is by definition the most flexible. Although it may be very important, it is not as important as the driver. And of course, the constraint that falls between these two extremes is called the middle constraint. Its importance and flexibility falls somewhere between the driver and the weak constraints, although not necessarily equidistant from the two. Figure 2.2 illustrates this point.

The constraint prioritization can and does change during a project. Not long ago, I planned to replace my company's computer system. There was no urgency. I was willing to settle for less than the latest hardware performance to save a little money. We planned on catching some items on sale and installing the new system ourselves, as our workloads allowed. Cost was the project's driving constraint. I wanted to get as much performance as possible without paying too much. Performance was the middle constraint and it was only slightly less important than cost. Because I was in no rush replacing an existing system, time was my weak constraint, the most flexible of the three.

**Figure 2.2**

*Understanding the triple constraints helps you understand project difficulty and risk, and deal with problems that may threaten the project.*

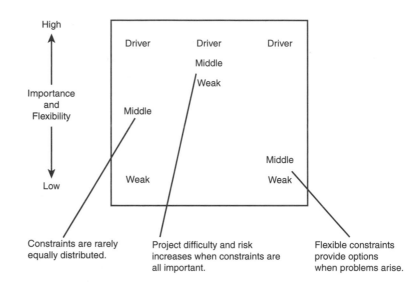

Constraints are rarely equally distributed.

Project difficulty and risk increases when constraints are all important.

Flexible constraints provide options when problems arise.

**Project Manager's Success Rule #2**

When problems arise, consider the triple constraints carefully before acting. Always protect the project's driving constraint—if it breaks, the project fails. Always identify the project's weak constraint—bending this may not be ideal, but it may save the project.

Then one sunny summer afternoon, a thunderstorm blew over and changed all that. With one bolt of lightning, our existing system was destroyed. Before the thundering crack had rumbled away, the triple constraints were turned upside down: To stay in business, we needed to get a system up and running fast. Cost was no longer the driver; it was now the weak constraint. Performance jumped into the driver status. Time followed closely in importance and became the middle constraint. In a flash, the project's original constraints of cheap and good had changed to good and fast!

I hope lightning never strikes your project. But be forewarned, the triple constraints are important and they can change quickly.

Good? Fast? Cheap? The constraint that drives the success of your project must be protected, even at the expense of the weak and possibly middle constraint.

## Who's in Charge Here: The Project's Manager, Originator, or End User?

After you understand the triple constraints, it becomes pretty evident that the project manager's role is to achieve the project outcomes while protecting the driver, and if possible, the middle and weak constraints as well.

There are three problems with this strategy (and probably what drives most project managers nuts). First, as we have seen, the prioritization of the triple constraints is not up to the project manager; only the project originator has that power.

Second, the end user is rarely asked to participate in this prioritization. Although their take on this issue is important, we must rely on the project originator to accurately identify and communicate the end user's point of view. Unfortunately for the project manager, the end user retains complete and full rights of project rejection.

Last (and perhaps, most absurdly), it is the rare project originator who even knows what the triple constraints are, let alone is able to verbalize their appropriate prioritization. This issue brings us to the following important skill.

## How to Question the Boss and Remain Happily Employed

Ask the project originator (the boss), "What is most important on this project, achieving the cost, the performance, or the time constraints (good, fast, or cheap)?" You know what the boss will say, "They're all essential! Give me all three, or else!"

Beware of projects where all three constraints are very important and must be achieved. These projects provide few alternatives for recovery if, and more likely when, you run into problems. Breaking any of the constraints makes the project a failure, and punches a major dent in your reputation. Fortunately, three drivers on one project is rarely the case.

If you look closely enough, there is usually some continuum of importance within the three constraints. Each may be important, but they are rarely equally important. Find out how each compares by asking the project originator a series of guiding questions. Try to find out what choices they would make, given a set of circumstances.

Early in the project definition stage, project originators aren't always aware of the triple constraints and certainly haven't given much thought to their prioritization. By asking questions, you will assist their understanding of the project, reveal their constraint priorities, and make it easier for yourself to achieve whatever their idea of project success is. You cannot be effective at planning or decision making unless you understand the project goals and the triple constraints.

**Secrets of Success**

**Being Your Own Project Detective**

Use comparative and open-ended questions to reveal the project originator's triple constraint priorities. Be sure priorities are clear before beginning the planning phase. Remain alert for changing constraint priorities during implementation.

31

Here are some of my favorite ways of interrogating the boss without getting fired. These questions have proven fruitful in many different types of projects, throughout many industries. This first set of questions is open-ended:

➤ Why are we doing this?

➤ What is the worst thing that could go wrong?

➤ If we had plenty of time, money, and resources, what would this project look like?

➤ If everything goes smoothly, what is the best possible outcome we can expect from this project?

➤ If everything went badly, what is the least acceptable outcome we must achieve with this project?

➤ In your opinion, what is the order of importance between the project's performance (describe this in their terms), the project's budget, and the time that is available to get it all done?

The next set of questions are designed to force a choice and help us prioritize. Use comparative questions with project-specific examples. Force choices by comparing two of the constraints at a time. This technique will help you establish the priorities of even the most incommunicative of project originators.

➤ If there are not enough resources to fully staff this project until project XYZ is completed, what would you want me to do?

➤ If it ends up costing an additional X dollars to complete the project within the targeted time line, how would that be?

➤ If we complete the project on time, except for objective XYZ, which we could finish within the next 30 days, would that be acceptable?

Keep in mind that your success is determined by how well the project meets the stakeholder's expectations. Understanding the underlying project physics (the triple constraints) sharpens your problem-solving tools to a fine edge. Planning becomes more effective. Implementation becomes easier. When problems arise, you'll be ready to cut, slash, or hack your way into the clear with the least amount of trouble.

Speaking of trouble, have you met my friend Murphy?

# Meeting Your Invisible Teammates, Murphy and Adam Smith

Some say you have to be a little bit crazy to be a project manager, so keep this quiet: I've got a couple of invisible teammates. And they can both be real problem makers when they're ignored. Please allow me to explain. (Project management really hasn't made me crazy, yet.)

### Murphy Joins the Team

Several decades ago, there was a project manager in New Mexico, who was testing the physiological effects of deceleration on the human body. The test subject was strapped into a rocket sled, blasted down a set of railroad tracks, and purposefully slammed into a water braking system. In the process, tremendous forces were sustained by the equipment, and of course, by the test pilot. If anything went wrong, somebody could easily be injured, or worse.

Project management lore has blurred from fact to fable at this point, so I'll continue with my version (albeit marginally plausible, it's infinitely more entertaining). Just imagine—what if the project manager knew the test pilot's spouse? Perhaps at a dinner party one evening, during a rare, serious moment, the concerned spouse stepped up to the project manager and asked: "What exactly are you doing to make sure my test pilot is coming home for dinner tomorrow?" We can only assume that the project manager would reply with the only correct answer in this situation: "We are doing everything that is possible and some things that aren't! We'll get him home safely. You can count on it."

I believe it was at that very moment the project manager (some say his name was Murphy, although this is not entirely clear) invented the most important, and now famous, law of project management. We call it Murphy's law: If anything can go wrong, it will go wrong. You can count on it!

This pessimistic point of view (although some consider Murphy to be an optimist) allowed the project team to maintain a perfect safety record on an extremely hazardous project. The test pilot came home for dinner, and project managers everywhere adopted a useful new teammate, albeit an invisible one.

Make Murphy and his law a part of your project team. He will be with you on every project, one way or another. You might as well make the best of it and invite him.

### Adam Smith Joins the Team

Speaking of uninvited guests, have you met my other invisible colleague, Adam Smith? He is only beginning to enjoy Murphy's notoriety, because he was first described as a project teammate by yours truly just a few years ago. Nonetheless, I have little doubt that he will become an increasingly popular colleague of project managers everywhere. See if you agree. This is his story:

I was engaged in a particularly difficult business turn-around project for a large electronics-manufacturing firm. There were many small projects being implemented to save this company (from itself, I might add). One of the key issues plaguing the company was that managers were not making good business choices. Science, technology, or engineering points of view were dominating the decision-making process. A broader business perspective was missing from their equations.

Project budgets were inaccurate, financial outcomes ignored, competitive forces scoffed at. The managers thought their technology was so good, so cool, so slick, that everyone would rush in and pay whatever they asked, on their schedule. Indeed, this had been the case in the past.

Project originators and project managers all agreed on the triple constraints. "Performance is most important. Cost and time will just have to be whatever it takes to deliver our superior technology," they reasoned. However, competitors were steadily winning away business, and the effects were becoming unacceptable. These seasoned project managers, buried up to their ears in "superior" technology, had been temporarily sheltered from the external forces of the competitive market.

As it usually does, the competition eventually caught up. Adam Smith's relentless and invisible hands, the laws of supply and demand, were at work.

First described in the late 1700's, the principles this observant economist discovered are timeless. They describe an environment of unlimited needs and limited resources. They predict that within a competitive environment, whoever provides the most value for the least cost will eventually become the victor, at least temporarily.

### Checking On Agreement

A short list is better than a long memory! Use a project initiation document to navigate quickly through the early portions of the definition stage. A signature line helps ensure that all project stakeholders are in agreement on these essential fundamentals.

The unforgiving nature of these laws reminds us that a little paranoia is a good thing. Stay sharp. Stay aggressive. Competition is everywhere. And when you think it isn't, you may be at the most risk.

In this dynamic, volatile business environment, his lessons are more important than ever. If you acknowledge Adam Smith as a teammate, you can avoid some potentially devastating judgment calls. Moreover, when your team whines about your insistence for accurate estimates, careful monitoring, speedy problem resolution, alternate plans of action, and performance excellence, you can do what all good executives do: blame the necessity on somebody else. In this case, you've got Adam Smith, and I'm sure that he would be honored to take the heat for you!

# Getting Started on the Right Foot: the Project Initiation Document

With so much to orchestrate, project managers often rely on checklists and forms. One of my favorites is the project initiation document. Its format changes a bit, depending on your industry and personal preferences. Project initiation documentation can be as short and sweet as a one-pager with the project originator's sign-off at the bottom, or it can run into volumes, depending on your needs.

The example in Figure 2.3 is effective for small- to medium-sized projects. Recreate this form in a word processor and customize it for your typical projects. If you are involved in large projects, such as building skyscrapers or placing a probe on Mars, the project initiation document can also serve as a checklist for other key project-specific requirements: quality metrics, safety considerations, regulatory requirements, and so on.

# PROJECT INITIATION DOCUMENT

| | |
|---|---|
| Project | Date<br>/ / |
| Goal Statement | |
| Outcomes and Deliverables | Time Frame |
| Assumptions | |
| Prioritization of Triple Constraints | |
| Threats and Risks | |
| Stakeholders          Roles          Responsibilities | |
| Project Approvals | |

Project Approvals

     /   /         /   /          /   /

Originator / Sponsor     User / Customer     Project Manager

**Figure 2.3**

*Create a project initiation document for each type of project you manage and use it as a checklist.*

## The Least You Need to know

➤ Specific, measurable, time-bound, realistic goals that are agreed upon by all stakeholders are essential to project success.

➤ The priority of the triple constraints—time, money, and performance—affects every decision you'll make as a project manager. Protect the driver to protect the project's success.

➤ Project risk increases as constraints become more important and therefore less flexible.

➤ Planning is a waste of time if you do not fully understand the goals and triple constraints of your project.

➤ The five-step project management process—define, plan, implement, control, and close—is effective for both small and large projects.

➤ A project initiation document keeps you focused on essential elements of the project definition process.

# Part 2
# Okay, Let's Plan Your Project

*You've arrived at the heart of the planning process; to succeed, you'll need a set of tools. Part 2 is just that—your very own collection of planning power tools. So, let's plug them in, turn them on, and build a schedule!*

*We begin by making sure you can get around in Microsoft Project 2000. With the program basics covered, you'll learn how to easily identify every single task that must be done to make your project a success. Then you'll learn the tricks of the trade for estimating how long each task will take to complete. Next, you'll enter the workflow sequence and before you know it, you've got a complete schedule! You'll know the start and stop times of the whole project and every task in it. All the whats and whens of your project will be lined up and ready to implement.*

*Grab your safety goggles—it's time to make the chips fly!*

# Chapter 3

# Getting Started with Microsoft Project 2000

---

### In This Chapter

➤ Installing and starting Microsoft Project 2000

➤ Moving around in the program, starting a new project file, and saving and retrieving your files

➤ Finding help and additional information when you need it

➤ Getting ready to plan your project with Microsoft Project 2000

---

Microsoft Project 2000 is a powerful program with many features designed to help you manage projects effectively. Its rich set of functions provides almost everything the majority of project managers could ever want. The first time you look at the screen, it can be rather intimidating. Don't assume you must master every detail of this complex program. Although it's nice to know these capabilities are there if you need them, most project managers never fully use its complete range of features.

## Everything the Beginning Project Manager Needs to Know About Computers

If you are new to project management, don't make the mistake of trying to control every detail of your project. The quest for perfection has been the undoing of many new project managers. What may seem like more control can turn out to be less control. Too much detail keeps you busy doing the wrong things—entering data, running reports, and updating diagrams—when you should be busy monitoring, communicating, and controlling.

Therefore, don't plan or control any project at a greater level of detail than is absolutely necessary. Carefully manage the items that can make a significant difference in the success of your project (yes, this is a judgement call) and ignore those items that do not make a significant difference. (For more information on how much detail you need, see the section "Keeping It As Simple As Possible," in Chapter 4.) Seek success rather than perfection.

Are you like most of us who manage projects? Is there too much to do and too little time to do it in? If so, then maximize the return on your time and energy. Use Microsoft Project's features in the order that I explain them in this book. We'll start with the essentials and move on to the exotic, ever mindful that your most important goal is project success.

If you have some experience with Microsoft Project and want to jump ahead, simply review each chapter's "The Least You Need to Know" section and go for it!

## Installing Microsoft Project 2000

If you haven't installed Microsoft Project 2000, you're in for a pleasant surprise; it takes only a few minutes. Most of that time, it does all the work while you watch. (That's the kind of work I like!)

Place the CD into your computer and close the drive. There is an autorun file on the CD that takes over as soon as the drive door closes. The install screen appears and leads you, step by step, through setup. For now, select **Install Microsoft Project 2000**, as shown in Figure 3.1. The next three options on the install menu are for exchanging project information using email and the Web. These options are covered in Chapters 18, "Publishing Projects on the Web," and 19, "Communicating with Teams via Email." If you decide to use these features, you can install them later.

### Autorun Files

An autorun file is a special file designed to make your life a little easier. Autorun files automatically launch a program when they are detected on a CD or disk that has been inserted into a drive. They are frequently used to start installation programs, as is the case with Microsoft Project 2000.

For now, choose the first option, **Install Microsoft Project 2000.**

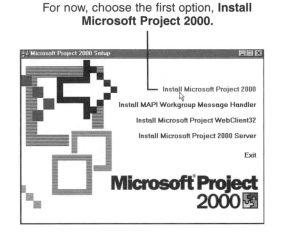

**Figure 3.1**

*You can run install at any time to add or remove program options.*

If for some reason the autorun installation program doesn't start when the drive door closes, you can run it manually. Select the Windows **Start** button at the bottom-left corner of your screen (see Figure 3.2), click **Run**, and then click the **Browse** button. Locate the folder **Autorun** in the CD drive, open it with a double-click, and find the **Autorun.exe** file. Double-click it, and you're off to the races! (I only *said* the install program does most of the work.)

To run install manually, click **Run**, then **Browse** to the Autorun folder on your CD drive, select **Autorun.exe**, click **Open**, and click **OK**.

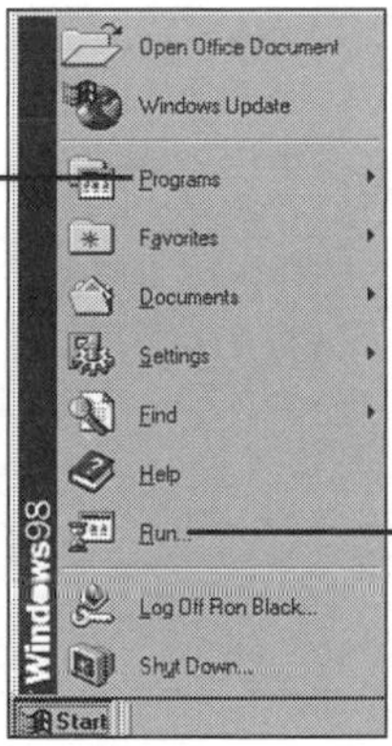

**Figure 3.2**

*The Windows Start button is found at the lower-left corner of your screen.*

To run Microsoft Project 2000, click the **Programs** menu and scroll down to **Microsoft Project**.

## Starting the Program

After Microsoft Project has been installed, you can start it by clicking the Windows **Start** button, pointing to **Programs**, and then clicking **Microsoft Project**. If you want to get a little fancier, you can create a shortcut icon and place it on your desktop. Then, anytime you can see your desktop, you're just a double-click away from all your project information. (Before computers it was the other way around—desktops couldn't be seen because of all the project information!)

**41**

To create a shortcut, open the folder **C:\Program Files\Microsoft Office** and right-click the **Microsoft Project** icon as shown in Figure 3.3. (The icons in your window may vary from those in Figure 3.3, depending on which Microsoft Office products are installed on your computer.) When the pull-down menu appears, click **Create Shortcut**. Find the icon labeled "Microsoft Project (2)" and drag it onto your desktop. If you want to rename it or get rid of the "(2)", right-click the icon and click **Rename**. Microsoft Project is now just a double-click away.

**Figure 3.3**

*To create a shortcut, right-click the Microsoft Project icon in the Microsoft Office folder, and then click Create Shortcut.*

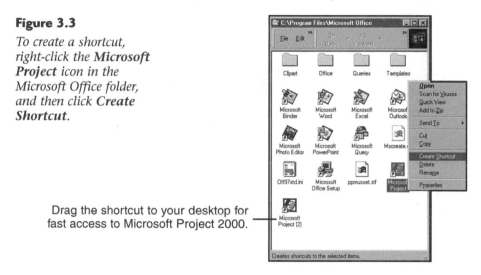

Drag the shortcut to your desktop for fast access to Microsoft Project 2000.

# What's All the Stuff on My Screen?

If this is your first look at Microsoft Project 2000, don't be alarmed. It really is easier than it looks.

First of all, if you've used any other Microsoft Office products, such as Word, Excel, Access, Outlook, or PowerPoint, you already know many of the basic commands. Secondly, the Microsoft Project 2000 commands most frequently used are available several ways: pull-down menus, shortcut keys, and toolbar buttons. Consequently, there really aren't as many commands to learn as it looks.

For some users it's easier to remember the menu words, and for others it's easier to remember the buttons. I, however, can rarely remember anything (as my colleagues will attest). Fortunately, no command memorization is required. There are plenty of descriptions and clues to help you navigate Microsoft Project 2000's commands. For example, place your mouse pointer over any button, hesitate for just a moment (as if you can't remember whether this is the choice you want) and notice what happens. Instant recall! A description of the button pops up, guiding your selection. I wish they could do something like that with my car keys.

You'll learn more handy tips in this chapter's section, "Getting Help in a Hurry." After using the program for a while, you'll develop your own favorite methods of accessing each command.

# *Mousing Around the Program*

The best way to get to know your way around Microsoft Project is to try it out. You can't hurt anything, so if you haven't already done so, start the program, take hold of that mouse, and make some tracks! (Sorry, bad pun.) See if you can identify all the features described in this section and shown in Figure 3.4.

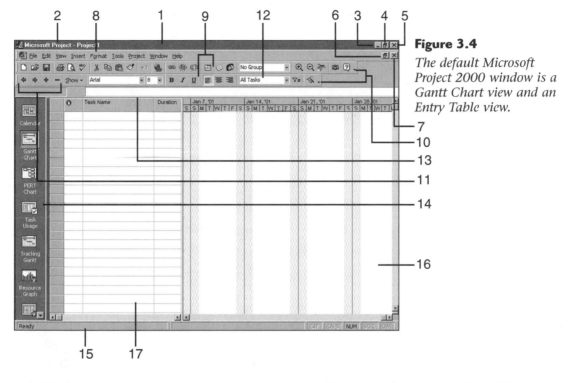

**Figure 3.4**

*The default Microsoft Project 2000 window is a Gantt Chart view and an Entry Table view.*

| 1 | Title bar | 11 | Changes outline levels on Entry Table |
|---|---|---|---|
| 2 | Current project filename | 12 | Filter restricts information viewed |
| 3 | Minimizes the program window | 13 | Type or edit a field's data in the Entry bar |
| 4 | Resizes the program window | 14 | View Bar provides fast access to the most |
| 5 | Exits Microsoft Project | | used views |
| 6 | Resizes the project window | 15 | Status Bar shows progress of processing |
| 7 | Closes the project | | and keyboard options |
| 8 | Menu bar | 16 | Gantt Chart view |
| 9 | Toolbars | 17 | Entry Table view |
| 10 | Add or remove toolbar commands | | |

A new project appears when you start Microsoft Project 2000. Try clicking, pointing, or hovering on fields, lines, buttons, and menu choices. Double-clicking opens additional information or definition windows whenever they are available. Right-clicking opens context-sensitive submenus.

You've probably noticed that the mouse pointer changes, depending on its location. Unless you understand what each of the pointers indicate, it can get a little frustrating. Don't memorize all the pointer styles in Table 3.1. Just keep your book handy in case you need to refer back to this page.

### Table 3.1   A Few Pointers on Mouse Pointers

| Pointer | Function |
| --- | --- |
| ↖ | What you see is what you get. The default pointer for selecting, clicking, dragging, and pressing on date spinners. |
| ✛ | Indicates your pointer is over a field in a table view. Clicking selects that field for data entry or editing. |
| ⌶ | Shows the location of the cursor in text, numeric, currency, or date fields. |
| ↔‖ | Indicates that the pointer is hovering over a vertical window separator and by pressing the left mouse button, you may drag it to adjust the size of the split. |
| ↕ | This does the same as the pointer above except it adjusts horizontal splits. When in the task table view, this indicates that you have selected a task for moving up or down within the task list. |
| ↔ | In column headings, drag this pointer to adjust the width of columns. |
| ↕ | In row headings, drag this pointer to adjust the height of rows. |
| ✛ | This pointer shows that you have selected an object, such as a network diagram node, and are ready to drag it to a new location. |
| ∞ | This pointer can be tricky, so be careful when you see it. It creates new links, and sometimes new tasks, in the Gantt and PERT Chart views. |

By default, the Entry Table and the Gantt Chart View are displayed as shown previously in Figure 3.4. Dragging the line separating the two views to the right reveals more of the Entry Table.

Much of Microsoft Project's power comes from its capability to store, retrieve, summarize, detail, and filter project data. There are 26 predefined tables, graphs, and charts that are called "views" in Microsoft Project. More than one view can be on the screen at once, and each view can be modified to meet your needs.

## Getting Help in a Hurry

With all these options, its nice to know there's help available no matter where you are in the program. From the moment you start to the moment you exit, there's ready help on everything from project-management practices to the details of printing a report. Best of all, navigating through all this information is easy.

The Help Home Page is an enormous smorgasbord of information. It greets you the first time you start the program. Thereafter, you can access this plethora of information in the pull-down menu on the menu bar by selecting **Contents and Index**, as shown in Figure 3.5 and later in Figure 3.6.

**Figure 3.5**

*A wealth of information is available through the Help Home Page.*

The following list describes the Help menu options:

➤ **What's New** helps you learn about the new features in Microsoft Project 2000 in case you've used a previous version.

➤ **Quick Preview** provides a brief overview of the program and its capabilities. It looks a little like a commercial, but it does provide a broad perspective of the program's features.

➤ **Tutorial** steps you through the process of entering project information, creating a schedule, tracking, and reporting progress. If you have a little time, these lessons are a good way to increase your program knowledge.

➤ **Project Map** is a good overview of using the program. It allows you to quickly navigate to the points you want to learn more about.

➤ **Office Assistant** is an information retrieval system in the form of an animated character. And oh, what a character he (she?) is! Check out the following section entitled, "Meeting Clippit, Your Personal Computer Tutor."

➤ **Reference** is an encyclopedic listing of the features and functions of Microsoft Project 2000. You'll find help on views, tables, filters, templates, troubleshooting, glossary items, features for disabilities, technical specifications, mouse and keyboard shortcuts, and more.

## Meeting Clippit, Your Personal Computer Tutor

Perhaps the easiest feature to use (and certainly the most entertaining) is your personal computer tutor, Clippit. To put him to work, click the **Microsoft Project Help** option in the **Help** menu. Clippit also pops to attentive assistance when you press the **F1** key.

**Figure 3.6**

*Clippit retrieves information and warns you of possible mistakes.*

Type in any words or phrases (it doesn't have to be a complete sentence), select **Search**, and Clippit retrieves a list of subjects for you to pick from. If you're like me, you'll be amazed at how well he gets the job done.

When you aren't using Clippit, he waits patiently, although not always quietly, for your next question. It can sometimes get a little rowdy, so if he distracts you with his playful antics or sounds, just give him the boot by right-clicking him and then selecting **Hide**. He'll be back, cheerful and eager as ever, when you press **F1**.

While you're learning Microsoft Project, it's a good idea to keep him on your screen. Most of the time, he will dodge out of your way. If he doesn't, just drag him to an unused portion of your screen. From his vantage point he can keep an eye on you. (Kind of scary, huh?) If you make a common error, he'll stop the process and ask you about it. All in all, Clippit makes a pretty good teammate!

## Other Sources of Help

If you have access to the Internet, help is available on the Web. On the **Help** menu, click **Office on the Web**. You'll be off on a trip through cyberspace to the latest information and support for Microsoft Project 2000.

## Starting a New Project File from Ground Zero

Before using Microsoft Project 2000 to plan an actual project, let's make sure you can create, save, and open project files. This way, you can be confident that your work is safe.

To create a new project, open the **File** menu and select **New**. In the window that appears, select **Blank Project** in the General tab, and click **OK**. (Later, in Chapter 17, "Too Many Projects, Too Little Time," I'll show you how to make and use project templates.)

In the Project Information window that pops up, enter either a **Start Date** or a **Finish Date**. If you know when the project must be completed, and you want Microsoft Project 2000 to schedule based on that date, enter the **Finish Date**. More frequently, project managers are interested in scheduling from a given date. If this is the case for you, enter a **Start Date**. Pick **Start** or **Finish**, not both, and click **OK**. You can always change this later, by clicking **Project Information** on the **Project** menu.

To save your new file, click **Save As** in the **File** menu. A file dialog box opens similar to the one in Figure 3.7. Select an appropriate folder for your project files. You'll have easy access to them if you select the **My Documents** icon, click new folder, and name the folder "Projects." Double-click the resulting folder to open it. Type the name of your new project file at the bottom of the dialog box and click **Save**.

All you need to do to open this project file is select **Open** on the **File** menu and double-click the file you want.

**Passing Time Around**

Determining when a project can be completed, given a starting date, is called a *forward pass*. Determining when a project must begin, given a finish date, is called performing a *backward pass*.

Up One Level          Create New Folder

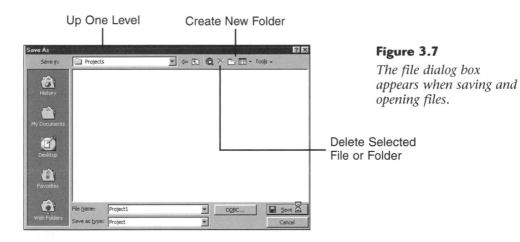

**Figure 3.7**
*The file dialog box appears when saving and opening files.*

Delete Selected
File or Folder

Congratulations! You've mastered the controls for Microsoft Project 2000, so it's time to put it to work planning one of your projects. Pick one out and let's get going!

**The Least You Need to Know**

➤ You may enter information and select views and commands with the mouse or keyboard.

➤ The mouse pointer changes shape in different locations of the program window to indicate its current function.

➤ Getting help is quick and easy with the Office Assistant Clippit, the Help Home Page, and Help on the Web.

➤ Creating, saving, and opening project files in Microsoft Project 2000 works like all other Windows programs.

# Chapter 4

# Thinking of Everything, Even If You Don't Know What You're Doing

## In This Chapter

➤ Identify every task that must be accomplished to make your project a success.

➤ Subdivide your project into logical, manageable segments with a work breakdown structure.

➤ Translate your project strategy into tactics you can implement.

➤ Increase your odds of success by eliminating unnecessary tasks.

➤ Make your project more manageable with summaries and milestones.

➤ Organize your project activities with Microsoft Project 2000.

To accomplish the project's goal, hundreds or even thousands of individual tasks must be identified and successfully completed. The process of identifying all required work is called *project decomposition*. This can be a chaotic process unless you understand the tricks of the trade.

## Creating Order Out of Chaos

Perhaps the most daunting challenge project managers must resolve is how to identify every activity required to accomplish the project goals and not leave something out.

Missing even a seemingly minor item can blow the project's chances of success. For example, which bolt, nut, or screw could be left out of out the space shuttle? I wager none of them could be—they're all essential. Every additional ounce of structure reduces the payload capacity. Therefore someone, somewhere along the line must have asked, "Is this essential?" about every fastener on the entire space shuttle.

If an essential item is overlooked, bad things can happen: subsequent work may be stopped; costs may exceed estimates, budgeted time and resources may fall short; the driving constraint may be impacted. (See the section "Understanding the Physics of Project Management" in Chapter 2, "The Project Management Process.") And if the driving constraint is at risk, so is the success of your project. Moreover, your reputation as a project manager can be permanently damaged.

The success of your project, and ultimately your success as a project manager, depends on how well you identify every essential activity, even when you've never managed a project like this before. Maybe our mothers were right, we should have been orthodontists!

## *Keeping It As Simple As Possible*

Attempting to accomplish too much is also risky. Encumbering a project with activities outside of the project's scope can turn a walk in the park into a jog on the freeway.

Trying to implement tasks that lie outside of the project scope can make bad things happen: the project may become difficult to manage; more resources must be found; and the sequence of work becomes more complex. Nonessential activities siphon time, money, and attention away from those tasks you absolutely must accomplish.

Why ask for trouble? Most projects are challenging enough already! Clearly, the key to successful planning is to identify all essential tasks while keeping your project as simple as possible.

To create order out of this chaos, project managers use a tool called the *work breakdown structure* (WBS). Like a safety net, the WBS helps you include every activity essential to achieving the project's goals and objectives. In addition, it helps protect your project from the nonessential activities that undoubtedly will try to creep in.

The WBS is a simple, flexible tool. It can take on several different formats, depending on the project manager's personal preferences. The traditional and most popular format is shown in Figure 4.1. Notice that it resembles an organizational chart.

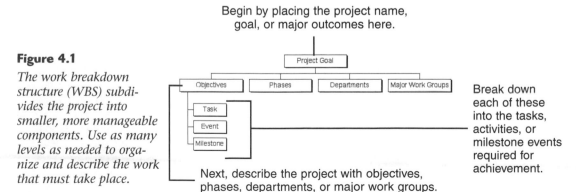

**Figure 4.1**

*The work breakdown structure (WBS) subdivides the project into smaller, more manageable components. Use as many levels as needed to organize and describe the work that must take place.*

50

Another frequently used format resembles an outline. This form is the one Microsoft Project 2000 uses. As you shall see, it becomes the backbone of all your planning and scheduling activity.

Whether you use the outline or the organizational chart format, the WBS is a visual tool used to organize what it takes to get a project done. In essence, the WBS is a hierarchy of goals, objectives, strategies, and tactics. Creating the hierarchy reveals how a project's major outcomes are supported by key objectives or strategies, and in turn, what tactics or activities are needed to implement them.

## Creating a Work Breakdown Structure Without a Nervous Breakdown

Trying to think of every task that must be completed on a major project is enough to push even seasoned project managers to the verge of a nervous breakdown. However, you can remain cool, calm and collected by following the procedure outlined in the following sections.

To create a WBS, you must have a clear understanding of the project's goals and objectives, the triple constraints, and the project assumptions. You probably already gathered this information when you created your project initiation document. (See the section entitled "Getting Started on the Right Foot with a Project Initiation Document" in Chapter 2.)

Begin creating your WBS by writing the project's goal at the top of a blank sheet of paper (this is "what" will be accomplished). On the next level, break the goal down into its major elements or supporting objectives ("how" it will be accomplished) as seen in Figure 4.2. When properly done, the second level describes your project implementation strategy. This level can then be broken down into the separate tasks required to achieve each major element.

### First Things First

Although it may be tempting, never skip or short-change the project definition step. Planning is ineffective without a clear understanding of the project's goals and constraints. The quality of your WBS depends on the quality of the information in your project initiation document.

For example, if the project is to create a new software application, begin your WBS with its goal, "To design, write, document, and train the users on an inventory management system by year end."

Obviously, there are as many strategies as there are project managers for implementing this project. I'll use a typical approach for illustration purposes.

**51**

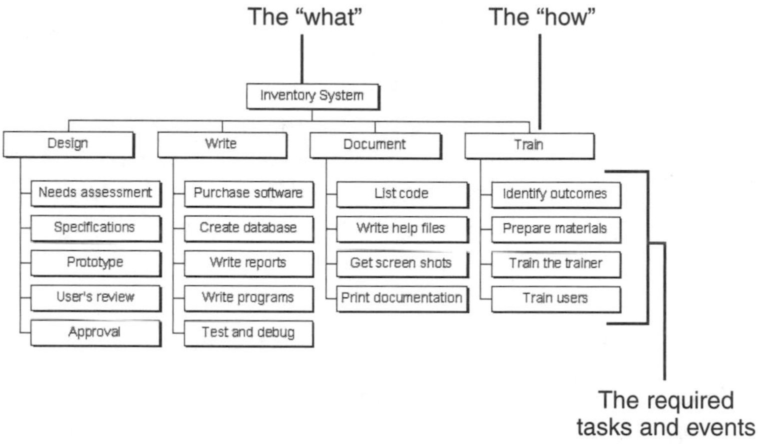

The "what"          The "how"

**Figure 4.2**

*Brainstorm your tasks and organize them under each phase of the project, without regard to their sequence of completion.*

The required
tasks and events

# Outline Your Project with Objectives, Phases, Tasks, and Milestones

You've just seen an example of the WBS formatted as an organizational chart. This same WBS can be depicted in an outline format as well. Here, the level of indentation indicates each lower level on the WBS. For example, an outline WBS for the inventory program project looks like this:

**Inventory system**

Design

      Needs assessment

      Specifications

      Prototype

      User's review

      Approval

Write

      Purchase software

      Create database

      Write reports

      Write programs

      Test and debug

Document

      List code

      Write help files

      Get screen shots

      Print documentation

Train

      Identify outcomes

      Prepare materials

      Train the trainer

      Train users

Although each project manager has a favorite WBS method, these two methods are especially helpful in different situations.

On simple projects and when you're working alone, the outline method is a fast and easy way to list all the major work groups, tasks, activities, and milestone events.

On complex projects or when facilitating a team session, the organizational WBS method is better suited.

After you've created the WBS, the information is entered into Microsoft Project 2000 in an outline form. You'll learn more about this process later in the "Organizing Your Project Tasks with Microsoft Project 2000" section.

## Going It Alone for Simple Projects

When the project is simple and you fully understand its nuances, the WBS is easily created without assistance. Choose the WBS format you prefer and get going!

Begin by placing the project name at the top of a blank sheet of paper. Then in an organizational or outline format, list the major work categories that must be accomplished. The next step is to brainstorm every task, event, or activity required to get the job done. Organize each item under a major work category as you go.

At this stage, capture every item that comes to mind. Creating the WBS is a learning process, and you want to uncover the best implementation process you can. As you proceed, alternative methods or approaches may appear. Don't reject anything, yet. Now is the time to turn your creativity meter on high and your judgment meter to low. Let the ideas roll!

When you think you've got it all, take a break and let your ideas soak in. It helps to regain a balanced perspective before continuing. When time allows, sleep on it. If you're in a time crunch, step away from your desk for at least a few minutes. better yet, take a break or go to lunch.

Then, with a fresh set of eyes, review your WBS and ask yourself these questions:

➤ Are lower-level items both necessary and sufficient for completion of project goals?

➤ Are there any items that are not essential to the project's success and that can be removed?

➤ Can adequate cost and duration estimates be developed at this level of detail?

➤ Is each element described in tangible, verifiable results?

➤ Can each item be appropriately scheduled, budgeted, and assigned?

Remember that planning is an iterative process. As you plan, you learn. Don't hesitate to return to a previous step in the planning process to improve your plan. Continue refining your WBS until you are confident that it adequately and as simply as possible describes the project. A minute spent now can save much frustration and many hours of implementation later.

## When the Going Gets Tough, Call for Reinforcements

As the project manager, you are ultimately responsible for the success of the project, so it falls on you to facilitate the development of a good WBS. However, in our complex project environment, no one person can possibly have all the experience, training, and knowledge needed to create a viable WBS alone.

Fortunately, your role as a project manager is not to think of everything yourself, but rather to make sure someone thinks of everything!

## Using Cross-Functional, Experienced Experts

The first step is to gather a team of "experts." Chances are no one is an expert on this project or they, rather than you, would be the project manager! However, what you can do is bring in people who collectively represent all the skills, knowledge, experience, and techniques your project requires. A group like this is called a *cross-functional team.*

Individuals who are willing and able to work in collaborative environments are most valuable. Some people prefer to work alone or are unwilling to work as part of a team. You'll make life easier on yourself and on them, and you'll improve your chances of success, by honoring each individual's work-style preferences. Allowing personal issues and self-serving points-of-view to infiltrate team decisions can be detrimental to the project's outcome.

In addition to cross-functionality, staff your team with open communicators and true team players—people who are able to commit to a common approach—an approach you agree with. You and your project's success have a great deal riding on this group's early work. In short, surround yourself with the talent you need and the personalities you trust.

## Organizing Your Project Tasks with Microsoft Project 2000

After you've established an initial WBS for your project, it's time to use the awesome power of Microsoft Project 2000 to organize, analyze, and further sharpen it. This step also paves the way for the next stages in planning: estimating task durations and sequencing the work.

### Creating a WBS That Sticks

When developing a WBS with a team, issue each participant a stack of sticky notes and a large marker. As they think of tasks, events, and milestones, have them jot down two or three key words describing each item. The notes can then be placed under each major work heading on a white marker board, flip chart, or conference table. This method makes it easy to interactively discuss, organize, and refine the WBS in a group setting. Using the same size and color of notes and markers helps to equalize each person's "voice" and improves participation levels.

With your WBS nearby, start Microsoft Project 2000 and open your project file. Make sure the Gantt Chart and Entry Table are shown. If not, select the **Gantt Chart view** from the View Bar. To enter a task, click the first empty field under **Task Name**. When selected, the field is highlighted with a dark outline, showing it is ready for data entry.

Begin at the top of your WBS with the project name, the first major workgroup, or task. Type its name into the selected field and press **Enter**. Microsoft Project automatically sets the task's duration to "1 day?" (the program populates this field and assumes this arbitrary duration is not correct) and its start date to today's date (or to the project start date you may have entered ear-

### Hooray for Computers!

Using software to create and organize a task list replaces the tedious hand process of creating a chart of activities over and over again until we got it right. Aren't you glad you have a computer?

lier). You'll change the project start or finish dates and each task duration later. For now, continue entering all tasks and major work groups. Then check your list and make sure nothing has been missed.

## Inserting, Deleting, and Moving Items on the Task List

Inserting an item that you may have missed, or adding one you just thought of, is easy to do in the Entry Table of the Gantt Chart view. For example, you might decide that inserting a short description of your project as the first line would help others understand the work breakdown structure. To do this, select the field where you want to insert the item and press the **Insert** key. Presto! Everything is magically shifted down and an empty row appears. Type in the description and you're finished. Notice—no eraser dust!

### Hooray for (Computer) Sticky-Notes!

By right-clicking anywhere on a task and selecting **Task Notes**, you have a handy storage place for any information you want, even pictures! A Task Note appears in the Information column so that you won't forget it's there.

Deleting an item or several items is also simple and fast. Just select the unwanted item and press the **Delete** key. Likewise, you can select a continuous series of items by clicking an item, moving to the last item in the series, and clicking it while pressing the **Shift** key. Alternately, by holding down the **Ctrl** key as you click on items, you can select a non-continuous list. But, be careful! Both the wanted and the unwanted can vanish with equally blinding speed.

Reorganizing your list is a breeze in Microsoft Project 2000 as shown in Figure 4.3. Click once on the row header to select the entire row. Now click and hold the mouse button down and drag the task to its new location in the list. Wow! Now that's living! (If you have trouble with this, be sure to pause just a moment between clicks so that the computer doesn't interpret it as a double-click.)

You may optionally enter and edit field data in the entry bar.

Drag the scroll bar box or click on the bar to move up or down in the list.

**Figure 4.3**

*Enter each major work category, task, and milestone event from your WBS into the Gantt Chart view in general order of task completion.*

Reorganize the list by clicking the row header and then clicking and dragging the row to a new position.

The highlighted field is ready to enter or edit.

New tasks default to "1 day?" duration and today as the start date.

# Making Your Project Task List Easier to Understand

Your project plan needs to be easily understood by everyone who relies on it for information. To get off to a good start, here are some things you can do (an explanation for each follows a little later):

➤ Use consistent naming conventions throughout your task list.

➤ Use an indentation system that visually communicates the WBS hierarchy.

➤ List the tasks in their general sequence of workflow.

➤ Add summary tasks and milestones to the task list to make the project easier to understand and easier to manage.

## Using Consistent Name Formats

Review your WBS naming conventions for consistency and clarity. Not only will your WBS communicate the strategy and tactics of your project more clearly to everyone who uses your plan, clear names will make many planning chores, such as structuring workflow logic, estimating costs, and estimating durations, much easier. Use these guidelines and examples when naming:

➤ **Tasks**—Tasks are the heart of your project. Describe tasks with clear and unambiguous wording in units that allow accurate cost estimates, accurate time estimates, and clear delegation of responsibilities. A *verb outcome* format is effective. Examples: Excavate footings; Survey users; Issue purchase orders; Debug code.

➤ **Milestones**—Arrival at a milestone confirms that all tasks it depended on (*successor tasks*) have been successfully completed. An *outcome verb* format is a good way to communicate a milestone's importance. Examples: Testing complete; Users trained; Approval received; System operational.

➤ **Summary tasks**—These items are subheadings within a task list. Tasks may be rolled up into the summary task, thereby greatly simplifying complex projects. Include a *grouping term* in these items. Examples: Mobilization phase; Needs assessment section; Training category; Production department.

## Adding Milestones

These events measure your progress and help you monitor and control the project. The careful placing of milestones in a large project can make it much easier to understand and manage.

Milestones are created in the task list exactly like tasks are with the exception that the task duration is set to zero. All zero-duration tasks are considered milestones in Microsoft Project 2000. In the Gantt Chart view they are denoted with a small diamond symbol.

You may occasionally want to use a task with a nonzero duration as a milestone. To do this, from the Gantt Chart view right-click the task to select it, click **Task Information**, and then select the **Advanced** tab. In the **Duration** box, enter the task duration and click the **Mark task as a milestone** check box (found in the bottom-left corner of the information dialog box).

## Showing Work Phases with Summary Tasks

Another method used to make a large task list more readable is the summary task. Major workgroups or phases are effectively communicated when shown as summary tasks in the task list. Lower levels can be rolled up into the summary task and hidden from view. Now you see it, now you don't!

### Oops! Where Did That Go?

Indenting and outdenting tasks is quick and easy, but it's also a bit tricky. A task's duration is easily lost when indenting tasks immediately below it. To minimize this problem, refrain from entering durations until you are satisfied with the WBS format.

### The Ins and Outs of 'Dents

Like many tasks in Microsoft Project 2000, there is more than one way to accomplish some things. You may also indent and outdent by clicking and dragging a task to the left or right.

You create summary tasks in Microsoft Project 2000 by indenting a task or group of tasks in the list. The item immediately above the indented items becomes a bolded summary task. The summary task's duration is automatically calculated, as the time required to complete the subtasks.

## Using Indentations to Convey WBS Hierarchy

Outlining your task list with indents and outdents has two main benefits. First, a graphic representation of WBS levels allows you to more easily spot which items are tasks, summaries, milestones, and the like. Second, task information may be compressed or expanded section by section with a click of the mouse. This allows you to focus on a group of items and hide the rest from view.

To indent or outdent single items, go to the Gantt Chart view as shown in Figure 4.4. Select the item you want to indent. On the Formatting tool bar, click the **Indent** or **Outdent** button.

Indenting a summary task or a task consisting of lower levels (such as subtasks) may cause the lower levels to indent one level too far. This can be rectified by selecting the effected tasks and clicking the **Outdent** button.

## Expanding and Contracting the List

You can display or hide any indented group of items in the task list. This is helpful in several situations.

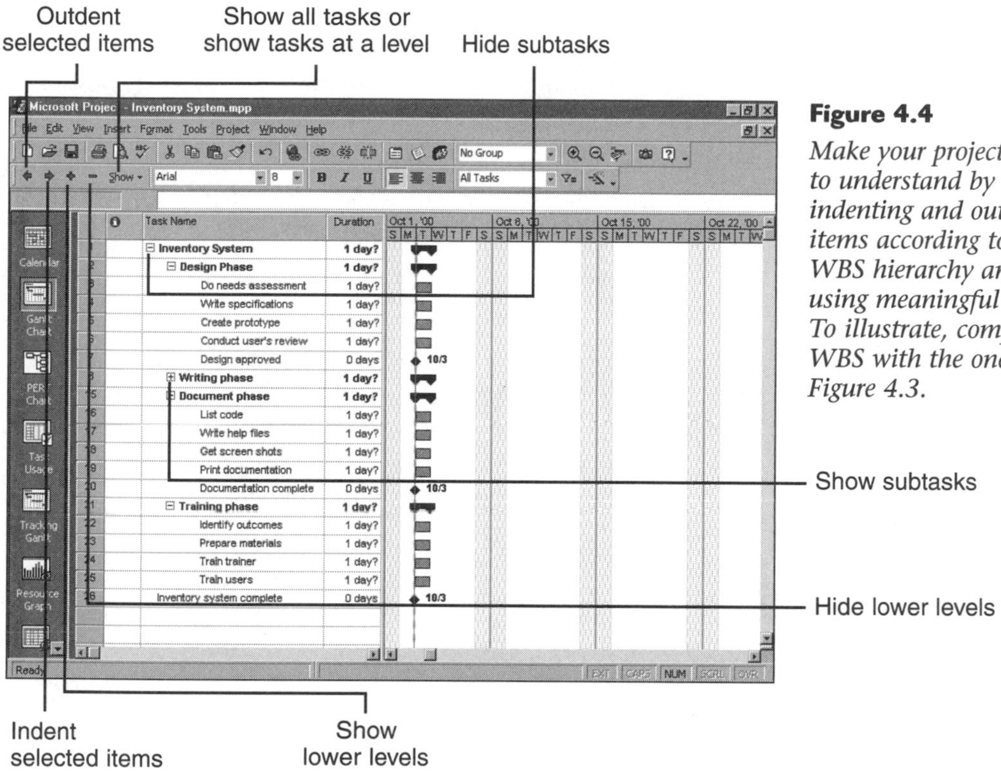

Outdent selected items

Show all tasks or show tasks at a level

Hide subtasks

Indent selected items

Show lower levels

Show subtasks

Hide lower levels

**Figure 4.4**

*Make your project easier to understand by indenting and outdenting items according to your WBS hierarchy and by using meaningful names. To illustrate, compare this WBS with the one in Figure 4.3.*

For example: you want to call attention to a team member's area of responsibility; you want a report without potentially confusing detail; or you want to limit what is displayed on your screen when working on large projects.

To expand or contact your list, select the **Gantt Chart** view. Click the **minus sign** or **plus sign** icons next to the name of the section you want to expand or contract. You can also select an item, and then click the **Show Subtasks**, **Hide Subtasks**, or **Show All Tasks** buttons.

## Printing Your List and Checking It Twice

A printed copy of the WBS listing is sometimes needed for the project's archives, for reports to management, and as part of contractually required documentation. While creating the WBS, I like having a fresh printout in my hand to mark changes on with a brightly colored pen.

A printout can also help determine if the WBS accurately and effectively describes the project's implementation. One way of facilitating this is to mark a copy "Final Review" (a bright red font is best) and circulate it for comment among your team members.

If you created the WBS alone, solicit comments from one or more knowledgeable colleagues. Successful project managers are adept at picking other people's brains! Unfortunately, Microsoft Project 2000 can't help you with the brain picking, nor can it print anything but a rather blasé rendition of the WBS listing.

However, if your printed listing doesn't need to be pretty, you're in luck! With just a few keystrokes, you can print the view that appears on your computer screen. The caveat is that you can't easily remove unnecessary columns, legends, or other items you might not want to appear.

You can print the WBS by using three methods:

➤ The first, and fanciest, is to export or cut and paste the list into another program, such as Word, Excel, or Access. You can publish a more presentable WBS with any of these programs. It is also easier to include it with other project documentation, distribute it via email, or the Web. (See Chapters 18–20, "Publishing Projects on the Web," "Communicating with Teams via Email," and "Sharing Information with Other Programs.")

➤ The second method is quick, but not so pretty: Select the **Gantt Chart** view and click the **Print** icon on the Standard toolbar. Bingo, your WBS arrives, complete with several columns of potentially confusing, meaningless information! I told you it wouldn't be pretty. This is fine for your own use, but if you need to share it with others, you'll want to at least hide the confusing information.

➤ This brings us to the third method (assuming we don't resort to scissors or white out), and no doubt, the most difficult. You'll want to save your project file before you make any of the following adjustments. When you are done printing the WBS, save it with a new name such as "Inventory System WBS Listing" and reopen the unchanged original.

In the Gantt Chart view, drag the vertical divider to the far right. Select all the column headers except the Task Name and right-click. Then select **Hide Columns**. Drag the column width to the right so you can see the complete tasks names. Select **Page Setup** on the **File** menu and change your page orientation to **Portrait**. Now you can click **Print Preview** and check it out. Choose **Header** in **Page Setup** and type in the project's name. When you're satisfied with how it looks, print it.

Figure 4.5 is the result of our work! Okay, okay. I know I promised you quick and easy. You didn't have to resort to white out or scissors, did you?

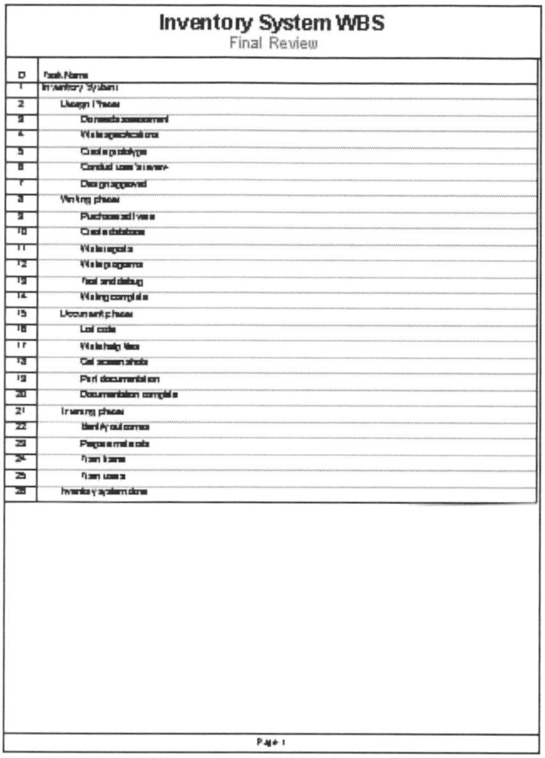

**Figure 4.5**

*A well thought out and presented WBS is an essential step in planning a successful project. Hide unrelated or potentially confusing information before distributing it.*

---

## The Least You Need to Know

➤ The work breakdown structure (WBS) is the best method for identifying every task or activity you need to make your project a success. An understanding of the project's goals, scope, and assumptions is a prerequisite.

➤ Eliminating tasks that are unnecessary reduces the drain on resources, makes the project more manageable, and improves the likelihood of achieving the project's key outcomes.

➤ Tasks are entered into a Microsoft Project 2000's Gantt View task view where they can easily be inserted, deleted, or rearranged. The task view supports summary tasks, milestones, and any number of sublevels required to document the WBS hierarchy.

➤ The WBS can be printed out for editing, review, reports, or project documentation purposes.

# Chapter 5

# Estimating Time with Science, Skill, and Fourth-Grade Math

## In This Chapter

➤ Why accurate time estimates are important to the success of your project

➤ The six methods project managers use to estimate the amount of time required to complete a task

➤ How to enter estimated durations in Microsoft Project 2000

➤ How Microsoft Project 2000 handles project time and calendar time

As a project manager, you're asked to see into the future on every project: How long will it take? How soon must we begin? Will we be done on time? It's as if you're expected to be a fortune teller!

And although you may sometimes wish you had their mystical powers of vision, you probably don't have their tools. Fortune tellers use crystal balls, wrap their heads in scarves, and use tents for offices. Furthermore, they have the good sense to leave town before their predictions can be proven wrong. (Maybe that explains the tent.)

But don't worry. You've got something better than a crystal ball and a head wrap. You're about to replace superstition with science, skill, and fourth-grade math. You're about to see into the future with such confidence and accuracy that you'll never have to use a tent for an office. I'll explain.

# How Long Will the Project Take to Complete?

One of the key questions on almost every project is, "How long will the project take to complete?" To effectively estimate the project's duration, you must know three things:

➤ What tasks must be accomplished?

➤ How long will each task take?

➤ In what order will they be accomplished?

If it is not obvious why order of task accomplishment is important, consider the following: Some tasks can only begin after others have been completed. Other tasks may run in parallel, that is, at the same time. The more tasks that are undertaken at once, the sooner the project will be done. Therefore, task sequence must be established before you can estimate a project's total duration.

**Sharpen Your Estimating Tools**

Your ability to estimate durations improves with experience and feedback. Practice estimating by breaking down your daily work into separate tasks. Estimate how long each will take, then track actual times and compare them to your estimates.

You've probably already completed the first step, identifying all the essential tasks, in Chapter 4, "Thinking of Everything, Even If You Don't Know What You're Doing." In this chapter, you'll establish time estimates for each of these tasks. Then in Chapter 6, "Sequencing Tasks to Fit Your Needs," you'll bring it all together and create a basic project schedule.

The whole process of scheduling depends on good duration estimates. The better you can estimate individual task durations, the more accurately you can answer these important questions:

➤ How long will the project take?

➤ When can we be finished?

➤ When must we begin?

➤ Is there any flexibility in the schedule?

# Answering Other Key Scheduling Questions

It would be nice if you could stop planning at this point. Unfortunately, you can't. Just because you created an accurate schedule doesn't mean the world will stop and politely let you execute your plan. (Although don't you wish it would!) As problems arise and situations change, you'll need to know where your plan is flexible and where it isn't.

An accurate schedule helps keep you in control. With an accurate schedule, you can adjust or adapt to meet current needs and conditions. For example, what if specialized equipment or specially skilled people needed on your project were busy elsewhere? What are your options? Should you get alternative resources, delay starting the work, or perhaps, change your approach altogether?

With an accurate schedule, you're more able to answer the key scheduling questions that will inevitably arise. You can manage individual tasks more effectively. You're more able to modify work sequence or methodologies to bring your project to a successful conclusion. With accurate information to base your judgement calls on, you'll be more able to act decisively. And equally important, you will be able to act with greater confidence.

# Estimating Task Durations

There are six fundamental ways to estimate task durations and needless to say, none of them are perfect! (That's why they're called estimates.) By using the most appropriate method for your situation, you can dramatically improve your accuracy. And with a little experience, people will begin to wonder where you're hiding your crystal ball!

## Using Historical Data

The most accurate and trustworthy data you can use is your own. Experience really is the best teacher. How long did your team take to accomplish a task like this last time? Although no two projects are ever identical, the similarities in tasks, skill levels, tools, and approaches form a solid base for accurate estimates. Whenever possible, rely on your own historic data as much as possible.

## Using References

If you can't use your own history, use someone else's!

In almost every industry that deals in projects, you'll find reference materials to help you estimate task durations. With a little research, you can find everything from how long it takes to pour a yard of concrete to how many lines of code a programmer can write in a year.

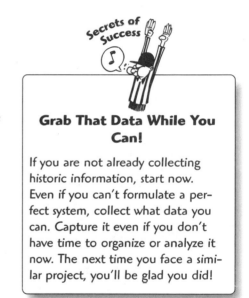

**Grab That Data While You Can!**

If you are not already collecting historic information, start now. Even if you can't formulate a perfect system, collect what data you can. Capture it even if you don't have time to organize or analyze it now. The next time you face a similar project, you'll be glad you did!

It is important to understand how the reference data was collected and what assumptions were made for its use. Don't assume someone else's methods are representative of your team or situation. Be sure to adjust the data for your team's skill level, working conditions, equipment, and any other factors you can identify.

References are rarely as good as your own data, but they are the next best thing!

## WAGing It

If you've been around estimating for long, you've probably heard the term WAG used in jest—the Wildly Aimed Guess (you may have heard another explanation for the acronym, as well). But it goes beyond jest. Sometimes a WAG is all you've got! You have no experience, no reference materials, and no clue where to start. So "WAG" describes an estimate that has little or no grounding in fact. It is simply a wildly aimed guess. Consequently, our confidence in the estimate's accuracy is low.

With that said, WAGs may be adequate. Consider a long series of tasks. If you WAGed the duration for each, it stands to reason that you would rarely hit any one duration exactly right (although you occasionally might get lucky). However, if you added up the total independent estimates, the high estimates are balanced out by the low estimates. The accuracy of the total is consequently better than the accuracy of any one estimate.

### Dividing and Conquering

Break large tasks into smaller tasks to improve estimating accuracy. For example, break Design Software into several smaller tasks. These could be Interview Users, Review Current System, Create Schema, Write Specifications, Prototype, and so on. On some projects, you may improve results by using the next smaller unit of measure—use minutes rather than hours, hours rather than days, days rather than weeks, or weeks rather than months.

Why not just flip a coin? Well, essentially you are. Pick heads or tails, flip the coin, and see what happens. On any one toss, your call is going to be one hundred percent right or one hundred percent wrong. The more you flip the coin and WAG the result, the more your actual results will approach your estimated fifty-fifty point.

If you are estimating a long series of tasks (twenty or more), it is likely that you will be over on some and under on some. Taken as a group, your accuracy is typically quite good. In other words, accuracy improves as the number of individual estimates goes up. Statisticians call this the law of large numbers. Non-statisticians call it the law of averages. In project management, we call it the WAG.

## SWAGing It

Add to a WAG one reference point, one similar experience, or one piece of data and your estimate greatly improves. We describe such an estimate as a SWAG, a scientific wildly aimed guess.

Although SWAGs are far from perfect, their accuracy is much better than WAGs. Over a series of estimates you have the law of averages balancing the individual errors. In addition, you now have at least one bit of information, experience, or data to guide your estimate. Consequently, SWAGs are generally far more accurate than WAGs.

The moral of the story is simple. Slight improvements in information can make large improvements in accuracy. If you can't use history, use references. If you can't SWAG it, then WAG it.

The last two methods are actual estimating methods that can use history, references, WAGs or SWAGs as their data basis. Let's take a look at how they work.

## The Delphi Approach

In Greek mythology, the Delphi Oracle was able to see into the future, answering all questions with ease. But rather than using a crystal ball, the Delphi Oracle relied on his ability to glean answers from the same people who were asking the questions. He used his abilities of query and observation to arrive at miraculously accurate conclusions.

Today, adept project managers use this same approach when faced with a difficult estimating task. Start by bringing together an appropriate collection of experts (called a cross-functional team). Ask each expert to independently estimate the task in question. Next, have each expert reveal their estimate and explain their reasoning to the group. Then with the benefit of one another's rationale, make another round of estimates.

Project Pitfall

### Building Better Estimates

A team member's willingness to accurately estimate task durations dramatically decreases in climates of fear or distrust. New teams are typically less trusting of one another than are mature teams. Therefore, they can't estimate as accurately as mature teams. For better estimates, build a climate of trust and respect. Let your team know that you expect an equal number of high and low estimates. Too many high estimates makes it look like they're padding. Too many low estimates makes it look like they're in over their heads. The goal is to minimize the estimate's variance to actuals. Posting estimates and actuals in the conference room sends a strong message that accuracy counts.

Usually, the second or third round reveals a strong consensus in opinion. And that consensus takes into consideration all the expertise and experience of your cross-functional team. The Delphi approach is part mythology, part science, and part statistics. And although it is somewhat cumbersome and time consuming, a highly skilled team can provide surprisingly accurate estimates in complex, multifaceted situations.

Okay, that pretty well covers the superstition and skill methods. I've saved the best for last. Here comes the science and fourth-grade math.

# PERT Analysis

PERT analysis uses the power of statistics and probability theory to improve the accuracy of your estimates. But don't be alarmed, it all boils down to fourth-grade math. And better yet, Microsoft Project 2000 does all the math!

Program Evaluation and Review Technique (PERT) was created to help the Navy manage the design and building of its nuclear submarine fleet. At that time, no one had ever powered a submarine with a nuclear reactor. Nor had anyone ever built the submarine's internal systems and then built a hull around it all.

Before this project, submarine hulls were completely assembled, then all the equipment was squeezed in through small hatches. Reversing this procedure was a radical approach. It created a high degree of uncertainty with individual task duration estimates. A better way of dealing with this uncertainty was needed.

To solve this dilemma, the Navy brought together the best minds from every area of expertise. Eventually, this cross-functional team of scientists, ship builders, engineers, statisticians, project managers, and others perfected this widely used estimating method we call PERT.

**Better Estimates Make Better Decisions**

Accurate task durations allow you to create accurate project schedules. Accurate project schedules reveal hidden resources such as slack and float (flexibility of starting or finishing a task). Remember, the better you plan, the easier it is to manage the project.

Although it sounds complicated, it really isn't. All you have to do is make three duration estimates for each task: an optimistic, a pessimistic, and a most likely (Microsoft Project calls this the expected duration). The optimistic estimate approximates the shortest expected duration over a theoretical one hundred trials. It answers the question, what is the fastest this task would be accomplished if it were undertaken 100 times? In a like manner the pessimistic and most likely durations are estimated.

Notice that the most likely duration is not necessarily a midpoint between the optimistic and pessimistic values. It can and frequently does tend toward either extreme. PERT's weighted average methodology allows for this and returns the duration estimate where the value is midway in likelihood.

For example, consider a task with 12 hours, 32 hours, and 100 hours as the optimistic, most likely and pessimistic values. PERT weighs the most likely value with four times the probability of either extreme. The PERT Estimate = ([Pessimistic + Optimistic + {4×Most Likely}])/6. In this case, PERT returns an estimated duration of 40 hours. The PERT estimate is midway in probability (40 hours), not midway in distance (44 hours), between the two extremes (12 and 100 hours). Because of this central tendency and the ability to take into consideration the extreme (although unlikely) possibilities, PERT is your most accurate method of estimating durations. Projects with as few as 20 tasks can benefit from this approach.

The more you're dealing with uncertainties in your project, the more you should consider using PERT. Microsoft Project 2000 makes it fast and easy, as you will soon see.

### The Expert Use of PERT

Program Evaluation Review Technique (PERT) was created to manage high-risk projects with a heavy research and development content. Now that computers manage the probability calculations so easily, PERT duration estimating is favored by many astute project managers even on smaller projects.

## Entering Task Time Estimates

Before you enter task durations, you should have already decided what tasks are necessary to complete the project. If you haven't done so, enter these tasks now. For complete instructions refer to Chapter 4. Notice that as each task is entered, the duration defaults to "1 day?"

### *Entering a Duration for Each Task*

Whether your duration estimates are based on a historical, reference, WAG, SWAG, or Delphi approach, it's easy to enter them into Microsoft Project 2000. From the Gantt Chart View, as shown in Figure 5.1, replace the default "1 day?" with your estimate. You may use minutes, hours, weeks, or months. Duration units may be indicated as shown in Table 5.1.

### Table 5.1 Duration Units and Their Abbreviations

| Unit | Abbreviation |
| --- | --- |
| minute | m, min, minute, or minutes |
| hour | h, hr, hrs, hour, or hours |
| day | d, dy, day, or days |
| week | w, wk, wks, week, or weeks |
| month | mo, mon, mons, month, or months |

**Figure 5.1**

*Replace the default "1 day?" with your estimated duration. Keep the "?" to show that it has not been finalized.*

| | | Task Name | Duration | Apr 9, '00 | Apr 16, '00 | Apr 23, '00 |
|---|---|---|---|---|---|---|
| 1 | | ⊟ Site Work Phase | 5 days? | | | |
| 2 | | ⊟ Earth Work | 3 days | | | |
| 3 | | Clear Vegetation | 12 hrs | | | |
| 4 | | Stockpile Topsoil | 16 hrs | | | |
| 5 | | Excavate for Retaining Wall | 3 days | | | |
| 6 | | Backfill Retaining Wall | 1 day | | | |
| 7 | | ⊟ Utilities | 5 days | | | |
| 8 | | Sanitary Sewer | 3 days | | | |
| 9 | | Storm Drains | 5 days | | | |
| 10 | | Water Service | 2 days | | | |
| 11 | | Natural Gas | 2 days | | | |
| 12 | | Electrical Service | 2 days | | | |
| 13 | | ⊟ Concrete Work | 3 days? | | | |
| 14 | | Footers | 1 day? | | | |
| 15 | | Pour Retaining Walls | 1 day? | | | |
| 16 | | Wall Curing Time | 5 edays | | | |
| 17 | | ⊟ Final Site Work | 1 day? | | | |
| 18 | | Curb and Gutter | 1 day? | | | |
| 19 | | Pavement | 1 day? | | | |
| 20 | | Landscaping | 1 day? | | | |
| 21 | | **Site Work Completed** | 0 days | ◆ 4/12 | | |

Project automatically calculates summary task durations. Their duration is equal to the difference between the earliest start date and the latest finish date of any task within the summary's subsection. Because we have not yet sequenced task workflow, the summary task durations are equal to the longest tasks in their subsections.

**Speak Like a Geek**

## What's That "?" All About?

The "?" associated with each default duration is Microsoft Project's estimated duration indicator. It's purpose is to facilitate team communications. When seeing this indicator, a team member is supposed to assume that the duration value is tentative—that a final estimate has not yet been established. This can be confusing. Because all durations are estimated durations, Microsoft Project 2000 could have come up with a better name for this indicator. I'll refer to it as the tentative estimate. To avoid confusion with your team members, I recommend that you do the same.

## Using PERT Analysis to Estimate Time

PERT estimates are equally simple to enter into the program. But before you proceed, it is always a good idea to save a copy of your project file. Then, from the **View** menu, point to **Toolbars** and click **PERT Analysis.** When the Pert Analysis toolbar appears, click the **PERT Entry Sheet** button. For each task, enter an **Optimistic, Expected** (the most likely), and **Pessimistic** value. Do not leave any of these three fields blank. The **Tab** key quickly moves you between fields when entering data in the PERT Entry Sheet view. Completed PERT estimates are illustrated in Figure 5.2.

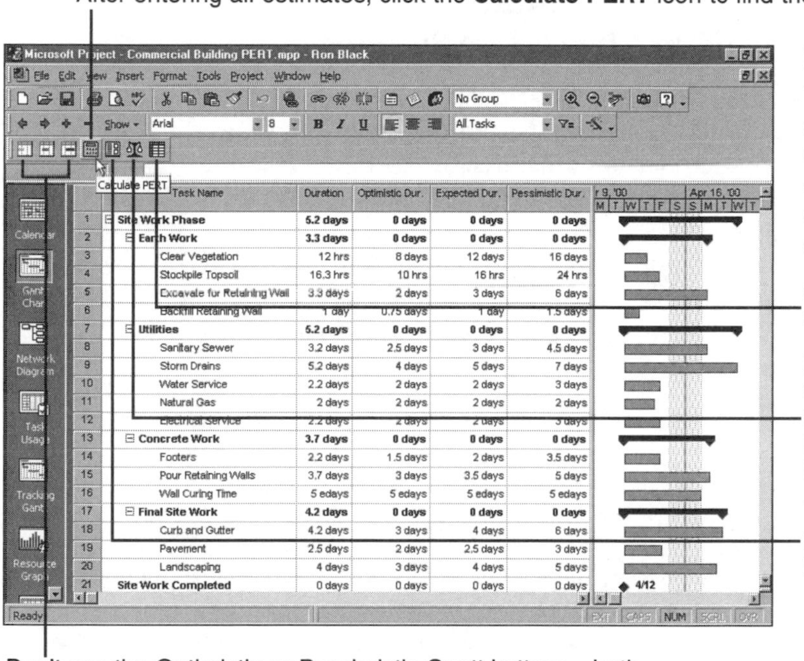

After entering all estimates, click the **Calculate PERT** icon to find the Duration.

**Figure 5.2**

*The PERT Entry Sheet allows you to enter the Optimistic, Pessimistic, and Expected (most likely) durations estimates as in a spreadsheet.*

Click for the PERT Entry Sheet view.

Don't change the PERT weightings from Optimistic = 1, Expected = 4, and Pessimistic = 1.

The PERT Entry Form provides an alternative method of data entry.

Don't use the Optimistic or Pessimistic Gantt buttons—both calculations result in inappropriate durations.

Alternatively, you may enter the estimates one at a time, using a form, as shown in Figure 5.3. The PERT Entry form pops up when you click the icon on the PERT Analysis toolbar.

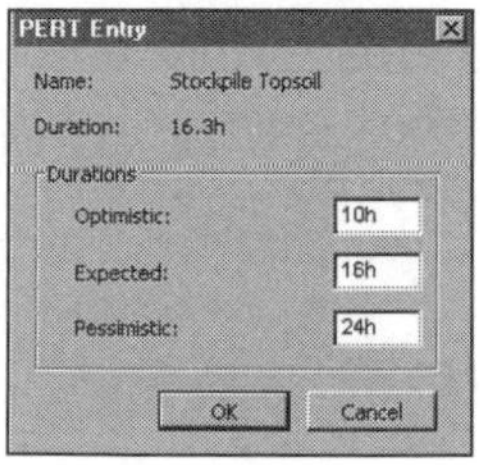

**Figure 5.3**

*The PERT Entry form provides an alternative method of entering duration estimates.*

71

After entering all the task estimates, click **Calculate PERT**. The weighted average esti-mate is calculated and placed into the Duration field. Congratulations! You now have an excellent set of time durations. Furthermore, you've overcome estimating fear and superstition with science, skill, and fourth-grade math! And, you're almost ready to create a project schedule.

*Project Pitfall*

### Don't Touch That Button!

Resist the temptation to calculate a project end date based on the pessimistic or the optimistic values. In PERT analysis, the central tendency toward the most likely duration (the Expected Duration in Microsoft Project 2000) is strong. The likelihood to experience either the pessimistic or optimistic extremes is weak. If you are not well-versed in statistical theory, it is easy to read too much into the Optimistic and Pessimistic project duration extremes. Both extremes are less likely than flipping a coin a hundred times in a row and having it land heads up every time. Rather, rely on the calculated estimate and carefully consider the few key tasks that could greatly influence the overall project duration.

## How Project 2000 Handles Project Time and Calendar Time

Before the days of Microsoft Project, project managers would laboriously calculate task and project durations as if every day were a working day. Then as the project was kicked off, each of these project days were placed on the organization's working schedule. In this way, holidays, work days, and shifts were factored into the schedule.

Microsoft Project handles all this for you. By default, each day consists of 8 hours, each week is 40 hours and each month is 20 working days in length. Workdays are Monday through Friday, from 8:00 a.m. to 5:00 p.m.. If you need to change these set-tings to match yours (or if you want to start working 20 hours a week instead of 40), from the **Tools** menu select **Options** and then click the **Calendar** tab (see Figure 5.4).

Some task durations occur during nonworking time. For example, consider a concrete retaining wall that must cure five days before being backfilled. If it was poured at 3:00 p.m. on a Wednesday, it would be ready for backfilling in five days, Sunday at 3:00 p.m.. It's completion is not dependent on the organization's normal work hours. To allow for situations like this, place an "e" at the beginning of the duration unit, for elapsed duration. These notations are shown in Table 5.2.

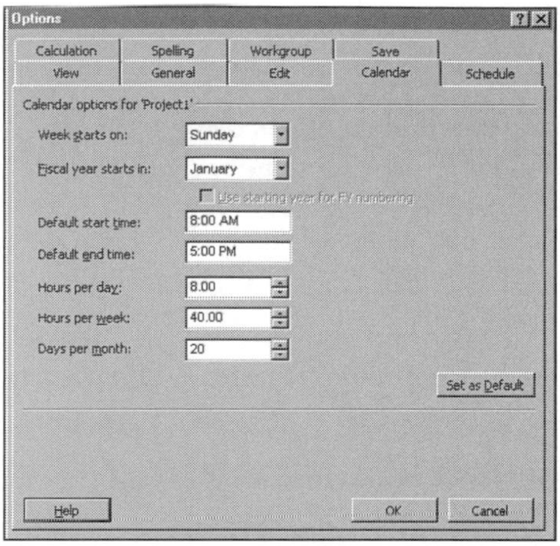

**Figure 5.4**
*Change these default workday settings to match your standard working days and hours.*

## Table 5.2    Elapsed Duration Units

| Unit | Description |
| --- | --- |
| emin | elapsed minute |
| ehr | elapsed hour |
| eday | elapsed day |
| ewk | elapsed week |

When you enter an elapsed duration, Microsoft Project 2000 ignores work calendars, workday settings, weekends, and holidays. Duration is continuous, based on a 24-hour, 7-day week. This is illustrated earlier in Figure 5.1. Notice how the five-day task, Storm Drains, begins on Wednesday, April 12, 2000 and is completed seven calendar or five working days later on Tuesday, April 19. The five elapsed day task, Wall Curing Time, begins on the same day, both five calendar and five working days later on Monday, April 17.

The next step is to establish the sequence of work order. So when you're ready, I'll meet you in Chapter 6.

## The Least You Need to Know

➤ Accurate duration estimates are essential to establishing how long the project will take to complete and when a project must be started in order to finish on time.

➤ Accurate duration estimates reveal where your project's schedule is flexible and where it isn't.

➤ Your ability to manage a project successfully increases with the accuracy of your duration estimates.

➤ In projects of 20 or more tasks, PERT estimating is generally the most accurate method.

# Chapter 6

# Sequencing Tasks to Fit Your Needs

**In This Chapter**

➤ Create a complete project schedule, with start and finish times for every task, using Microsoft Project 2000.

➤ Find out how long your project will take to complete.

➤ Choose the best scheduling strategy to make sure your project is completed on time.

➤ Learn how to identify and maximize the hidden resource, schedule flexibility.

➤ Find out what constraints are and how to use them to make the schedule fit your needs.

Wow! Think of all you've accomplished thus far. You've defined the project with goals and triple constraints. You've identified all the essential tasks, phases, and milestones. You've entered the work hierarchy into Microsoft Project 2000 and estimated the task durations. Your project plan has come a long way. And no doubt, so has your understanding of the project.

Now, you're plan is about to really take shape. As soon as you sequence the workflow, you'll have a project schedule! And when that's done, you'll have an excellent understanding of how long the project will take, where the schedule is flexible, and where it isn't. Your understanding of the project is about to go into warp drive!

# A Good and Simple Approach

Microsoft Project 2000 can handle many facets of even complex projects. That's good when you need it. Unfortunately, some new project managers think they must put every feature of the program to work to have a good plan. Fortunately, this is not the case.

In fact, too much effort spent pursuing pinpoint accuracy can be detrimental to your project's success. Fussing with the detail (which can never be absolutely perfect) can take your attention away from managing the project.

### Keep It Simple

To get the most out of your planning effort, do as little as possible! Of course, you need a goal, an understanding of the triple constraints, and an accurate work breakdown structure. Everything after that is a judgment call. On medium to large projects or those of high importance or risk, create an accurate schedule. If resources are scarce, add resources to your plan. If you must calculate earned value billings, add material and resource costs to the project plan. Avoid hourly task reporting when possible. Rather, estimate progress based on tasks not started (0%), started (50%), or completed (100%). In this way, you'll manage the actual accomplishment rather than the reported progress. Moreover, you'll be managing the project, not the software.

Don't let your plan get in the way of accomplishing the project! Keep your plan as simple as possible. It will be easier to understand, easier to communicate, easier to monitor, and easier to manage. Later, when you fully understand the plan's "big picture" you can always resort to greater levels of detail if you must. For now, to make your plan good, keep it simple.

## Workflow Sequence Strategies (Your Mother Was Right!)

The logic of your project's workflow and the duration of each task determine how long your project will take. The more tasks that are done at once, the sooner the project will be done. Consequently, good project managers take their mother's advice and "Never put off until later what can be done now."

### Perfect Plans Aren't

Seek success rather than perfection! Astute project planners draw a careful balance between precision and simplicity. Too much precision encumbers planning, monitoring, and decision making. Not enough precision limits the plan's effectiveness and your ability to control project progress. Accept the fact that there is always some ambiguity in a project. Make sure your time is spent on managing the project rather than managing the plan.

Therefore, the first scheduling strategy is to do everything you can, as soon as you can. In this manner, when a task takes longer than you expect, you can minimize the impact on the project's completion. On the other hand, if a task takes less time than you expect, you can use the extra time to accomplish something else.

The second scheduling strategy is to do everything you can at the same time. As long as this approach does not hinder the quality or completion of other tasks, concurrently running tasks shorten the overall project duration.

For example, consider the project of preparing a pasta dinner. While you wait for the water to a boil you can prepare the salad (two concurrent tasks). While the pasta cooks in one pan and the sauce simmers in another, and the bread warms in the oven, you can set the table (four concurrent tasks). On the other hand, some tasks need to be done individually, such as chopping the garlic—you're probably too early in the project to have anything else going, and you'd better not be distracted while handling the knife!

Generally speaking, the more tasks you run concurrently, the more scheduling flexibility you have. Schedule flexibility is a hidden resource. What if the pasta isn't ready when you are? The astute project manager would throw a load of clothes into the washer, help the oldest with his math, and stop the twins from fighting. Project managers call concurrent tasks *parallel* tasks. (Busy parents call concurrent tasks survival.)

To shorten the project and provide greater flexibility, follow your mother's advice! Do everything you can, as soon as you can.

## Finish-to-Start Dependencies

When a task can't begin or end until another task begins or ends, the workflow has a dependency. Recalling the earlier example, you can't start your sauce until you've chopped the garlic. The task that affects the dependent task is called the *predecessor* task. The fewer dependencies you have in your schedule, the fewer chances you'll have of encountering work stoppages and bottlenecks. The fewer dependencies you have in the schedule, the more tasks can run in parallel, and the shorter your project will be.

The sequence of work and the amount of time required to complete the project is largely determined by task dependency relationships (see Figure 6.1).

**Figure 6.1**

*Project duration depends on task durations and dependencies.*

Parallel tasks shorten the project's duration.

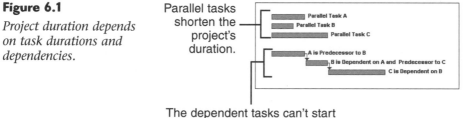

The dependent tasks can't start until their predecessors finish.

The most common task relationship is when a task (the dependent) can't start until some other task (the predecessor) has finished. This is called a *finish-to-start dependency*. The last two tasks in Figure 6.1 have finish-to-start dependencies with their predecessor tasks. Consider again your pasta dinner project. The dependent task, cooking the pasta, can't begin until its predecessor task, boil water, has been accomplished.

In most projects, the majority of all task dependencies can be described with the finish-to-start relationship. Use it unless it obviously violates workflow logic. If you need to, you can change the relationship to a more appropriate one later. For now, go with as simple a workflow as possible.

## Going with the Flow of Dependencies

As you enter task dependencies into Microsoft Project 2000, it creates a workflow logic link. The tasks are scheduled based on this link, starting as soon as possible. The easiest way to schedule is to list your workflow logic (as described with the dependent tasks predecessor) in the table of the Gantt Chart view, and let the program do its job.

Task relationships that aren't obvious are easier to see when the Gantt Chart begins to take shape. These relationships can be modified later, as we better understand the project's workflow. Now's the time to go with the flow! Let's try it out.

There are multiple ways to enter dependencies. It's easiest to see your cause (the dependency) and effect (the schedule), in the Gantt Chart view. Drag the vertical divider to the right until the Predecessor column is visible. To provide more working space, hide unused columns by right-clicking the column head and selecting Hide Column.

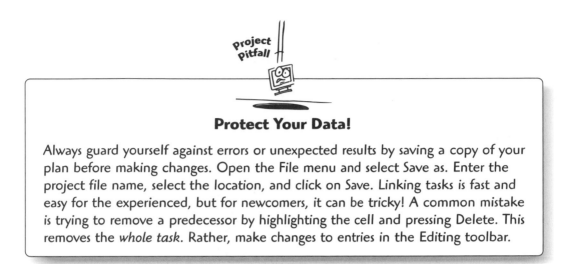

### Protect Your Data!

Always guard yourself against errors or unexpected results by saving a copy of your plan before making changes. Open the File menu and select Save as. Enter the project file name, select the location, and click on Save. Linking tasks is fast and easy for the experienced, but for newcomers, it can be tricky! A common mistake is trying to remove a predecessor by highlighting the cell and pressing Delete. This removes the *whole task*. Rather, make changes to entries in the Editing toolbar.

Begin at the top of your task list and consider what task must immediately precede the current task. If there are none, leave the column blank. Place the predecessor's ID number into the Predecessor field. If more than one predecessor must immediately precede this task, separate their ID numbers with a comma. A partially completed plan is shown in Figure 6.2.

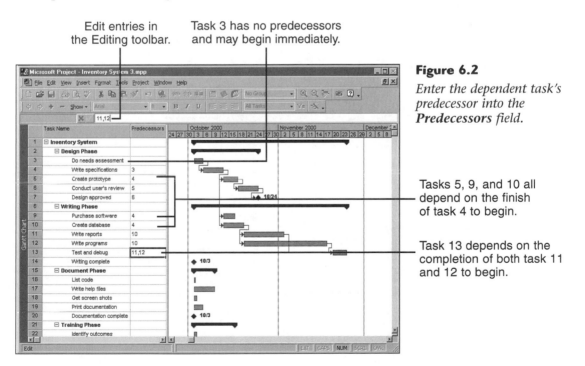

**Figure 6.2**

*Enter the dependent task's predecessor into the **Predecessors** field.*

The Gantt Chart instantly shows the changes you have made to the schedule. The dependencies are shown with an arrow between each task by default. If your chart doesn't show the dependency links, choose **Format**, and then **Layout** from the menu bar. Select either of the linking arrow options as shown in Figure 6.3.

**Figure 6.3**

*Task dependency links can be modified in the Layout dialog box.*

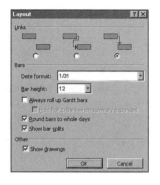

You may also link tasks by clicking the predecessor taskbar and dragging to the dependent task. A window pops up to ensure the results are what you want, as shown in Figure 6.4. When you release the mouse button, the dependent task jumps to its new location. This process can be somewhat confusing when you first try it. Check the logic of your new workflow carefully!

**Figure 6.4**

*To create task dependency, click the predecessor task and drag to the dependent task.*

When dragging to link tasks, a text box pops up to describe the new dependency.

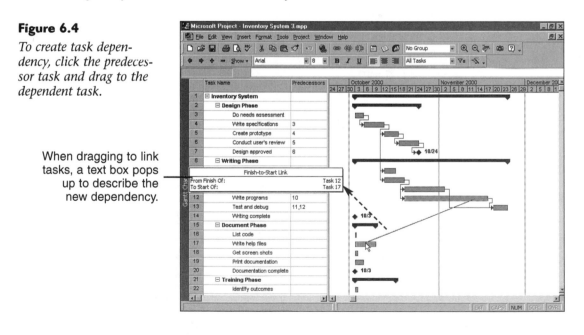

As soon as you have entered all necessary task dependencies, your schedule is complete. You should now review it for workflow, overall project duration, and possible work bottlenecks. To examine a link more closely, hover your pointer over a link until the description appears. This pop-up description is shown in Figure 6.5.

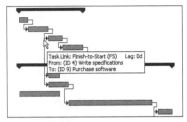

**Figure 6.5**

*Each dependency link can be checked by pointing at the link until a description box appears.*

The person who coined the phrase, "A picture is worth a thousand words," must have been a project manager! Our understanding of the project dramatically increases as the work sequence is shown in a network diagram—in this case, a Gantt chart. Chances are you'll want to make a few adjustments in your schedule. If you must, you can tune it up with the following tactics.

# When Simple Isn't Good Enough

Not all relationships can be adequately represented with finish-to-start dependencies. You may need to use other relationships to get the schedule you want. These include the start-to-start, start-to-finish, and finish-to-finish task relationships. All of these describe special kinds of parallel task relationships, as you shall see.

## Start-to-Start Dependencies

Consider the project of building a high-speed commuter rail line between two cities. Using a finish-to-start dependency, you would have to wait for the entire roadbed to be finished before placing the first tie!

It would obviously be better to give the crew preparing the roadbed a head start on the tie placing crew. Then as soon as the tie crew had a head start, the rail placing crew could begin. Roadbed, ties, and rails should all run concurrently, with a slight staggering of the starts. This type of dependency is a start-to-start dependency with a time lag. The start of the dependent task lags behind the start of the predecessor task, as shown in Figure 6.6.

To speed the completion even more, you might decide to build the line from both ends at once. The east and west construction teams could then work in parallel on the converging lines. (Okay, so I had to sneak a geometry pun in there. You still get the point, right?)

**Figure 6.6**

*When using a start-to-start dependency, adjust when the dependent task will begin with lag time.*

## Finish-to-Finish

In the finish-to-finish relationship, the dependent task can't finish until the predecessor task finishes. This sounds like a classic case of, "Which came first, the chicken or the egg?" It becomes more apparent if you use the example of scrambling a dozen eggs for breakfast. You can't finish scrambling the eggs until you have finished cracking them and putting them in the pan. If you used a standard finish-to-start and cracked all the eggs before you began scrambling, you'd risk burning the first egg or two. Okay, okay so you don't like to cook. Consider the project tasks in Figure 6.7. A new fiber optic cable has been installed in a building. The project manager knew they could begin testing two weeks after the installation begins. However, the finish of testing is dependent on when installation finishes.

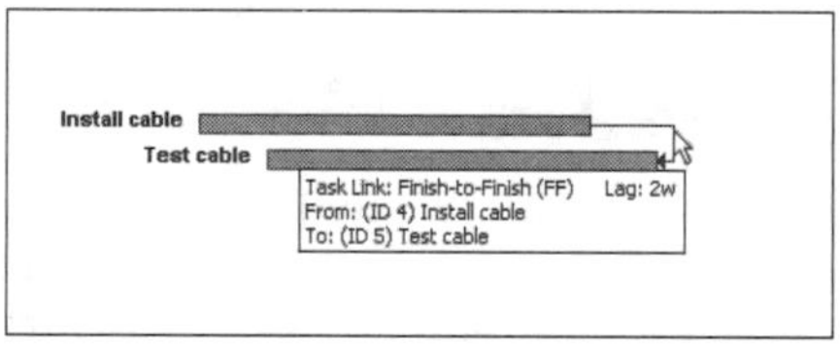

*Finish-to-finish dependencies are useful in some situations. Use lag to off-set the scheduled finish.*

## Start-to-Finish

Another occasionally helpful dependency is the start-to-finish. This is when the dependent task can't finish until its predecessor has at least started.

Consider the project of installing new equipment on several assembly lines. Training the operators could not be completed until the predecessor, install new equipment, has at least been started. The operators need at least one machine to train on. This is illustrated in Figure 6.8.

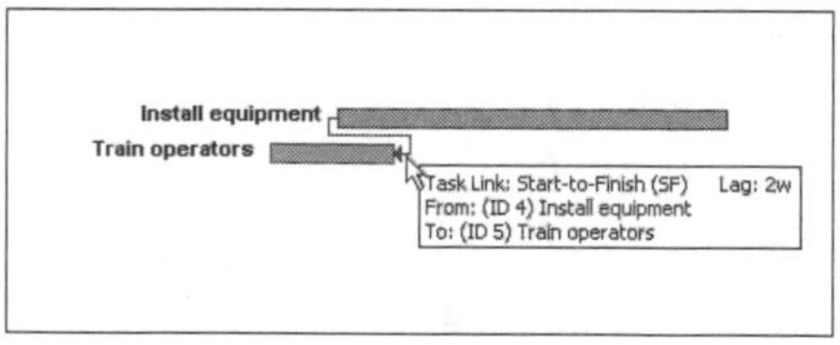

**Figure 6.8**

*Start-to-finish tasks are rare, but great when you need them. Use lag time to vary task overlap.*

## *Using the Task Information Dialog Box*

To change a task's dependency, predecessors, or lag time, use the Task Information dialog box. Right-click the task, click **Task Information**, and choose the **Predecessors** tab as shown in Figure 6.9. Lag time can be set in duration time units or as a percentage.

The default value
is finish-to-start.

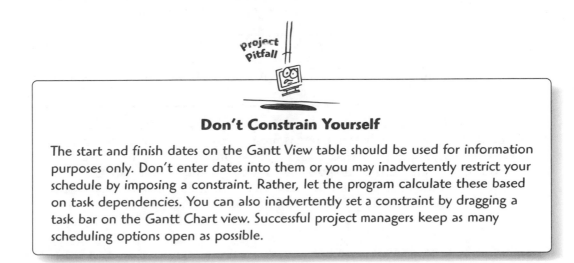

**Figure 6.9**

*The Task Information dialog box gives you complete control of task durations, dependencies, predecessors, and lag time.*

Lag time
adjusts
the
task's
overlap.

In addition to setting task dependencies, there are eight powerful constraints to make sure your tasks are scheduled the way you want. These are described next.

# More Good and Simple Tricks

Let's suppose we can't use our mother's or Microsoft's default scheduling method, and start every task as soon as possible (ASAP). Sometimes we just have to start or finish tasks with some other logic. In project planning we call this logic a *constraint*.

Project
Pitfall

### Don't Constrain Yourself

The start and finish dates on the Gantt View table should be used for information purposes only. Don't enter dates into them or you may inadvertently restrict your schedule by imposing a constraint. Rather, let the program calculate these based on task dependencies. You can also inadvertently set a constraint by dragging a task bar on the Gantt Chart view. Successful project managers keep as many scheduling options open as possible.

The eight constraints available in Microsoft Project 2000 are shown in Table 6.1. All of these except As Soon As Possible (ASAP) and As Late As Possible (ALAP) severely restrict the schedule's flexibility (and flexibility is good). Use the others only when you absolutely must.

## Table 6.1    Using Constraints to Restrict the Schedule

| Constraint | Description |
| --- | --- |
| ASAP (As Soon As Possible) | This is the default constraint for projects scheduled from a start date. The schedule remains as flexible as possible. |
| ALAP (As Late As Possible) | This is the default constraint for projects scheduled from a finish date. The schedule remains as flexible as possible. |
| FNLT (Finish No Later Than) | Use for tasks which must finish on or before a date. Useful for including contractual obligations into a schedule. Automatically used when a finish date is typed in for a task in projects scheduled from a finish date. |
| SNLT (Start No Later Than) | Used to schedule tasks around a latest possible start date. Automatically used when a start date is typed in for a task in projects scheduled from a finish date. |
| FNET (Finish No Earlier Than) | Used for tasks which must not be finished any earlier than a certain date. Automatically applied on projects scheduled from a starting date when a finish date is typed in. |
| SNET (Start No Earlier Than) | Prevents a task from beginning before a certain date. Automatically set when a task start date is entered on projects scheduled from a project start date. |
| MSO (Must Start On) | Restricts the task to a single starting date regardless of dependencies. |
| MFO (Must Finish On) | Restricts a task to being completed on a specific date. |

Don't anchor tasks with constraints unless you must. When you must use a constraint, consider carefully which one is most appropriate. Then as shown in Figure 6.10, right-click any task, select **Task Information**, and choose the **Advanced** tab. Select the constraint from the pull-down menu. Then enter the date in the **Constraint date** box. A small calendar icon in the Indicator column shows that your constraint is set. If it has a red dot, the constraint may be very restrictive.

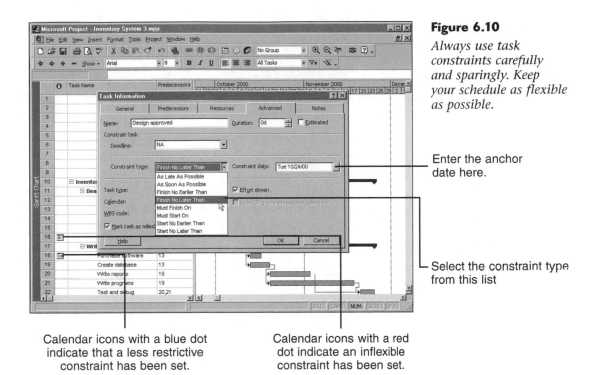

**Figure 6.10**

*Always use task constraints carefully and sparingly. Keep your schedule as flexible as possible.*

Enter the anchor date here.

Select the constraint type from this list

Calendar icons with a blue dot indicate that a less restrictive constraint has been set.

Calendar icons with a red dot indicate an inflexible constraint has been set.

To make the project easier to manage and more likely to be successful, follow your mother's and my advice:

➤ Start everything as soon as you can.

➤ Keep workflow logic as simple as possible.

➤ Use constraints carefully, and only if you must.

➤ Keep your plan as flexible as possible.

➤ To make a good schedule, make it good and simple!

**The Least You Need to Know**

➤ Projects are normally scheduled for completion in the shortest possible timeframe. The schedule depends on task durations, sequence of workflow, and constraints placed upon the tasks.

➤ Of the four task dependency relationships, the finish-to-start is the most frequently used and easiest to manage.

➤ Using parallel tasks helps to accomplish the project in a shorter timeframe.

➤ There are eight available constraint types in Microsoft Project 2000. These can be selected or in some cases they will automatically engage. Care must be taken in their use.

➤ Attempting to control a project too closely can result in reducing your managerial effectiveness.

➤ Experienced project managers try to maintain as much schedule flexibility as possible.

# Chapter 7

# Getting a Handle on Your Resources, Costs, and Budgets

---

## In This Chapter

➤ Create a resource list of people, equipment, facilities, and material

➤ Customize calendars for your project and resources

➤ Create resource groups to speed reporting and tracking

➤ Set pay rates, costs, and availability for each resource

---

You can't do it all alone! It takes people, equipment, and material to accomplish any significant project. And the larger the project, the harder it is to coordinate and control the vast resources you need to get the job done. Microsoft Project 2000 offers many powerful features that can help you control your resources and use them most effectively.

Setting and tracking resources in your project allows you to accomplish several important things:

➤ You can schedule according to resource availability, in addition to work sequence and task duration.

➤ You can identify work bottlenecks caused by resource limitations.

➤ You can budget and track costs of the entire project, each task, and each resource.

➤ You can distribute workloads fairly throughout a team.

Before you can put Microsoft Project 2000 to work coordinating resources, it needs to know what resources are available, when they work, and how much they cost. You'll set up your resources in this chapter. Later, in Chapter 8, "The Resourceful Use of Resources," you'll assign resources to the project tasks.

# Defining Resources and Costs

The first step in setting up your resource list is to decide how much detail is best for your project. You may want to enter each member of your team by their name as a resource. You could alternately enter each of the job titles, such as Programmer I, Senior Analyst, Electrician, or Apprentice Electrician. Whenever possible, opt for the least restrictive choice. Remember that unneeded precision places a heavy burden on you and doesn't necessarily improve your control.

There are four basic types of resources: people, facilities, equipment, and materials. People, facilities, and equipment resources have similar parameters, so Microsoft project combines them into a category called *work resources*. Here you would find such items as scientists, carpenters, laboratories, air compressors, and electron microscopes. In the material resources category you would find all the consumable goods used to accomplish a task. These might include concrete, nails, chip sets, and gallium arsenide wafers (or in my case, iced mochas and pistachios).

### Keep It Good and Simple!

Keep your plan as simple as possible! Don't assign and track project resources unless you must. The more detail you track, the less time you'll have for other important project management duties. Just because Microsoft Project 2000 allows you to control resources with precision doesn't mean you should. It's better to execute a good plan now than a perfect plan later.

### Spreading the Numbers Around

Don't try to control too many cost details in Microsoft Project 2000. It's primarily a scheduling system, not an estimating, bill-of-material, or labor-control program. For these tasks, you will discover that attaching spreadsheets is frequently more convenient and effective. And when your team members are spreadsheet users, you can delegate some of these tasks to them. For additional information, see Chapter 20, "Sharing Information with Other Programs."

## Creating a Resource List

To create a resource list, select **Resource Sheet** from the **View** menu. Point to **Table** (also in the View menu) and click **Entry**, as shown in Figure 7.1. Each of the columns of the resource sheet is described in Table 7.1. Notice that many fields have pull-down menus to make data entry fast and easy. You can see an example resource sheet in Figure 7.2.

**Figure 7.1**

*Open the Resource Sheet from the View menu.*

## Table 7.1    Resource Sheet Columns

| Column | Description |
| --- | --- |
| Indicator | Column used to alert you to special information. A note icon indicates additional comments are available in the resource dialog box. These may include spreadsheets, pictures, documents, or other items associated with this resource. Resource overallocations are indicated here with a caution sign icon. |
| Resource Name | Text or numbers used to identify the resource. The name should be distinct from all other resource names. For example, the name may be an individual (such as Bill Smith), a type of resource (electrician), a job title (senior analyst), a department (accounting), or a vendor (Good and Fast Company). |
| Type | Select either work or material as the type of resource to allow Microsoft Project to correctly calculate costs and usage. (For example, if the type of resource is *material*, Project ignores calendar restrictions because material items are theoretically always available.) |
| Material Label | For material items, enter the unit of measure for costing, such as each, foot, meter, ton, cubic yard, kilogram, and so on. |
| Initials | Add or edit the initials to provide a space-saving name for use on Gantt charts. |

*continues*

## Table 7.1   Continued

| Column | Description |
| --- | --- |
| Group | Enter a group name to allow filtering and reporting by groups. The resource may be added to more than one group by separating each group name with a comma. |
| Max. Units | Enter a percentage to indicate how much of this resource is available for the project. The default is 100%, but it may range from 0% to 6,000,000,000%. One full-time programmer would be indicated with 100%. If the programmer is only available for this project one-quarter of her time, enter 25%. Five full-time available programmers are shown as 500%. |
| Std. rate | This is the cost per unit of the resource. The default work unit is per hour (h), but year (y), week (w), day (d), or minute (m) may also be used. Simply type in the rate, a forward slash, and then the unit abbreviation. For example, 45,000/y ($45,000.00 per year) or 1,500/d ($1500.00 per day). Microsoft Project converts all amounts to an hourly rate for calculations, using a 52-week year and 40-hour week. These defaults may be changed in the Options dialog box. |
| Ovt. Rate | Enter the overtime rate for the resource in this column. If left zero, no charges will accrue for overtime work. Be careful! This may (or may not) be appropriate for salaried employees who are not paid overtime. |
| Cost/Use | This is a one-time charge for the resource. It may be used in addition to the standard rate and overtime rate. It accrues each time a work resource is used and only once when assigned to material resources. |
| Accrue At | This selection allows you to change when the program charges the resource to the task. The default is prorated, so the cost is accrued on a percentage of completion basis. You may also select **Start** if, for example, a vendor must be paid upon arrival. Select **End** if the vendor will be paid upon completion. |
| Base Calendar | There are three default base calendars in Microsoft Project 2000: Standard, Night, and 24 hours. You may set up other base calendars if your project uses other work shifts. |
| Code | You may place any text or numbers in this column. A frequent use is to enter accounting codes for integration with other applications. |

Alternately, you may add new resources in the Gantt Chart entry table view. This trick is especially useful when you are attaching resources to tasks (see Chapter 8) and you realize the resource you need is not yet listed on the Resource Sheet. Simply enter the new resource in the task's **Resource Name** column. Be sure to go back to the Resource Sheet to enter complete resource costs and availability information.

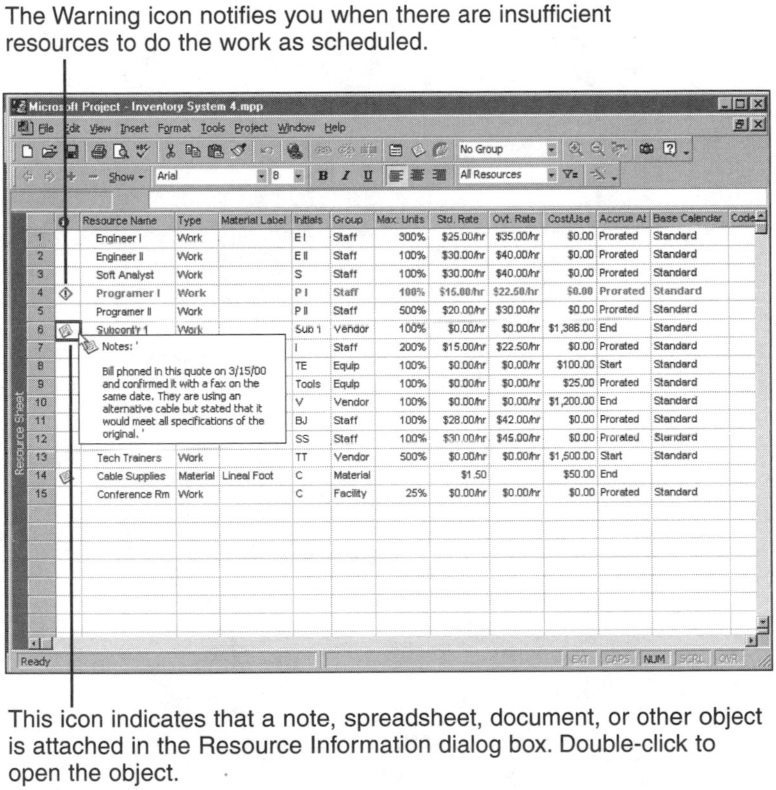

The Warning icon notifies you when there are insufficient resources to do the work as scheduled.

**Figure 7.2**

*The Resource Sheet provides a spreadsheet-like table for easy data entry.*

This icon indicates that a note, spreadsheet, document, or other object is attached in the Resource Information dialog box. Double-click to open the object.

If you have more than one project that uses the same resources, they don't have to be entered all over again. Rather, you can share them with a resource pool. To learn more about resource pools, go to Chapter 17, "Too Many Projects, Too Little Time."

Resources may be customized further in the Resource Information box. Right-click anywhere in the Resource Sheet and select **Resource Information** from the resulting pop-up menu. A dialog box appears, as shown in Figure 7.3. This dialog box contains several tabs for date entry, including the Costs tab shown in Figure 7.4.

Allows you to send email messages from
within Microsoft Project. See Chapter 19,
"Communicating with Teams via Email."

**Figure 7.3**
*Some resource information
can be accessed only in
the dialog box.*

Allows project team members
to communicate among one
another via email or the Web

Limits the dates a
resource may be used

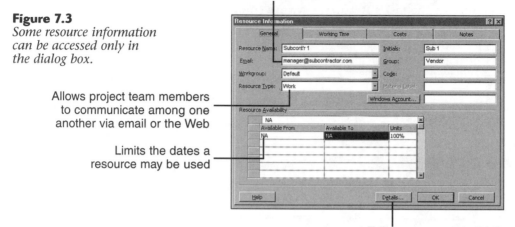

Edit resource contact information in
your email address book.

**Figure 7.4**
*Future changes in resource
costs may be entered under
the Costs tab in the Resource
Information dialog box.*

Alternate rate tables
may be used.

Enter the date the
new rate takes effect.

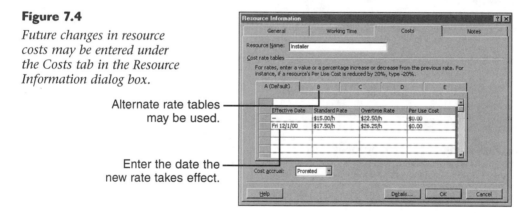

## Using Fixed Costs

Another method of adding costs to your project schedule is by entering a fixed cost
to each task. These costs are not dependent on changes in work durations. Fixed costs
may be used in addition to resource costs. Any fixed cost will be added to the
resource costs to calculate total cost for the task.

To enter a fixed cost, on the **View** menu click **Gantt Chart**. Again on the **View**
menu, point to **Table** and click **Cost**. Select the task for which you want to set a
fixed cost, and type a cost value in the **Fixed Cost** field. Use the **Fixed Cost
Accrual** field to control whether costs will be realized at the beginning of the task
or prorated over its duration.

# Calendars, Resources, and Time to Ponder

Creating a project plan and scheduling tasks, resources, and costs requires a robust understanding of when each item is needed and available. Microsoft Project 2000 solves this problem by building several calendars into the program. These include standard calendars, base calendars, project calendars, and resource calendars.

Fortunately, you don't have to find space on your office walls for all these calendars! And you won't have to ponder which day you'll set aside to figure all these out, either. They're really simple after you get the hang of it. Just think of them in terms of a work calendar hierarchy. The resource calendar is based on a project calendar, which is based on a base calendar, which is based on a standard calendar. Got it? Let's take a closer look.

The standard calendar is just that, a standard annual calendar without holidays. It includes all the days of the year and all the working hours set up in three different work schedules: a standard day shift, a night shift, and a 24-hour continuos schedule. (The last one is perfect for project managers, eh?)

Of the three calendars that come with Microsoft Project 2000, the standard day shift calendar is most frequently used. It consists of an eight-hour day (8 a.m. to 5 p.m.), Monday through Friday work schedule. The night shift calendar is an eight-hour (11 p.m. to 8 a.m.), Monday through Friday work schedule. And the last one is a 24 hours a day, 365 days a year calendar. (This one is pretty much reserved for equipment, machines, robots, and people who need better union representation.)

No holidays are preset in any of these three calendars. You may add holidays or other nonworking times (such as plant shut-down periods) to each of these. If none of these calendars describes your normal working hours, create a new one by copying the most similar and editing it as shown in Figure 7.5. From the **Tools** menu, select **Change Working Time**, and then click **New** on the Change Working Time dialog box.

**Your Hidden Resource**

Flexibility is the project manager's greatest asset. There are three keys to unlocking this hidden resource: a thorough understanding of the project's work sequence; an accurate estimate of each task's duration; and a finely tuned accounting of resource availability.

Select each day you want to modify (such as national holidays or your birthday). Then click either **Nonworking time** or **Nondefault working time** to edit the day. To revert back to the original, click **Use Default**. To edit all days of the week, as shown in Figure 7.6, click on each weekday column heading while pressing **Shift**.

**Figure 7.5**

*Create new calendars for your company's standard shifts and holidays.*

**Figure 7.6**

*Edit the new calendar's working days and hours to match your company's.*

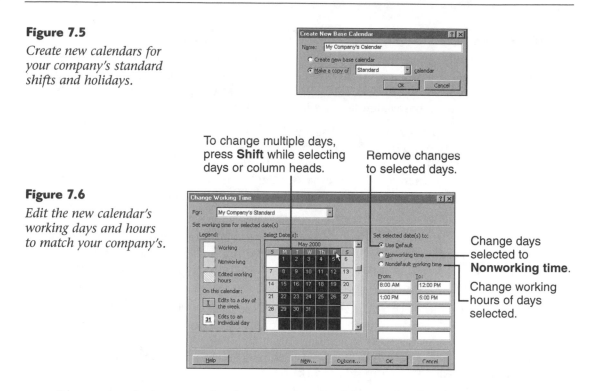

To change multiple days, press **Shift** while selecting days or column heads.

Remove changes to selected days.

Change days selected to **Nonworking time**.

Change working hours of days selected.

It's easy to select a new calendar as your project's base calendar (to make sure the company doesn't work on your birthday). First, select **Project Information** from the **Project** menu. Then click the **Calendar** option in the Project Information dialog box, as shown in Figure 7.7, and select a base calendar for your project.

**Figure 7.7**

*Set the project to your base calendar.*

Good job! Now that your project is running on your company's base calendar, you're ready to look at each of your resource's availability. In the Resource Sheet table, select the appropriate calendar from the pull-down menu in each resource's Base Calendar field. (Refer to Figure 7.2 for an example.)

If the selected base calendar doesn't perfectly match the resource's availability, customize each resource's calendar. For example, if resource Bill Johnson is going on vacation during the project, modify his calendar to prevent Microsoft Project from scheduling him then. To keep Bill happy, right-click his row in the Resource Sheet, select Resource Information, click the Working Time tab, and make your adjustments as shown in Figure 7.8.

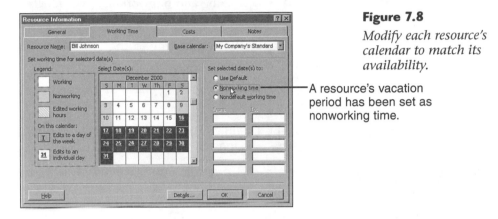

**Figure 7.8**

*Modify each resource's calendar to match its availability.*

A resource's vacation period has been set as nonworking time.

Although it is not frequently used, there is one other calendar you should be aware of—the task calendar. Occasionally it may be important to limit when a task can be undertaken. For example, if you are upgrading equipment on an assembly line, it's important not to impact normal operations. It would be useful to limit when Microsoft Project 2000 would schedule working on these machines.

You can assign any base calendar a task. In this case, the night shift calendar is appropriate. Otherwise create a new base calendar, and then from the **Gantt Chart** view select the task and right-click to open the Task Information dialog box. As shown in Figure 7.9, select the **Advanced** tab and choose a calendar from the pull-down list. Checking the **Scheduling ignores resource calendars** box overrides any resource availability restrictions.

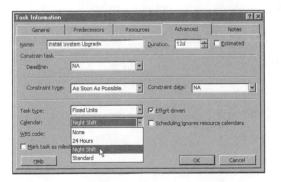

**Figure 7.9**

*Assigning a calendar to a task restricts when work may take place.*

Congratulations! You've just given Microsoft Project 2000 all the cost and calendar information it needs to successfully schedule resources and track costs. And if you were clever about it, you won't have to work on your next birthday! (There has to be some benefit in being a project manager, doesn't there?)

## The Least You Need to Know

➤ The project's base calendar sets working and nonworking times for the entire project.

➤ Individual work resources are available according to the calendar selected for them in the Resource Sheet table.

➤ Calendars are easily adjusted to match working and nonworking times of the organization, project, or individual resource.

➤ Costs for people, equipment, facilities, materials, and supplies may be entered and tracked in Microsoft Project 2000.

# Chapter 8

# The Resourceful Use of Resources

### In This Chapter

➤ Assign one or more resources, full or part time to each project task

➤ Balance workloads and responsibilities throughout the project team

➤ Identify where resources are over- and under-allocated

➤ Make the best use of your limited resources

How long a project takes to complete and the results it ultimately achieves are largely dependent on the quality and quantity of the resources used on the project. Better trained, more experienced people turn out better work. Better materials, equipment, and supplies facilitate better results.

But as you well know, project managers don't always get the quantity or quality of resources they want. Don't blame me (or your boss for that matter). Blame our old friend Adam Smith. You remember that prankster don't you, Murphy's buddy? (See the section in Chapter 2 called "Meeting Your Invisible Team Mates, Murphy and Adam Smith.") It's his laws of supply and demand that make us squeeze all the good (and a little more) out of every last penny. (That guy is, no doubt, the world's biggest cheapskate!) Thanks to Adam Smith, you'll never have all the resources you want for a project. You're forced to make do with what you have. The good news is, you're not the first one to face this dilemma. Project managers who came before you developed sound principles of resource usage and control. We call this process *resource loading* (assigning resources to tasks) and *leveling* (optimizing resource utilization).

Microsoft Project 2000 automates much of this process. In this chapter, you'll learn how to put all this power to work on your project. Trust me, some of the stuff you're about to see would amaze even Adam Smith!

# Resource Allocation—Loading

In the project management environment, it is important to make the best use of all resources. Before assigning resources to tasks, consider the following:

➤ How important is quality in this task?

➤ How critical is time in this task?

➤ Does overall project workflow depend on this task's successful and timely completion?

➤ What levels of skill are needed to accomplish this task?

➤ If more resources are applied, can the task be accomplished faster? better? safer? cheaper?

➤ Can this task be accomplished slower, later, or incrementally without an adverse effect?

You compiled a resource list in the last chapter. Now is a good time to review it with the previous list of questions fresh in your mind. Are all the skills, experience, materials, facilities, and supplies that you need available? For even the smallest of projects, this is not an easy question to answer. However, by the time you've completed loading your project with resources, you'll have a clear understanding of how your resources really stack up.

### Performance Attracts Performers

Make it easy on yourself! Get the best people. Most of your colleagues like having an accurate schedule to plan their work responsibilities around. As your reputation for well thought out, realistic, and consistently accurate schedules grows, the people who value doing a good job will seek out your projects. On the other hand there are some who prefer to lurk in the shadows, hiding their inadequacies in projects with inaccurate schedules, weak performance measures, and anemic control. Rest assured, those folks will avoid your team like the plague!

# Effort-Driven Scheduling

Project's *effort-driven* (its default method) scheduling assumes that your tasks take less time to complete if more resources are applied to them. That is, overall task duration extends or shortens as the required work is completed faster or slower. This is true for tasks that have either fixed units (also the default) or fixed work task types.

For example, you're putting a new sprinkler system into your yard. Digging the ditches (ugh!) will take one person (you) 40 hours of pick and shovel work (ouch!). You could look at this as fixed units (so many feet of ditch or yards of dirt to move) or fixed work (40 hours of digging). When you add resources (a teenager with shovel and work gloves) to a fixed unit or fixed work task type, you'll complete the total work in half of the original duration (now 20 hours). With eight equipped teenagers, you could reduce the task duration to five hours. In both cases, the units and work remained fixed as the duration changed.

Project
Pitfall

### Socking It to Durations

When calculating effort and durations, just because the math works doesn't mean the resources will! Be careful to allow for the law of diminishing returns when loading a task. For example, if it takes one person four days to knit a pair of socks, you might assume that two equally talented knitters could accomplish the job in two days. In reality, they may be slower. If neither knitter is familiar with the pattern, both have to overcome the same learning curve, thereby increasing the actual work performed! In addition to learning curves, another problem plagues the effort to shorten task durations. Every task has an optimal work force. Four knitters, no matter how qualified, can't shorten this task's duration. There isn't room for them to work.

Effort-driven scheduling works great for fixed work and fixed unit tasks.

On the other hand, some tasks do not respond to the addition of resources. These task types are called *fixed duration*. For example, hiring that same energetic teenager to help you watch new grass grow will not speed the greening of your yard. Growing grass, drying paint, and waiting for the Food and Drug Administration to approve a new formulation are all examples of fixed-duration tasks.

Effort-driven scheduling doesn't work so great for fixed-duration tasks.

Fixed-duration tasks are not as responsive to the addition or removal of resources. Therefore, while assigning resources to tasks, be sure to mark fixed-duration tasks as such. (We'll do that when we assign resources.) This helps Project 2000 do a better job scheduling tasks.

### Getting the Resources You Need

When the resources you need don't report directly to you, it's easy to come up short. Help prevent this shortfall by establishing open and frank communications with the resource holder early on. Provide an accurate schedule of when you'll need their resource and when you'll return it. When all else is equal, the person with the most credibility (an accurate plan) wins the resources. Ask for the resource holder's personal commitment, and make your communications as public as possible. They will be less likely to go back on their word when it has been publicly acknowledged. The project manager with the best planning and communication skills is the one who consistently wins the scarce resources.

## Taming the Duration, Units, and Work Formula

As the sprinkler system example demonstrated (a fixed unit or fixed work example), a task's duration is equal to the amount of work that must be done and the number of resources doing that work. Project 2000 uses the following formulas (and a little algebra) to describe this relationship:

| | |
|---|---|
| Duration = Work / Units | (Used when first assigning a resource) |
| Work = Duration × Units | (Used when reassigning a resource) |
| Units = Work / Duration | (Used when reassigning a resource) |

There is a problem, however. Anytime you change one of these numbers, Project 2000 has to choose which of the other two should be balanced. Although it does a pretty good job of this, you can't expect it to always make the right adjustment. Be alert and make sure the changes are having your desired effect.

It's best to see for yourself how this works. Open a project you can experiment with, and let's assign some resources to your tasks.

## Assigning Resources

The best way to understand how Project 2000 responds to your resource assignments is with the Task Form in combination with the Gantt Chart. This combined view is shown in Figure 8.1. To open it, select the **Gantt Chart** from the **View** menu. Now split the window by selecting **Split** from the **Window** menu. Click your mouse anywhere in the bottom pane to activate it, choose **Details** from the **Format** menu, and then click **Resources & Predecessors**. You're ready to put your team to work!

Gantt Chart view

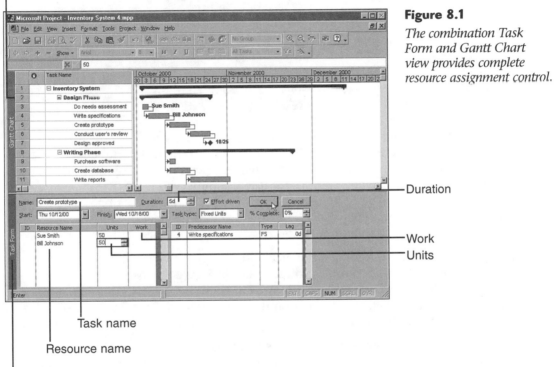

**Figure 8.1**

*The combination Task Form and Gantt Chart view provides complete resource assignment control.*

Task name

Resource name

Task Form view

At first glance this view may look intimidating, but closer inspection should reveal that you're familiar with most of the selections from use in other views. The top and bottom panes are synchronized by task. Regardless of which columns are hidden in the top pane, notice that Duration, Work, and Units are always in view in the bottom pane, right where you can keep an eye on them!

When the program is set to automatically calculate (the default), the Gantt Chart instantly responds as you assign resources and make changes. It's a good idea to use the Automatic calculation option until project size makes it unwieldy. Check this setting before you continue. From the **Tools** menu select **Options**. When the dialog box appears select the **Calculation** tab and make sure **Automatic** is selected under the Calculation options for Microsoft Project area, as shown in Figure 8.2.

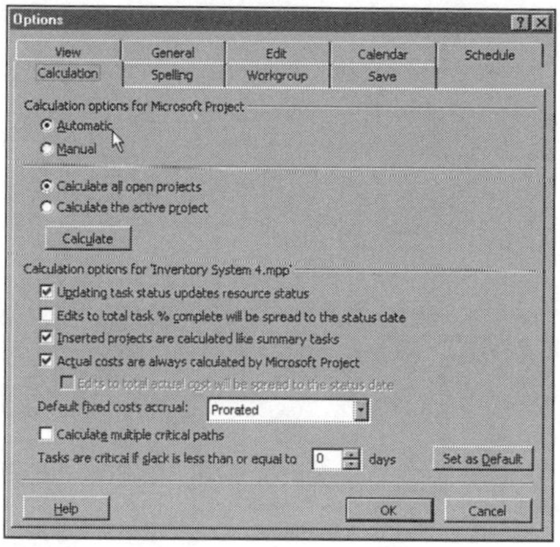

**Figure 8.2**

*To stay in control of your resource assignment changes, set the program to automatically calculate.*

To assign resources, select the task in the top pane. You may also do this with the **Next** and **Previous** buttons on the Task Form. Now, in the task form, click in the **Resource Name** field. If you've defined resources, they'll all pop up in a list. If you haven't, or if the resource you want is not listed, simply type it in. (If you add new resources here, go back to the Resource Sheet view and finish inputting rate and availability information.) It's usually best to select from the menu. This way you won't inadvertently enter the same resource with two different spellings.

Select a task and begin assigning a resource to it. Choose the Resource name. Now click the **OK** button on the Task Form as you saw back in Figure 8.1. Notice that resource Units defaults to 100% (as Scotty would say, "I'm givin' her all she's got, Captain!") and the work is calculated as the Duration times the Units. With a Duration of 2 days this results in Work of 16 hours. That's all pretty straightforward, so far....

In a like manner, if you enter 50% in Units (perhaps the resource only needs to work half time to complete this task), work is calculated as the Duration times the Units. So, the result might surprise you—it produces eight hours of work for the task. The math is the same, but we've revealed what may be a surprising effect of the effort-driven scheduling approach.

It turns out to be a good way of handling many situations. If you wanted to share the task responsibilities, add each resource, enter each Unit of resource percentage, and click **OK**. In our example of a 2-day Duration, with 2 resources at 50% Units each, work for each is 8 hours. And, the total work for the task is 16 hours.

The program's behavior really isn't as weird as it first sounds. Just remember that Project 2000 makes it easy on us (most of the time) by making assumptions. The more it assumes, the less we have to enter! The missing elements of the Duration, Work, Units formula is calculated based on which items are entered before you click the OK button.

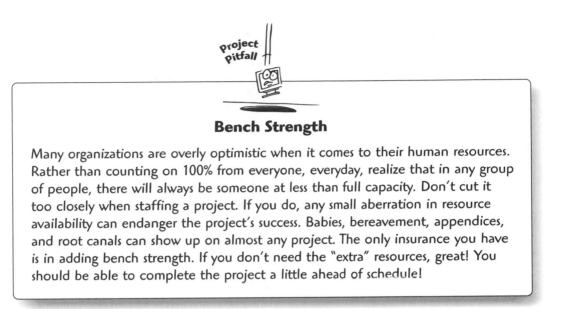

## Bench Strength

Many organizations are overly optimistic when it comes to their human resources. Rather than counting on 100% from everyone, everyday, realize that in any group of people, there will always be someone at less than full capacity. Don't cut it too closely when staffing a project. If you do, any small aberration in resource availability can endanger the project's success. Babies, bereavement, appendices, and root canals can show up on almost any project. The only insurance you have is in adding bench strength. If you don't need the "extra" resources, great! You should be able to complete the project a little ahead of schedule!

You'll get the results you want most of the time. When you don't, it will be instantly apparent with automatic calculation turn on. In that case, adjust your entries and click away until you're happy!

As shown in Figure 8.3, other important scheduling elements are accessible in the combination Gantt Chart and Task Form view.

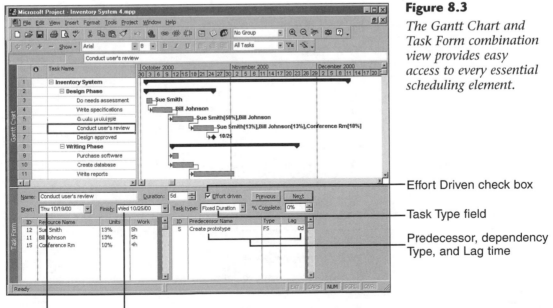

Start date or constraint date

Finish date or constraint date

Effort Driven check box

Task Type field

Predecessor, dependency Type, and Lag time

**Figure 8.3**

*The Gantt Chart and Task Form combination view provides easy access to every essential scheduling element.*

Notice that the Task type field is readily accessible in this view. From time to time you'll need to change Fixed Units to Fixed Duration or Fixed Work. And if you must rethink workflow based on resource availability, work sequence is easily modified from this view. A word of warning—don't modify the Start or Finish dates unless you want to set a scheduling constraint. (Workflow and constraints are covered in detail in Chapter 6, "Sequencing Tasks to Fit Your Needs.")

# Resource Reallocation—Leveling

When you don't have enough units of a resource to accommodate the required work and duration of a task, you've got a problem! Somehow, you need to get the project done. Generally, there are three things you can do:

> Get more resources.
>
> Reduce the scope of the project.
>
> Work longer with the resources you have.

Assuming that the project originator (your boss?) and the project end user (your customer?) are the last people you want to impact, Project 2000 tries to do the right thing. It automatically slides the work out in time based on your resource assignments, task dependencies, and durations. This is usually a pretty good solution. But if the project pushes out too long, you may not be able to get everything done in time. In that case, you'll need some fancy project management footwork. Table 8.1 shows a checklist of solutions to consider.

### Table 8.1    When the Schedule Isn't Working

| If You're Short on... | Try This... |
| --- | --- |
| People | Schedule tasks later. |
| | Ask for more project time. |
| | Balance skills with tasks more accurately. |
| | Break tasks into simpler activities and then give senior people helpers. |
| | Add part-time, temporary, or full-time staff. |
| | Use outside services. |
| | Purchase rather than make. |
| | Limit project scope. |
| Time | Assign more resources. |
| | Work overtime. |
| | Rethink workflow sequence to schedule tasks sooner and parallel more tasks. |
| | Use outside services. |

| If You're Short on... | Try This... |
| --- | --- |
| | Purchase rather than make. |
| | Limit project scope. |
| | Provide assistance by adding junior people to work with senior people. |
| Materials | Rethink workflow sequence to schedule tasks later and parallel less frequently. |
| | Use alternate vendors. |
| | Reconsider make or buy options. |
| | Ask for a time extension. |
| Facilities | Rethink workflow sequence to schedule tasks later and parallel less frequently. |
| | Work additional shifts. |
| Short on everything | Stop project planning and revisit the project definition stage to choose a more realistic strategy. |

## The Least You Need to Know

➤ Microsoft Project 2000 uses an effort-driven scheduling method to compute the amount of work based on task duration and resources assigned.

➤ The schedule adjusts automatically based on workflow sequence, constraints, duration, effort, and resource availability when automatic calculate is on.

➤ Work can be planned around individual resource issues such as vacations, downtime, and full- or part-time commitments.

➤ The combination Gantt Chart and Task Entry view provides excellent control when assigning resources to your project.

# Part 3
# Optimizing Your Plan

*When you have too much to do and too little to do it with, you need some project management magic. And that's what this part is all about—pulling rabbits (in this case people, materials, machines, and money) out of the hat.*

*Part 3 shows you how to put your resources to work where they'll do you the most good. You'll learn to create resource pools and calendars, allocate work, smoothe workloads, shorten your schedule, and work around resource shortages. Making do with what you have has never been easier. And that's the kind of magic that makes a project manager successful!*

# Chapter 9

# What You Must Know About Microsoft Project 2000

---

### In This Chapter

➤ Understand how Microsoft Project 2000 schedules so you can make the best choices for your project

➤ Schedule your project to start as soon (or as late) as possible

➤ Use constraints effectively in your project schedule

---

By this time, your project plan holds a wealth of interrelated details about your project. Microsoft Project 2000 uses many of them to schedule. A small change in one detail can have major effects as it ripples throughout the schedule. An understanding of what goes on behind the scenes will help you avoid any unexpected scheduling results. After all, there are probably already enough surprises in your workday!

When you understand how Project schedules, you're more able to plan and get the results you want. You can, for example, place interim deadlines for phases of work, schedule tasks based on resource availability, safely delay the start of tasks or projects, or balance workloads throughout the project team. And most importantly, you'll realize the ultimate achievement of all professional project managers—making sure your vacation starts on time!

## How Microsoft Project 2000 Schedules Your Projects

A good schedule is your most important project management tool. You probably realized this when you decided to use Project 2000. If you're new to project management, you may have expected the software to take care of all these messy scheduling details.

For the most part, it does. However, no two projects are exactly alike, and no two project managers want a schedule exactly alike.

What you may not have realized is that Project's flexibility requires a potentially confusing array of features and options. What started out as a way of simplifying and speeding up your work can have the opposite effect. It can bog you down in details. In truth, Project 2000 gets the easy part of the scheduling job.

You're the one who collects, analyzes, edits, and enters everything that you decide is important. You're the one who decides how much detail is enough. Project 2000 just provides a place to store all these details, performs a few simple calculations, creates tables with the data, and draws a picture of the results. It does the stuff you would delegate to any good assistant. However, in the scheduling department, you're the boss.

To make sure you never have to reschedule your vacation, it's important to understand how Project 2000 schedules your work and calculates start and finish times.

**Scheduling to Manage**

The schedule is the centerpiece of everything you do as a project manager. Be sure it's valid and as accurate as possible. But don't make it any more complex than it has to be to get the results you want. Remember that you're not managing a schedule, you're scheduling to manage.

# Start Date or Finish Date Scheduling

One of the first things you want to decide when creating a project schedule is whether the project should be scheduled based on a completion deadline or on a start date. If you use the default, Schedule from Project Start Date, Project attempts to start each task as soon as possible, depending on each task's duration and predecessor dependencies. Working from the start date forward (called a forward pass), each duration in the longest sequence of tasks (the critical path) is added together. This determines when the project may be completed (the early finish date).

When scheduling from a project finish date, tasks on the longest sequence of tasks (the critical path) are started as late as possible. To use this scheduling method, select **Project Information** from the **Project** menu to open the Project Information dialog box (see Figure 9.1).

When scheduling from a finish date, Project 2000 adds the duration of each predecessor task, working from the project deadline (late finish date), back to the first task. This calculation (a backward pass) determines when the first task must begin (late start date) to finish the project on the date entered. Tasks that do not fall on the longest sequence of tasks (the critical path) are scheduled to begin as soon as possible without beginning before the first task's start date. The results of scheduling from a finish date are shown in the bottom example in Figure 9.2.

Dates may be adjusted to suit your project's timeframe.

Choose Project Finish Date or Project Start Date to base schedule calculations.

Establishes days, shifts, and hours of work available for scheduling

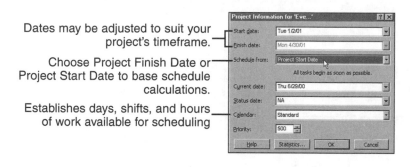

**Figure 9.1**

*You may choose to schedule tasks as soon as possible or as late as possible depending on the start or finish date option.*

### Critical Dates

An accurate schedule is your most important project control tool. It shows when every task must start and finish to complete the project on time. The four key control dates are *early start, late start, early finish,* and *late finish.* The early start specifies how soon a task may begin according to its predecessor's finish. The late start specifies how late a task may begin according to its successor's start. In a like manner, the early and late finish dates specify when a task may or must be completed. The difference in the early and late start dates (or finish dates) is called *slack.* Slack is flexibility in your schedule. When a task has no slack, it is called a *critical task*—it has no flexibility in time. Manage critical tasks carefully.

For more information on the critical path and its effect on the project's schedule, see Chapter 10, "Shortening the Schedule."

**Figure 9.2**

*Individual tasks and task sequences (paths) that are shorter than the longest sequence (critical path) are scheduled as soon as possible in both Start Date and Finish Date scheduling options.*

The longest sequence of tasks sets the overall project duration.

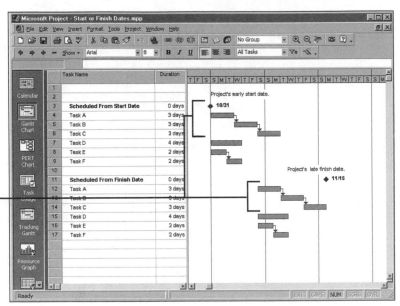

# Project Calendar

Tasks are scheduled according to the workdays, holidays, shifts, and hours of work described in the project's base calendar. Select your project's base calendar in the Project Information dialog box, as shown previously in Figure 9.1. Resources may also have calendars that restrict their availability. For more information on using resource calendars, see Chapter 7, "Getting a Handle on Your Resources, Costs, and Budgets."

# Task List Placement

Project 2000 begins all scheduling calculations with the first task in the Task Name field and proceeds down the list, as you can see in Figure 9.3. With all other things being equal, the higher on the list the task resides, the sooner it will be considered for scheduling and resource assignments. Try to place tasks that will be performed early in the project high on the list. This also makes the schedule easier for others to understand. Chapter 4, "Thinking of Everything, Even If You Don't Know What You're Doing," describes in detail how to create and enter the task list.

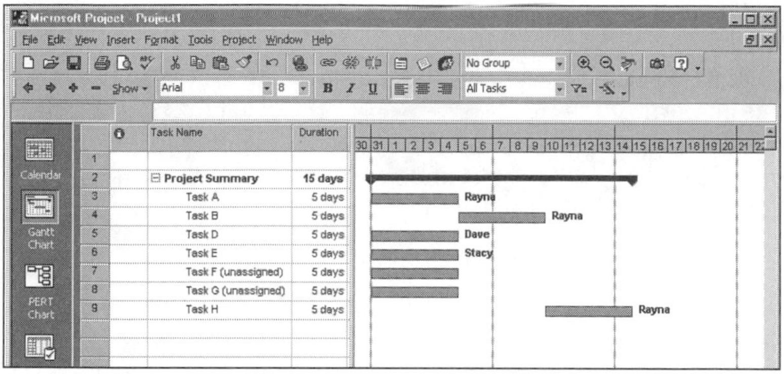

**Figure 9.3**
*Project begins scheduling from the top of the task list and then applies dependencies, resource assignments, and other constraints.*

# Task Duration

Duration is handled in a straightforward manner when resources are not assigned. The longer the duration, the longer a task will take to finish. However, as soon as you assign a resource to the task (assuming it is not a fixed-duration task), the duration/work/units formula kicks in with what sometimes can be unexpected results. Depending on task type (fixed-units, fixed-work, or fixed-duration) and the resources assigned (work or material), duration can be dramatically changed. Each of these elements is checked by Project 2000 when it calculates the schedule.

Establishing accurate durations is essential to creating effective project schedules. Chapter 5, "Estimating Time with Science, Skill, and Fourth-Grade Math," provides all the tools you need to get the job done.

# Task Dependencies

The sequence of workflow is set with task dependencies. Much depends on the task-to-task relationships within a project schedule. Workflow sequence becomes the backbone of all scheduling activities. Frequently the greatest decisions the project manager can make lie within the realm of workflow sequencing.

Alternative approaches may speed completion, reduce resource requirements, minimize project risk, reduce project costs, or increase schedule flexibility. Generally speaking, the fewer dependencies in a project, the more options you have.

Chapter 6, "Sequencing Tasks to Fit Your Needs," shows you how to use task dependencies most effectively.

# Task Lag Time

When two or more tasks with the same workflow sequence are undertaken in the same timeframe, lag time is the amount of the head start given to the predecessor. Lag time adds to the project's overall duration when it is applied to a task on the longest (the critical) path. It forces the dependent task to start and finish later than it would without lag time. To shorten the schedule, use lag time as sparingly as possible.

# Task Constraints

Constraints confine the scheduling of a task in some way. The more restrictive constraints anchor tasks to specific dates, thereby restricting scheduling flexibility. There are eight constraint types in Project 2000 (see Figure 9.4). For projects that are scheduled from the start date, the ASAP (As Soon As Possible) constraint is used.

The first task is scheduled to begin as soon as possible. It may be delayed (has slack or float time) for 17 days without affecting the project's completion.

**Figure 9.4**

*Eight constraints are available to limit when a task may be scheduled. All, except ASAP (As Soon As Possible) and ALAP (As Late As Possible), greatly restrict the schedule's flexibility.*

Constraints that are more restrictive are indicated with a red-dotted calendar icon.

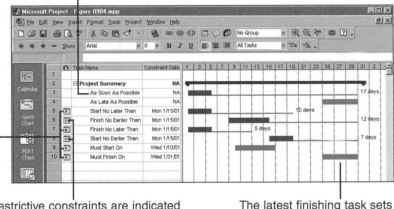

Less-restrictive constraints are indicated with a blue-dotted calendar icon.

The latest finishing task sets this project's total duration.

When scheduling from the finish date, the ALAP constraint is used. The ALAP and ASAP constraints allow flexibility and are the least restrictive. All others greatly confine the capability of Project to schedule tasks. For example, these restrictive constraints include the FNLT (Finish No Later Than), which can be used to ensure a contract requirement is met. Use the six restrictive constraints when you must, but use them sparingly. See Table 6.1 in Chapter 6 for more information on using constraints to restrict the schedule.

## Beware of Accidental Constraints

Project 2000 sets a constraint when you type a start or finish date into the schedule or drag a taskbar from the Gantt chart to a new location. To avoid inadvertently reducing your scheduling options, allow Project to calculate all start and finish dates. A small calendar icon appears in the indicator column when restrictive constraints are set. Double-click the icon and select the Advanced tab in the Task Information dialog box to review or modify the constraint.

# Resource Availability

As mentioned previously in "Task Duration," when resources are assigned, duration shortens or extends according to the duration/work/units formula. The task type and scheduling method are also taken into consideration as the schedule is calculated. Generally, adding more resources to the project helps reduce overall project duration, as shown in Figure 9.5.

Better use of resources on critical tasks (the longest sequence of work) may help shorten the project duration. See Chapter 11, "Leveling Workloads," for more information.

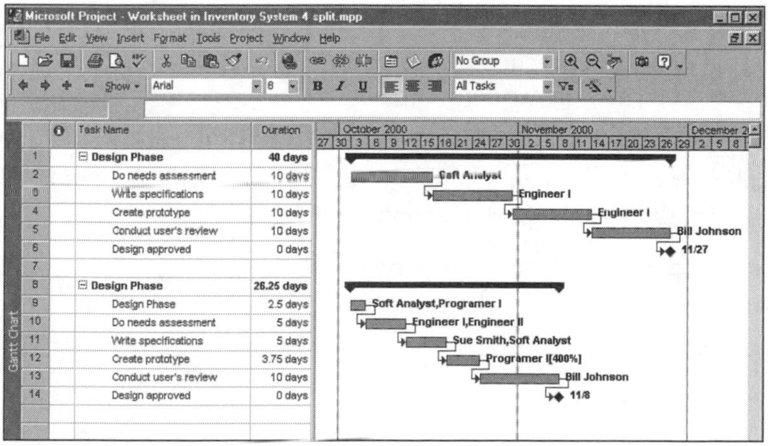

**Figure 9.5**

*Assigning additional work resources to effort-driven tasks shortens the path's duration.*

# Task Work

The amount of work that is done on a task is calculated with the duration/work/units formula. The formula is called into play to determine a task's duration when resources are assigned to an effort-driven, fixed-units or fixed-work task.

# Effort–Driven Scheduling Options

This is the default scheduling method for Project 2000. It affects the schedule calculations as soon as a work resource is assigned to a task. Task duration is calculated based on the initial loading of resources to the task. The version of the formula used (where duration = work / units), depends on which factor is entered and which of the remaining factors Project 2000 assumes it should calculate. When additional resources are assigned, you usually prefer work to remain constant and task duration to shorten. When effort-driven scheduling is turned off, total duration remains constant even as you assign more resources.

# Task Type Options

There are three task types in Project 2000. Tasks, which are either fixed-work or fixed-units type, are affected by the assignment of work resources. When more work resources are applied, task duration shortens. Adding or removing resources does not affect the length of fixed-duration tasks.

Well, there's the big picture of how Project 2000 schedules. Talk about a plot within a plot! You might want to keep a bookmarker in this section. Then if you get unexpected results, just double-click on the task and check out those settings. Think of it as your not-the-last-one-at-work-again insurance policy.

---

### The Least You Need to Know

➤ The schedule is the most important managing and control tool available to project managers.

➤ Microsoft Project 2000 calculates schedules based on the project's start or finish date, task durations, task dependencies, resource assignments, and constraining dates.

➤ It uses the critical path method in all schedule calculations, where the longest sequence of tasks determines the overall duration of the project.

➤ Minor changes in any planning element can ripple significant changes throughout the schedule.

# Chapter 10

---

# Shortening the Schedule

## In This Chapter

➤ Making the most of your project's time

➤ Finding the hidden resource slack time and putting it to work

➤ Understanding the critical path and why its management is essential to project success

➤ Techniques to speed up a slow project

Successful project managers are known for their ability to get things done on time with limited resources. What many of their amazed colleagues don't realize is that these successful project managers are just taking their mother's advice. They understand the significance of "never putting off anything that can be done now." They've learned through experience, training, good parenting, or the school of hard knocks, that time is a precious commodity.

Of all the resources, time is the only one that is absolutely inflexible. No matter what you do or who you are, additional time can't be purchased, borrowed, or even (excuse me, Mom) stolen. To make matters worse, time goes away whether it's used or not.

Okay, okay. You know that! And that's why you're improving your project management skills, right? After all, project management techniques were developed with one primary focus: to effectively use that most precious resource of all, time.

# Hustling While You Wait

Some of the techniques project managers use to get more done in less time are almost magical. Thomas Edison was one of the most prolific project managers of our century. He summed up those techniques nicely when he said that all things come to those who hustle while they wait. Hmmm...as the mental whiplash subsides, ask yourself these questions:

➤ Where can I pick up the project's pace?

➤ What resources do I have that are not being used at this moment?

➤ Where should I focus my limited resources if I want to shorten the project's duration?

➤ What can I afford to do later to free up more resources and accomplish the time-important tasks?

It's important to know which tasks, if accomplished more quickly, will shorten the project schedule. In addition, it's important to know which tasks can be moved around in the schedule, freeing resources for use elsewhere. The body of knowledge that we call project management carefully discriminates between these tasks—those with time flexibility and those without.

Hustling while you wait has become a science!

# The Critical and Noncritical Paths to Success

If there is one word that is misunderstood in project management, it is the word *critical*. People tend to use it as a way of describing tasks that are important. However, as you may recall from Chapter 4, "Thinking of Everything, Even If You Don't Know What You're Doing," every task we choose is important. In fact, every task we choose is essential!

## Essential Tasks Aren't Always Critical

When a task is critical, it must be accomplished on time or the project duration increases. When a task is critical, it has zero flexibility. Therefore, although every task is essential to the project's success, not all of them have inflexible time lines. Not all essential tasks are critical. Some may be accomplished anytime before the project is done.

Fortunately, in most projects many tasks can be delayed without delaying the project. The timeline for accomplishing these tasks (essential as they may be) is flexible. This flexibility is the project manager's biggest tool.

### The Impossible Project

Beware the impossible project! Contrary to the popular saying that all things are possible given enough time and money, some projects just can't be accomplished. Watch out for pet projects, projects with overly optimistic goals or assumptions, and projects without slack time—especially those that someone else has already failed on. It takes only one impossible project to destroy your reputation as a successful project manager.

## The Hidden Resource and Key to a Project Manager's Happiness

When you stop and think about it, project managers don't get that many choices. Frequently they don't get to pick their teams, set their budgets, or even negotiate the project's goal. The biggest managerial tool at the disposal of the project manager is their authority to decide who does what, when. And depending on how those decisions are made, a project manager can find the all-important hidden resource: flexibility.

Noncritical tasks have some flexibility when they can start without delaying completion of the project. This extra time is called *slack* or *float*.

Hidden within every project lies the resource, slack. It can be used to adjust the availability of resources to shorten the project's overall duration. How much slack you can find depends on your creativity and your scheduling skill. Those who understand how to create and use slack to their best advantage have found Project Management Nirvana!

## Identifying the Critical Path

Project managers use the word *critical* to describe a task that has no flexibility in time. Critical tasks must be accomplished as planned or the project will not be completed on time. Critical tasks have no flexibility. They, therefore, have zero slack or float.

The critical path can also be described as the longest sequence of tasks in a project. Every task on this longest chain of events is, by definition, a critical task. To determine the longest path in the project, one must first identify every chain of events within the project. This was established by the way you entered the workflow logic. (See Chapter 6, "Sequencing Tasks to Fit Your Needs," for more information on task dependencies and workflow logic.)

119

## Critical, Essential, or Important Tasks?

To improve communications on the project team, be careful how you use the words *critical, essential,* and *important.* Use *critical* only to describe those tasks which, if not completed on time, will cause the project to finish late. *Essential* tasks are those required to achieve the intended results of the project. Use *essential* to remind your team that even tasks that are not glamorous or interesting are still essential to the project's success. Finally, when using *important* to describe a task, always include your reasoning. Although all tasks are important, some are more important than others. For example, a task may be important because its completion opens several paths of work or because it has high visibility to stakeholders.

Next, the duration of each task is added for each path. Whichever path has the longest duration is the critical path. The reasoning is this: If there is time enough to do the longest path, the shorter paths will fit in. For an example, see Figure 10.1.

**Figure 10.1**

*The critical path is the longest sequence of tasks within a project. All other paths have flexibility expressed in days of slack.*

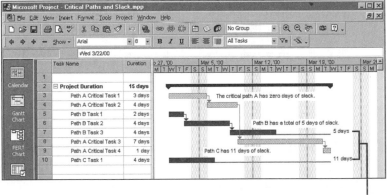

Slack, the hidden resource, is revealed as a small line in the Detail Gantt view.

Microsoft Project 2000 makes identifying critical tasks and those with slack quick and easy. From the **View** menu, click **More Views**, and then select **Detail Gantt** (see Figure 10.2). Every change you make to the critical path is instantly revealed.

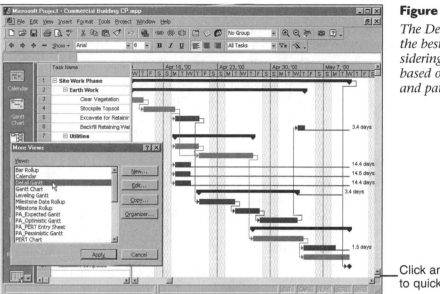

**Figure 10.2**
*The Detail Gantt view is the best choice when considering scheduling options based on the critical path and paths with slack.*

Click and drag the Split bar to quickly open a lower pane.

## Identifying Slack (or Float)

The Detail Gantt view is also good for identifying task and path slack time. As shown earlier in Figure 10.1, slack time appears as a small bar trailing out from the last task on every path that has slack. You can visualize how much flexibility is in the path by mentally sliding the tasks down the slack line. If it looks like you may be able to make some improvements, save a copy of your current plan.

Let's see if you can hustle while you wait!

## A Need for Speed? Load Up on Resources

To speed up a project, place additional work resources on any fixed-work or fixed-unit tasks. If those tasks lie on the critical path, you'll be shortening the entire project's schedule. Of course, the critical path changes as task durations change, but the first area to hustle on is always the critical path.

## Resource Allocation in a Critical World

When a task can be delayed without affecting the start of another task, the slack is called *free slack*. And it really is free. Free slack doesn't cost the project any time, anywhere. *Total slack* is the total amount of time a task can be delayed without affecting the project's completion date. Using total slack probably won't hurt anything, but you may have additional schedule juggling to do.

There is a lot to watch when you juggle resources and tasks. The critical path can change rapidly. Project 2000 makes it easy to stay in control. Opening a pane in the bottom of the window and displaying the Resource Sheet is the best way. You may

**121**

need lots of room to view a complex project's paths, so be ready to switch back and forth between views a lot. Here's the best trick for this: To open a lower pane quickly, click the **Window Split Bar** and drag open a lower pane. Then right-click in the lower pane and select the **Resources & Predecessors** view.

The split bar you saw in Figure 10.2 appears just below the vertical scrollbar. To quickly close the pane, just drag it out of sight to the bottom of the window. This trick is helpful when you're moving resources from one task to another.

# Adding Resources

The problem with adding resources to speed up a project is that you may not have any to add! When was the last time you saw someone standing around complaining that they didn't have enough to do? One of the options is to hire additional people. However, if that's not in the budget, what's a project manager to do? Well, it's time to steal (oops, sorry Mom!) er, borrow, some resources.

About the only place to find extra resources is on tasks that have some slack. Certainly, reducing a task's resources may slow it down, but that's okay, as long as there is enough slack so nothing goes critical.

# Increasing a Resource's Available Time on Task

Another way of applying more effort to a task is by increasing the resource units. For example, in lieu of having people work a quarter of their time on a task and taking four weeks to complete it, schedule them for half of their time and complete the task in two weeks. Better yet, convince the resource person that it's easier to do a good job when they're focused on a single task. Then schedule them full time and reduce the task to a week! As you might guess, when you need to shorten a project, persuasion skills are as important as scheduling skills.

## Assigning Overtime Work

Overtime usually costs more, so it isn't always in the budget. However, there are times when the financial cost is actually lower with overtime. For example, consider the salaried employee who is paid the same for 40 hours as for 50 hours of work. If the person's productivity, quality, and judgement (not to mention health, family, relationships, and so on) isn't adversely affected by the long hours, the more she works, the less it costs the project. (And the more it costs the resource!)

### Don't Change the Resource Calendar More Than Necessary

Although you can use Project's resource calendar to increase the number of hours a resource is available, you might notice I don't discuss that approach much. Some specific resources, such as mainframe computers, might be available 24 hours a day, but in most cases I consider that approach a good way to make a schedule work and a project fail. Changing a resource's calendar beyond their 40 or 50 "standard" hours may be illegal in some areas—it causes burn-out when used as a standard approach, it can create resentment, and it most likely will reduce productivity. I try to avoid extending the work calendar in all except the most desperate of business situations.

### Focusing on the Team

People are our most important resource. Effective team leaders assume that every team member is capable of making a positive contribution. Find a challenging, meaningful role for every member of your team. Helping them succeed is good for the team members, good for the project, and good for you!

There are situations when it makes sense to work overtime, even if it is more expensive. Consider a time-sensitive project where the completion of a single task opens several other paths of work, such as "Design approved" in the project shown in Figure 10.3. We call a situation like this a *work burst*. It is often strategically important to accomplish a work burst as soon as possible. Time savings made on or before a work burst translate into time savings for each subsequent path. In those cases, paying a little more to open the workflow may be smart.

## Manage Those Work Bursts!

Two or more paths of work opening up behind a task is called a *work burst*. These points in the workflow sequence are important to identify and carefully manage. When negotiated sooner than planned, work bursts can create slack time on all subsequent paths. On the other hand, work bursts can also be a dangerous work-flow bottleneck. If not successfully negotiated, all subsequent work will be delayed and the project's progress may be severely hindered. To identify work bursts in a Gantt chart view, be sure the workflow links are selected in the Gantt chart layout dialog box. Alternatively, view your project in the Network Diagram view.

When reassigning resources, leave a margin of error on those tasks that are especially difficult, risky, or out of the team's realm of experience.

**Figure 10.3**

*The Gantt Chart helps you consider the critical path, slack time, and resource use from a strategic point of view.*

Watch for tasks that hold a strategic importance to the workflow, such as this work burst.

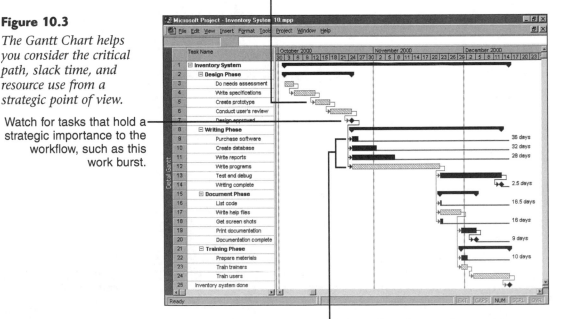

Reschedule tasks with long slack times to free up resources.

To assign more resources, increase their available time on task, or to assign overtime work, use the combination Gantt Chart and Resource Sheet view. Follow the steps on how to assign resources in Chapter 8, "The Resourceful Use of Resources."

# Other Speedy Tricks

In addition to shortening tasks with the thoughtful use of slack time and resources, another key strategy is to compress the schedule: Move as many tasks as far forward in time as possible. This takes on two basic forms, as discussed in the following sections.

## *Breaking Critical Tasks into Subtasks*

The first of these tactics is to break critical tasks down into smaller work units. It is often possible to then move some of these smaller tasks off the critical path. In the project you saw in Figure 10.3, task number 17, *Write help files*, could be broken into *Write overview*, *Write glossary*, and *Write help files*. Presumably, both the glossary and overview could be started as soon as the design had been approved. This would take some time off the critical path and shorten the project.

## *The Parallel Approach*

Another fruitful tactic is to parallel more tasks; that is, run more tasks in the same timeframe. This usually takes more resources, but if they are available, the parallel approach can be very productive.

Consider the task Test and debug shown previously in Figure 10.3. It may be possible to begin testing as soon as some of the program has been written, rather than waiting for its total completion. Changing Test and debug's dependency on Write programs to a Start to Start Relationship and creating a 25% lag time (a 25% head start for Write programs) creates additional slack for Test and debug. That could be very handy if there happen to be any problems with program code.

The same effect can be achieved in Finish to Start dependencies by using a negative lag time in the dependent task to "reduce" the lead time of the predecessor task. The project has been rescheduled with these changes in Figure 10.4. In doing so, the project duration was reduced by 15.5 days, and slack time was thereby increased for every task in the project.

Now that's what I call hustling while you wait! Mom would be proud.

Reducing lead time (using negative slack on a Finish to Start dependency or lag on a Start to Start dependency) compresses the critical path.

**Figure 10.4**

*Schedules can be improved by using slack time, shortening task durations with better resource use, and through the creative use of task dependencies, lead time, and lag time.*

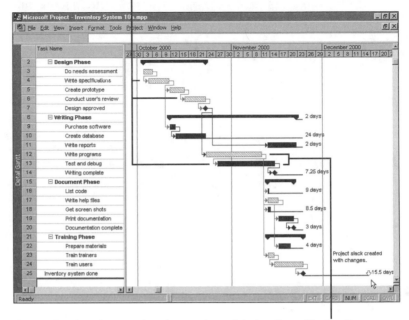

Dependencies that can be changed to minimize the critical path are easy to spot using the Detail Gantt view.

# Reducing Project Scope

What if it all fails? You've used every trick, stretched every resource and negotiated for more time. Nonetheless, your project is still too long.

There are two options that may help in this predicament. The first is to go ahead and hope something changes. It just might! Your insight to the situation is probably the best there is. So make a judgement call and if you decide to go forward, try to hedge your bets!

Perhaps the better option is to revisit the definition stage. Not all projects are possible, even if the resources you need are available. It's far better to know that now than later. Try to reduce the scope of the project. Failing that, look for another strategy that will solve the problem this project was intended to solve. Alternately, you may be able to break the project into smaller phases and engage in what can be accomplished.

### The Least You Need to Know

➤ Understanding the critical path is the key to unlocking a project's hidden resource—slack.

➤ Project durations may be decreased by applying three primary strategies: reducing task duration; removing tasks from the critical path; and running more tasks in parallel.

➤ The Detail Gantt view in combination with the Resource & Predecessor view provides a powerful method of applying each of the project shortening strategies.

➤ Not all projects can be accomplished in the desired time frame with the resources that are available. Be alert for the impossible project. Be ready and willing to revisit the definition stage of the planning process.

# Chapter 11

# Leveling Workloads

## In This Chapter

➤ Locating resource overallocation problems

➤ Using manual leveling techniques to solve resource overallocation problems

➤ Using contours to better match workloads with tasks

➤ Using Microsoft Project 2000's automatic leveling features to solve resource overallocation problems

The process of leveling resources has one primary purpose: to create a schedule that works with the resources you have available. When assigning resources to scheduled tasks, chances are problems will slip into the schedule. You may find that you've overallocated a resource—tried to accomplish too much, too soon, overly taxing it. Or you may find you've underallocated a resource—someone is standing around without his or her full capacity being used. (Wouldn't that be nice for a change?) In most projects, there are just too many complexities and interrelationships to get the resource loading right the first time.

In addition, as the project is implemented, changes from the original plan are almost inevitable. People come or go. Some tasks finish earlier, and others later, than expected. You may have vendors that don't show up at all! In the dynamic project environment, eventually, you'll have to adjust the project's resource loading.

This adjustment process is called *leveling*. In general, there are two types of allocation problems you'll be dealing with: overallocations and underallocations. Having too many resources is seldom viewed as a problem by most project managers. It's usually obvious that those resources can be given additional work somewhere. It's the overallocation problems that are difficult to deal with. We'll take a close look at these.

## Planning to Learn

Don't try to make a schedule perfect on your first pass. Planning is an iterative learning process. At first, go for an approximation of a workable schedule. Only after a reasonable workflow sequence has been established should you begin to apply resources. Don't stop planning when you've created the first workable schedule. Continue to adjust tasks, resource usage, and work sequence until you minimize risk, maximize slack time, finish on time, and effectively use your resources. The schedule is often the only thing a project manager truly controls. Master it.

## The Lowdown on Leveling

Having the right number of people on a project is almost always a challenge. Having too many resources causes cost overruns; too few resources causes time overruns. *Leveling* is the term project managers use for reducing over- and under-allocations of project resources. Two basic leveling strategies are used. The first is to change the number of resources available on a project. This strategy can't always be used because of worker shortages, budget considerations, or the demand for resources on other projects. The second strategy is to move work around to fit resource availability. This method is usually the best approach, as long as the project's completion date is not pushed out. To make the best leveling decisions, project managers must have an accurate schedule and a thorough understanding of the project.

# Solving Resource Overallocation Problems

As resources are assigned to tasks, Microsoft Project 2000 checks the resource's calendar to make sure it is a working resource. It doesn't however, check to see whether the resource is being used anywhere else in this same timeframe. It lets you overassign resources all you want. In other words, you can assign more work to one resource than that resource can possibly accomplish in a given time. (I'm not talking about your supervisor, honest!)

Allowing more work to be assigned to one resource than can be done may sound a little mean-spirited at first. However, some projects are scheduled from a different point of view. For example, you may want to schedule a project in the shortest possible timeframe, and then go back and add extra resources where a shortage becomes apparent. Allowing overallocations gives you more creative freedom as you build an optimal schedule.

To avoid placing someone in an overloaded situation, you'll probably want to fix overallocation problems as soon as possible. However, to fix them, you must first find them. Project 2000 makes this quick and easy.

## Finding Resource Overallocations

Overallocations are easy to find. Indeed, they almost jump off the page to get your attention. To find overallocations, open the Resource Sheet view, the Resource Usage view, or the Resource Allocation view. As shown in Figure 11.1, a bright yellow caution sign icon appears in each task's indicator column when resources are over-allocated. Wouldn't it be nice if a large one of these popped up on your office door when your boss overallocates you?

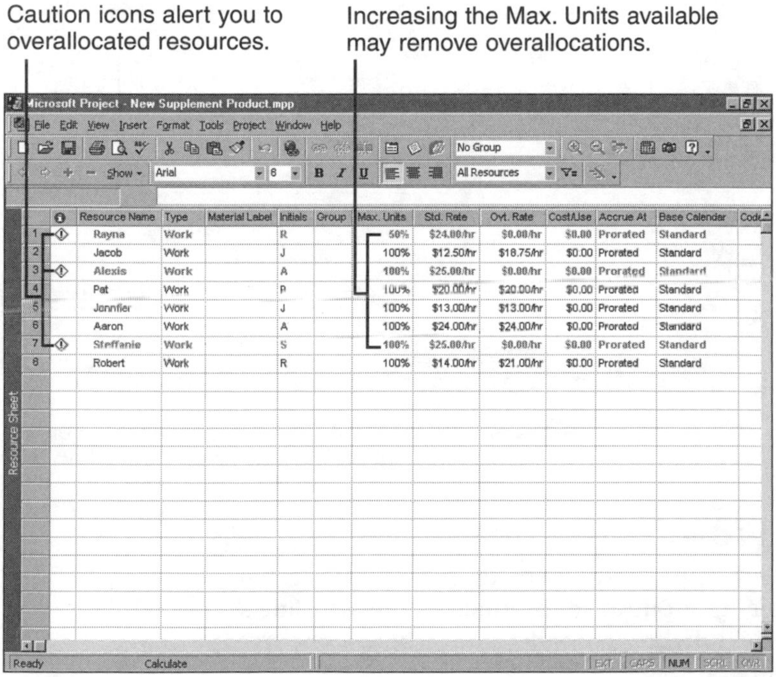

Caution icons alert you to overallocated resources.

Increasing the Max. Units available may remove overallocations.

**Figure 11.1**

*The Resource Sheet view can be used to spot over-allocations. Select it from the View menu or View Bar.*

131

## The Resource Sheet View

The Resource Sheet view is shown in the previous Figure 11.1. If you planned your project with less than a resource's full capacity being used, this is a handy view. It's easy to change a resource's maximum available units here. Raising a person's half-time availability (50%) to three-quarter-time availability (75%) might be all you need to do.

Open this view by clicking **Resource Sheet** in the View Bar or by selecting it from the View menu. In addition, while you have this view open, check to see that the overtime rates are set correctly. Later, you may want to add overtime to reduce an overallocation.

## Resource Usage View

To see how many hours of overallocation exist for a given resource, use the Resource Usage view. It may be opened from the View Bar or from the **View** menu. Add the Overallocation field to the view by selecting **Details** from the **Format** menu. The view appears in Figure 11.2.

**Figure 11.2**

*In the Resource Usage view, tasks are grouped by resource.*

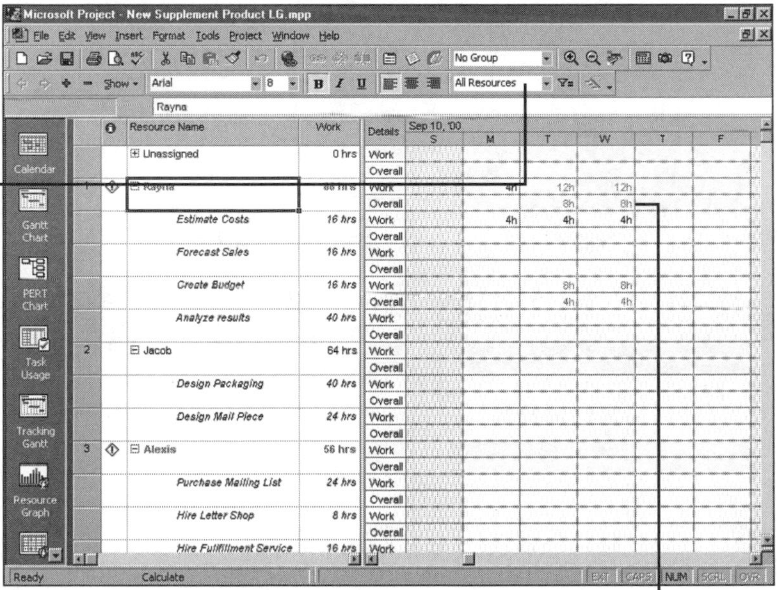

View may be limited to overallocated resources by applying a filter.

Resource Rayna is overallocated eight hours on Tuesday and Wednesday.

## Resource Graph View

The Resource Graph view helps show where a single resource is over- or under-allocated. You can zoom in or out to see as much of the schedule as needed. This view, shown in Figure 11.3, helps you understand where a resource may have available time for reallocation.

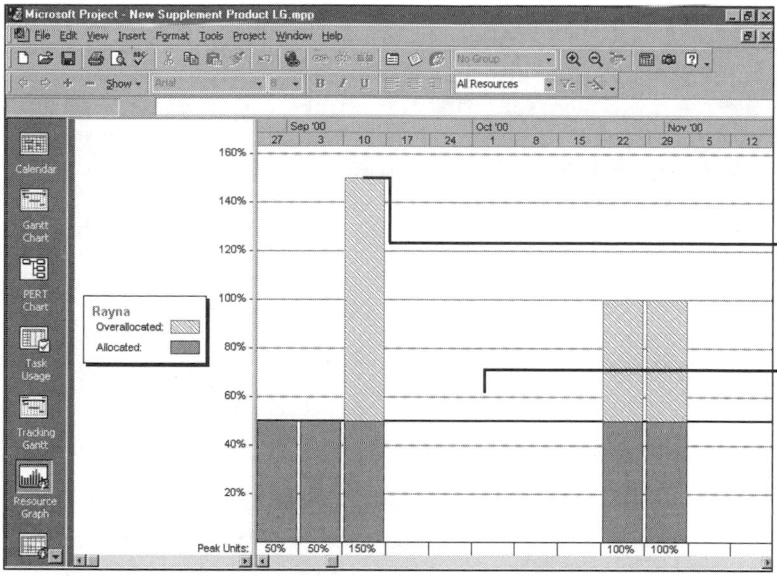

**Figure 11.3**

*The Resource Graph provides more detail to help you understand where allocation problems and options may lie.*

Allocation for Rayna peaks at 150% during the week of September 10, 2000.

Resource Rayna's maximum units available are 50%.

# Manual Resource Leveling

On smaller projects, those with perhaps 6 to 12 resources and up to 30 tasks, the fastest way to level your resources is to do it manually. There are no priorities to set or choices to think through. You simply make changes until you get the results you want.

To begin, turn automatic leveling off. You get the same results when automatically calculating, but it's easy to miss seeing what happens. Until you're more experienced with Project 2000, use the manual calculation setting. Then just before you click **Calculate**, your eyes have a chance to focus on the areas that will be changed. From the **Tools** menu, select **Resource Leveling** and click the **Manual** option, as shown in Figure 11.4.

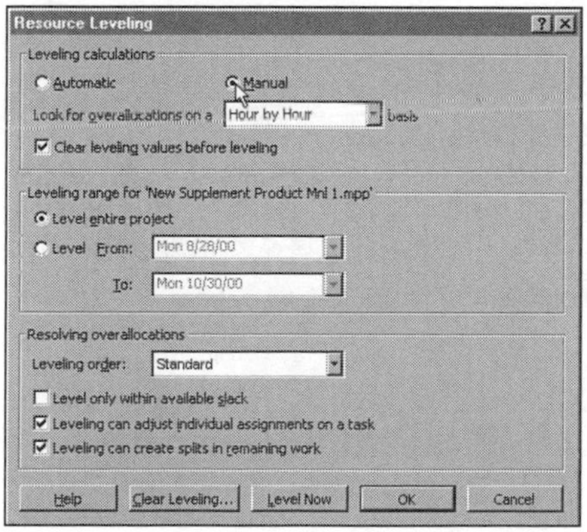

**Figure 11.4**

*For manual resource leveling, adjust the settings in the Resource Leveling dialog box.*

For best results, the remaining choices should be set as shown in Figure 11.4.

133

# *Delaying the Start of Noncritical Tasks*

First, try to move tasks around within their available slack time. You could add resources to a task to reduce overallocation problems, and that is probably the easiest thing to do. However, adding resources usually means adding costs, and adding costs isn't always an option. Using a task's slack doesn't require additional resources, costs, or time.

### Slack Is Your Friend!

Tasks on the critical path cannot be slowed down or delayed without causing the entire project to finish later than originally planned. However, tasks that don't fall on the critical path have slack. Delaying these tasks, up to the point of using all their slack time, won't impact the project's scheduled completion date. By sliding tasks back in time (delaying their starts), overallocations may be reduced. Slack is a hidden resource that only an accurate schedule can reveal. Wise project managers build as much slack as possible into their schedules.

Always look for opportunities early in your resource leveling process to use slack time to reduce resource overallocations. Using slack usually has the least adverse impact and is the easiest to accommodate within the confines of the schedule.

The Resource Allocation view is a good way to see your adjustments and their impact on each task's related resources. However, it also shows leveling that has already been accomplished. This can cause some information overload! The Resource Allocation view appears in Figure 11.5.

To avoid this problem, use the Detail Gantt view. To see which resources are over-allocated and on which days, create a combination view with the Resource Usage table in the bottom pane. The other benefit of using your own combination view is that you can see how your adjustments affect the rest of the schedule. Critical tasks and slack is shown for all tasks.

Select **Detail Gantt** from the **More Views** choice in the **Views** menu. Split the window by dragging the Split bar up or selecting **Split** from the **Window** menu. Click in the lower pane to make it active. Then select **Resource Usage** from the **View** menu.

You'll want to be able to quickly calculate to see your adjustments. Add the Calculate Now button to the Standard toolbar by clicking the **Add or Remove Buttons** arrow on the toolbar and selecting **Calculate Now**. You'll see something similar to the screen shown in Figure 11.6. If you make an adjustment and the resulting schedule change is not satisfactory, return to the before calculated stage by selecting **Undo** in the **Edit** menu.

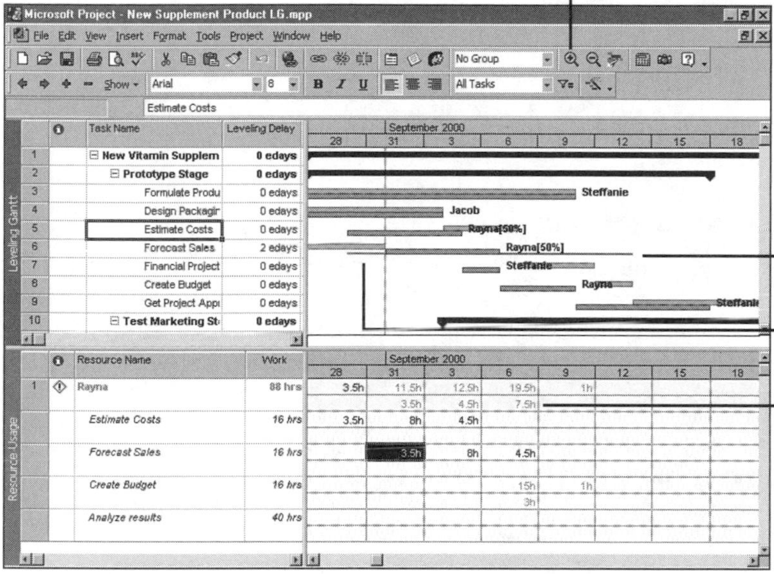

Zoom to see hours, days, weeks, months, quarters, or years.

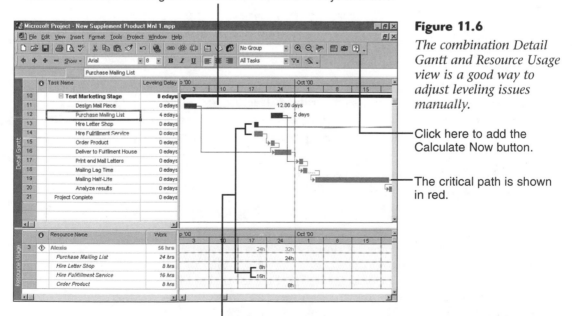

**Figure 11.5**

*The Resource Allocation view shows tasks that are overallocated in the Leveling Gantt pane.*

Additional slack time is available here.

This task has already been delayed to level resources.

Overallocations are shown in red.

Slack is indicated with a green line and the number of days available.

**Figure 11.6**

*The combination Detail Gantt and Resource Usage view is a good way to adjust leveling issues manually.*

Click here to add the Calculate Now button.

The critical path is shown in red.

Notice that resource usage correlates by date with the task bars.

To level tasks within available slack time, select the first task in your schedule. As the resource it uses appears in the lower pane, notice whether it is overallocated. If it is, zoom out so you can see the relationship this task has to the rest of the schedule. If there is available slack, it shows up as a green line to the right of the task with the total days available noted.

Place your cursor in the task's Leveling Delay field and add or subtract delay. Click outside of the field. Watch the Detail Gantt view and click the **Calculate Now** button. The schedule snaps into the new shape. Check out the effects and if they are acceptable, go to the next overallocated task. If they are not acceptable, reverse the procedure—remove the changes in delay and recalculate.

## The Nonparallel Approach

Another strategy to reduce overallocations is to remove parallel tasks. This requires some careful consideration of workflow logic. Running tasks in sequence that were originally in parallel has the effect of lengthening the time it takes to accomplish that path. Typically, lengthening a noncritical path is not a problem. The project can still be accomplished according to the original schedule.

If tasks on the critical path are changed from parallel to sequential, overall project duration increases. This may or may not be acceptable, depending on your situation.

### Changing Workflow Logic

There is always more than one way to accomplish any project. Experienced project managers are adept at getting results by making the best strategic and tactical choices. In an environment of resource shortages, it is often the best choice to run tasks in sequence even if they could be run in parallel. Although this strategy may increase the project's duration, it also reduces the number of resources needed to accomplish the project. In addition, this approach can help you manage expectations by overly optimistic stakeholders. Build a schedule that rigs your project for success!

To change workflow sequence, right-click the task in Detail Gantt view or its entry table. Select **Task Information** from the pop-up menu. Go to the **Predecessor** tab and change the **Predecessor, Type**, or **Lag** that describes the parallel relationship. You'll recall that negative lag on a task with a standard Finish to Start relationship produces a parallel relationship. (See Chapter 6, "Sequencing Tasks to Fit Your Needs," for more information.)

## Adding Overtime

When all else fails, you may decide to work resources overtime. In most labor situations, this is a more expensive option. Overtime work usually comes only at a premium price. However, for salaried employees or in some cases subcontracted services, overtime work is essentially free. We may pay for the first 40 hours of work each week that a salaried employee works, but every productive hour thereafter costs no additional money. One should not forget, however, that even salaried employees have a life outside of work!

In a like manner, the conditions of a subcontract agreement might not mention the timeframe within which work must be completed. Subcontractors in this case might be required to pay premium overtime rates to their people to keep the project moving forward. The prime contractor would therefore see no additional costs for requiring a resource to work overtime.

To add overtime, click in the lower pane of our combination view to make it active. Select the **Resource Form** from **More Views** in the **View** menu. Now right-click in the lower pane and select **Work details**. Adjust the overtime hours as needed, as shown in Figure 11.7, and click **OK**. Be sure to click the **Calculate Now** button you have automatic calculation turned off.

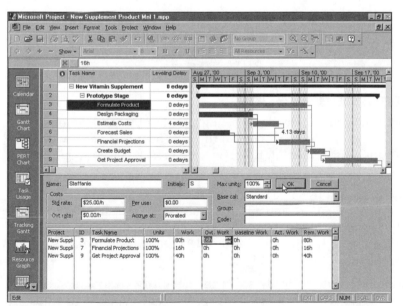

**Figure 11.7**

*Open a combination view with the Gantt Chart and the Resource Form to modify overtime used on an overallocated task.*

## Splitting Tasks

In the real world, one of the options a project manager has is to partially complete a task, finish a more important one, and then return to the original task. You may call it multiplexing, but Project 2000 has made it legitimate! It's called *task splitting*.

It's easy to use this feature. Right-click a task bar in the Gantt Chart view and select **Split Task** from the pop-up menu. Place the mouse at the split point, as shown in Figure 11.8, and drag the remainder of the task to the right. To remove this adjustment, drag the split bars back together. Now that's multiplexing with style!

**Figure 11.8**

*Right-click the task and select **Split Task** to divide a task at any point.*

Drag a portion of the task to a later time.

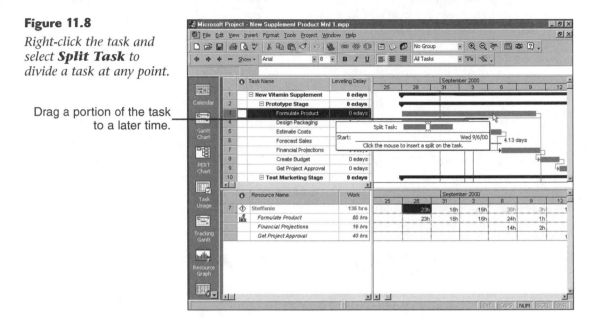

## Automatic Resource Leveling

After all the hard work you've just completed leveling a project by hand, automatic resource leveling probably sounds like a wonderful thing. When the time available for your project isn't too tight, it is wonderful. However, care must be taken to get the results you want.

Project 2000 takes into account a resource's working capacity, its assigned units, the resource's calendar, the task's duration, and any constraints that may be in place. It pushes tasks out in time until resources are no longer overallocated. It does this by using available slack, splitting tasks, and adding start delay time. Your project's duration can easily be extended, so be careful.

To begin leveling your project automatically, select the **Leveling Gantt** view. Then from the **Tools** menu, choose **Resource Leveling**. A dialog box appears (the one you saw earlier in Figure 11.4). To level, save your current schedule. Then, select the options you want as described in Table 11.1. Click **Level Now** and presto! Be sure to carefully check the results.

## Table 11.1    Resource Leveling Dialog Box Options

| Option | Description |
|---|---|
| Automatic | Automatic leveling constantly levels all resources when a task or resource is entered or adjusted. This option is not normally selected. |
| Manual | This default leveling option requires you to click the **Level Now** button to induce automatic leveling. |
| Look for over-allocations on a __ basis | Day by Day is the default and works best for projects scheduled in hours or day units. Sets the point at which leveling is induced. |
| Clear leveling values before leveling | When automatic leveling is selected, clear this box to speed up leveling. The default for manual leveling is to enable this option. |
| Level entire project | Selected is default. When cleared you may choose a date range to level. |
| Level from | Enter a date range of tasks to level. |
| Leveling order | Choose **ID** to level tasks in ID number order. Choose **Standard** (usually the best choice) to level based on dependencies, slack, dates, priorities, and constraints. Choose **Priority, Standard** to first check task priorities and then undertake the Standard leveling order. |
| Level within available slack | When Selected prevents the project finish date from being extended. Depending on the schedule's slack, there may little or no leveling performed. |
| Leveling can adjust individual assignments on a task | This selection allows leveling to adjust all resources on any task. To set this feature on an assignment by assignment basis, add a Level Assignments Field to the Task Sheet and set it to Yes or No. |
| Leveling can create splits in remaining work | This selection allows leveling to split all tasks. To set this feature on a task by task basis, add a Leveling Can Split Field to the Task Sheet and set it to Yes or No. |
| Clear Leveling | This button clears all leveling on all tasks. |
| Level Now | Click this button to level when Manual Leveling calculations has been selected. |

# Contouring Work Assignments

Project 2000 provides one other important method to distribute resource loading over the task's duration: a work contour. The default is a flat contour, where work is equally distributed throughout the task's duration. The Back Loaded, Front Loaded, Double Peak, Early Peak, Late Peak, Bell, and Turtle contours all distribute work on a preset percentage. The duration of the task is broken into 10 equal divisions and the resource's work is distributed over the task according to the table in Figure 11.9.

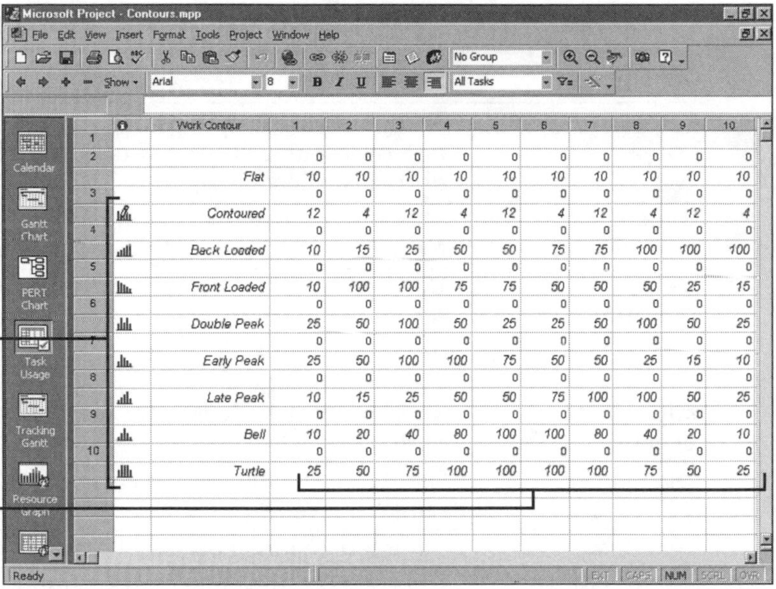

**Figure 11.9**

*Tasks with 100 hours of work over a 10-day duration and 10-hour workday were created to demonstrate the available work contours.*

Icons indicate the type of contour selected.

The resource's effort is distributed over the task as a percentage of the daily total assignment.

| Work Contour | 1 | 2 | 3 | 4 | 5 | 6 | 7 | 8 | 9 | 10 |
|---|---|---|---|---|---|---|---|---|---|---|
| | 0 | 0 | 0 | 0 | 0 | 0 | 0 | 0 | 0 | 0 |
| Flat | 10 | 10 | 10 | 10 | 10 | 10 | 10 | 10 | 10 | 10 |
| | 0 | 0 | 0 | 0 | 0 | 0 | 0 | 0 | 0 | 0 |
| Contoured | 12 | 4 | 12 | 4 | 12 | 4 | 12 | 4 | 12 | 4 |
| | 0 | 0 | 0 | 0 | 0 | 0 | 0 | 0 | 0 | 0 |
| Back Loaded | 10 | 15 | 25 | 50 | 50 | 75 | 75 | 100 | 100 | 100 |
| | 0 | 0 | 0 | 0 | 0 | 0 | 0 | 0 | 0 | 0 |
| Front Loaded | 10 | 100 | 100 | 75 | 75 | 50 | 50 | 50 | 25 | 15 |
| | 0 | 0 | 0 | 0 | 0 | 0 | 0 | 0 | 0 | 0 |
| Double Peak | 25 | 50 | 100 | 50 | 25 | 25 | 50 | 100 | 50 | 25 |
| | 0 | 0 | 0 | 0 | 0 | 0 | 0 | 0 | 0 | 0 |
| Early Peak | 25 | 50 | 100 | 100 | 75 | 50 | 50 | 25 | 15 | 10 |
| | 0 | 0 | 0 | 0 | 0 | 0 | 0 | 0 | 0 | 0 |
| Late Peak | 10 | 15 | 25 | 50 | 50 | 75 | 100 | 100 | 50 | 25 |
| | 0 | 0 | 0 | 0 | 0 | 0 | 0 | 0 | 0 | 0 |
| Bell | 10 | 20 | 40 | 80 | 100 | 100 | 80 | 40 | 20 | 10 |
| | 0 | 0 | 0 | 0 | 0 | 0 | 0 | 0 | 0 | 0 |
| Turtle | 25 | 50 | 75 | 100 | 100 | 100 | 100 | 75 | 50 | 25 |

To use this feature, go to the sheet portion of the Task Usage or Resource Usage views. Right-click on a task assigned to a resource and open the Assignment Information dialog box. This is shown in Figure 11.10. Select the contour you want and click on **OK**. The Indicator column displays a Work Contour icon. If you manually adjust the work contour, the icon changes to an Edited Contour icon.

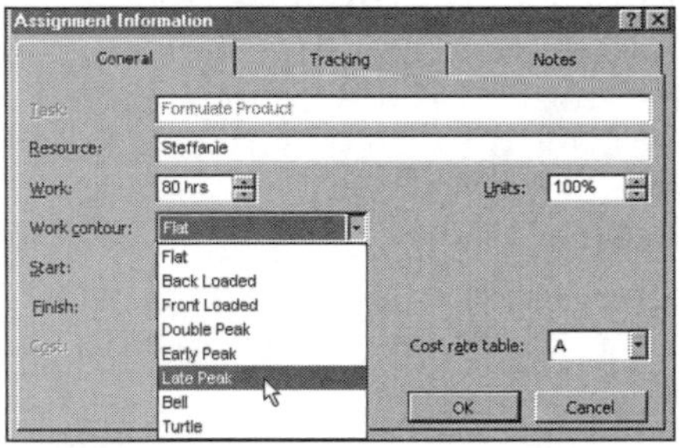

**Figure 11.10**

*Change the Work Contour in the Assignment Information dialog box.*

---

## The Least You Need to Know

➤ Resource overallocation can be leveled manually or automatically with Microsoft Project 2000.

➤ Leveling resources on the critical path may extend the duration of the project.

➤ Resource overallocations should first be reduced by using available slack time.

➤ Resource contours can be used to fine tune resource usage within a task.

# Part 4
# Managing for Success

*Unfortunately, you can't do everything alone. It takes a lot of other people, resources, and information to bring in a successful project. And it doesn't take a very big project to create a large problem controlling all this. Microsoft Project 2000 really comes to the rescue in the control department.*

*In Part 4, you'll learn how to use your project plan and Microsoft Project 2000 to monitor and control every important aspect of your project. A good plan helps you get and stay in control. It helps you understand where the project is flexible and where it isn't. You'll learn how to identify potential problems, plan alternative courses of action, and use your resources most effectively. You'll learn how to use reports, views, and charts. You'll learn how to gather and publish all the information you need to take action with confidence—and manage for success.*

Looking Good!

# Chapter 12

# Monitoring Progress

## In This Chapter

➤ Collecting project actuals—task start and finish dates, durations, and costs— and updating the plan

➤ Understanding why tracking project progress doesn't always reveal project achievement

➤ Establishing a baseline to monitor project performance

➤ Uncovering hidden problems before they can sidetrack your project

Creating a project plan provides three major benefits, the first of which is that planning is a learning process. The more you plan, the more you learn about the project, the possible problems, and the most effective implementation strategy. Secondly, the plan provides the basis of all communications to the project team and the project's stakeholders, both before and during implementation. Finally, the plan provides a scale to gauge project progress. And at that point, the race is on!

## When the Plan Is Complete and You're Ready to Go

Now comes the process of moving the project forward until you've achieved success. Staying in control of a project requires information—a lot of it! However, the last thing you need is busy work. You already have enough to do, don't you? So the information needs to be in a format that's easy to collect, easy to enter, and easy to understand.

In this chapter you'll gather the information you need to measure project progress. You'll learn how to use the hard data on completion status, resource use, and budget compliance. However, projects are about more than just data. Projects are about people. It takes high levels of communication, cooperation, and motivation to bring a difficult project in successfully. With Microsoft Project 2000, you'll be able to stay in touch with the data and still have time to stay in touch with your most important resource—the people.

Project 2000 facilitates your ability to understand what's happening quickly. And with better information, you're able to act more decisively and with greater confidence. Better, faster information means better, faster decisions. And that means better, faster project results!

What could be better?

### Avoiding the Myth of the Perfect Plan

If you're a rookie project planner, there's a common mistake you'll want to avoid. In fact, it's a perfectly common mistake to make. It's the belief that with foresight and skill, a plan can be created that, if closely followed, will ensure project success. Alas, the myth of the perfect plan! Need I remind you that Murphy, uninvited guest though he may be, is on your project team?

When your plan is complete and you're ready to go, remember, the plan is never actually finished. You're dealing with the unknown, so be ready and willing to change the plan as you must. The perfect plan is only as perfect as your willingness to adapt it to changing conditions. Adjust, amend, and improve it as you proceed.

There is no such thing as a perfect plan. The closest thing you can get is a perfectly adaptable plan.

## Chaos Control for Project Managers

To maintain control of a project, the project manager must have an understanding of the project's state of forwardness. As the phrase "state of forwardness" implies, the true status of a project goes beyond the percentage of completion, units achieved, or budget compliance. Although all these measures of project progress are important, none of them, whether considered alone or together, tell the whole story.

# Measuring Progress

Collecting and measuring progress data, as set forth in typical project plans, may ignore essential indicators of achievement:

➤ Is the implementation strategy producing the expected results?

➤ Are problems being effectively dealt with as the project unfolds? Or are problems being avoided, perhaps piling up, only to block progress at some point in the future?

➤ Is the project team staying focused, positive, and productive?

➤ Is stakeholder interest remaining at satisfactory levels or is their interest waning?

➤ If the project is a success, will it achieve the desired results?

Measuring progress solely against a plan has other problems as well. Even the best plans are only estimates of how the future will unfold. No one gets the future right all the time. Even the best planners occasionally overlook essential elements or critical phases, or fail to realize the significance of unexpected difficulties.

For example, consider a major health care company's project of developing a revolutionary new medical device. For over a year, the project was on budget, on time, and according to the project plan, progressing well.

There was, however, one flaw in the project's progress. The results of this device, as predicted in the initial laboratory research, couldn't be replicated in the prototype stage. Literally millions of dollars had been spent. The project team was under pressure to show results. They pressed on, hoping this stumbling block could be resolved. All the while, the project was on track and on budget, according to the plan. But rather than picking up speed on the way to success, the project was picking up speed on the way to disaster!

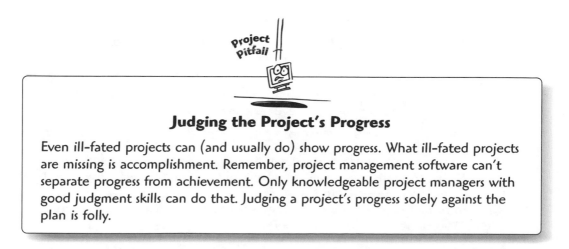

Project Pitfall

### Judging the Project's Progress

Even ill-fated projects can (and usually do) show progress. What ill-fated projects are missing is accomplishment. Remember, project management software can't separate progress from achievement. Only knowledgeable project managers with good judgment skills can do that. Judging a project's progress solely against the plan is folly.

In retrospect, the plan had overlooked one small, but essential element. In this case, a milestone that should have signaled go or no-go hadn't been noted in the plan. As the project manager related this oversight to me, I couldn't help but recall a sign I once saw while driving across a desolate part of the western United States. It read, "You might be lost, but you're making good time."

## Minutiae to Milestones, What Should You Monitor?

Determining how much detail to track can be a difficult choice. Greater amounts of detail don't automatically increase your control. More detail does however, increase your workload and the workload of your team.

When deciding how much detail to track, keep it as simple as possible. Consider the experience level of your team, the difficulty of the project, and the priority of the triple constraints. Also check to see whether the contract documents require any specific progress reporting. Many organizations have a set policy for reporting progress. You'll want to keep your project in compliance with all contractual and organizational procedures.

In all cases, monitor everything that you decided was important enough to include in your plan. This usually includes workflow progress, task durations, and milestone accomplishments. In addition, you may want to include resources, equipment, material usage, and expenditures.

Secrets of Success

### Focus on Success, Not Perfection

In the dynamic world of projects, you may be forced to veer from the original plan frequently. Teams, durations, equipment, and resources may be in constant flux. In this environment, keeping the plan perfectly up-to-date may prove impossible. Nonetheless, by selecting the right milestones and focusing on this achievement, you can complete even the most chaotic project successfully.

Don't however, get trapped in the detail. Successful project managers monitor achievement and attitude as well as budgets and durations. The best way to do that is to make sure your project plan identifies all key achievement milestones. For additional information on setting milestones, see Chapter 4, "Thinking of Everything, Even If You Don't Know What You're Doing."

Manage your milestones with an obsession! They are the key to achieving success.

**Measuring Real Progress**

Seasoned project managers realize that progress reported by hours of work or percentage of completion can be grossly misleading. Difficulties may arise, or worse yet, the person responsible for the task may not accurately report his progress. To avoid these problems, rely on observed achievement rather than reported progress. With this approach, the project manager gauges three checkpoints for each task or milestone—not started, in progress, or completed. This progress information should be weighted heavily in all management decisions.

# Collecting the Information

The fastest way to collect project information is to have the person in charge of each task provide status updates. With a little work, this can be input directly into the project plan via email or the Web. These methods are described in Chapters 18, "Publishing Projects on the Web," and 19, "Communicating with Teams via Email."

These methods work great in some situations, but for most projects, progress reporting is still done the old-fashioned way—people talking to people.

Whether it's done electronically or person-to-person, remember that until a task is completed, progress is always a judgment call. Furthermore, when asked to evaluate progress, some team members are naturally optimistic (perhaps overly so), and others may be pessimistic. Always consider the source and quality of the progress information you're relying on. Whenever possible get out of your office. Go see for yourself!

**M.B.W.A. Lives On!**

There was a time when M.B.W.A. (managing by walking around) was in vogue. Managers were encouraged to get out of their offices and see what was going on. That's still good advice. The game is won or lost on the field of play, not in the bleachers. The closer you get to the work and the people doing the work, the better your perspective will be.

## *Finding the Bad News Is Good News*

Effectively managing a project requires the ability to find out what's not going well, and then fix it. Moreover, spotting the problem early is important—that's when you have more options available to solve the problem. (For problem solving techniques see Chapter 14, "When the Going Gets Tough, the Tough Get Creative.")

Unfortunately, the natural tendency in most project teams is to delay announcing problems or to minimize a problem's significance. In fact, good news travels faster than bad news in the project environment! Because bad news won't come to you, you've got to go to it! Seek it out. When you find bad news, that's good! Now you can fix the problem.

The best way to uncover problems is to ask open-ended questions. Don't wait for trouble; ask your team probing questions on an ongoing basis. You'll get best results with a polite and gracious demeanor, so keep rapport levels high. The following list of questions is effective:

➤ What problems have you encountered thus far?

➤ What problems do your foresee?

➤ What is your biggest concern right now?

➤ How might this change in the future?

➤ How is the project going?

If you receive a one-word answer such as "fine," continue probing with this, my all time favorite probing technique:

➤ Tell me about it.

   You needn't stop after using it once. In fact, it becomes increasingly useful as you continue:

➤ Tell me about that!

Open-ended questions uncover essential information that your plan does not directly address. When using these probing questions, remain emotionally neutral. Don't send messages of mistrust, fear, or condemnation with your tone or demeanor. Make sure they see you as a project manager who seeks the good and the bad news with equal candor and professionalism.

## Collecting Progress Information

You need a steady stream of information to monitor project progress. As a rule, collect data on everything included in your plan (tasks, durations, resources, equipment, budgets, and milestones). This may include the actual start and finish dates of tasks, the percentage of work completed, and the actual costs incurred. We refer to these experienced values as *actuals*.

You'll get the best results if the actuals are collected at set intervals of time. On projects a year or more in duration, collecting data monthly is probably sufficient. For projects two or three months in duration, you may want to collect data weekly. In fast moving projects with a duration of a few days to a month or two, you may need daily updates. Collect actuals often enough to identify problems early.

# Establishing a Baseline

To provide an easy reference point for comparing actuals against the plan, Project 2000 enables you to set a baseline. Key information about tasks, resources, and assignments is captured and stored for comparisons.

To set a baseline, open the **Tools** menu, select **Tracking**, and then choose **Save baseline** and **Entire project**. The dialog box appears as shown in Figure 12.1. Your baseline is set that easy!

If the Planning Wizard is active, it prompts you to set a baseline when you save the project file. (You can turn the wizard on or off by selecting **Options** from the **Tools** menu and going to the **General** tab in the dialog box. Then check or uncheck **Advice from Planning Wizard**.)

**Figure 12.1**

*Setting a baseline after the plan has been completed and just before the project begins allows you to compare actuals against the plan.*

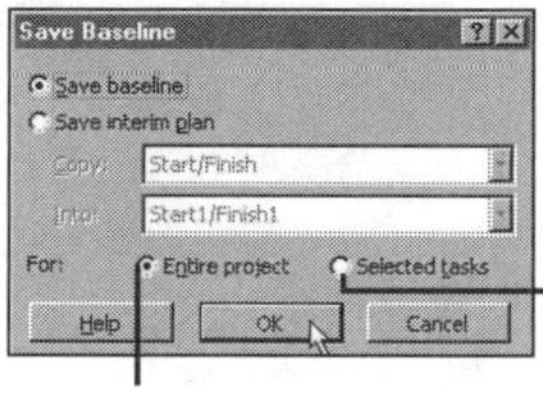

To set a baseline for tasks added after the original baseline has been established, select **Selected tasks**.

Select **Entire project** to establish the initial baseline.

If you add or change a task after you've set the initial baseline, don't worry. You can always set new baseline information for them. First, select the tasks for which you want to set a baseline. If the tasks are next to one another, click the first one, then press **Shift** and click the last one. If the tasks are not adjacent, click the first one, then press **Ctrl** while you click each additional task. After they are all highlighted, select the **Select tasks** option in the Save Baseline dialog box and click **OK**.

Now that your baseline is set, you can begin recording the project's actual performance.

# Updating Your Project Plan

Entering actuals can be as complex or as simple as you want to make it. At a minimal level, you can track the start and finish dates of each task. If you need to track more, there are many options available. Project 2000 allows you to track durations, work, resources used, and costs incurred.

# Entering Task Start and Finish Actuals

Tracking the start and finish dates of tasks helps you keep the project on schedule. As we have seen, if tasks on the critical path finish late, the entire project will finish later than planned. Always keep a close watch on all critical tasks' start and finish dates.

The easiest way to enter the actual start and finish dates is in a combination view. Open the Tracking Gantt view by selecting it from the **View** menu. Now open a lower pane by clicking and dragging on the split bar in the bottom right of your screen, just below the vertical scrollbar. Click in the lower pane to make it active and open the More Views dialog box. Find the Task Details Form view and apply it. Your screen should now look like the one in Figure 12.2.

Top of bar shows current plan.

Bottom of bar shows plan's baseline.

Panes are coordinated so that the current task is shown in the bottom pane.

Task's percentage of completion

**Figure 12.2**

*The combination Tracking Gantt and Task Details Form view makes it fast and easy to update the task's basic tracking information.*

Changing the Current plan inserts a Start No Later Than or Finish No Later Than constraint.

Baseline may be adjusted here.

Change actual Start and Finish dates.

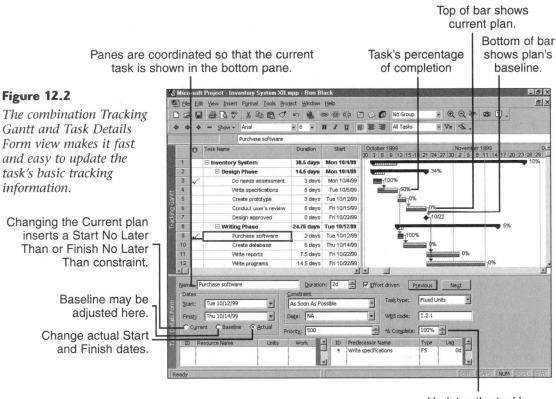

Updates the task's percentage of completion

# Entering the Task's Actual Work or Duration

Every once in a while, Project 2000 does so much that it can become a little tricky. Remember how Project calculated work, duration, and units in Chapter 8, "The

Resourceful Use of Resources"? When you update work or duration actuals, these relationships are at it again. It's easiest to understand how duration and work affect one another by reviewing their definitions:

*Actual duration* is the amount of time the task has been in progress.

*Actual work* is the amount of work that has been accomplished.

Obviously, work may proceed better or worse than planned. Therefore, Actual Duration and Actual Work may not always be in direct proportion to one another. For example, if resources were assigned to an effort-driven task (the default), you should ignore Actual Duration and enter Actual Work completed. Project 2000 then calculates Remaining Work as Work (planned) minus Actual Work. It also calculates Percent Work Complete as Actual Work divided by Remaining Work.

When you update a task's Actual Duration, Project 2000 calculates the Percentage of Completion as Actual Duration divided by Duration. Remaining Duration is calculated as Duration minus Actual Duration.

The easiest way to enter updates for Actual Duration or Actual Work is to use the Tracking table in the Task Sheet view. Open the **View** menu and select **More Views**. Now find **Task Sheet** in the **More Views** dialog box and apply it. To make the Tracking table active, open the **View** menu, select **Table**, and then choose **Tracking**. This view is shown in Figure 12.3.

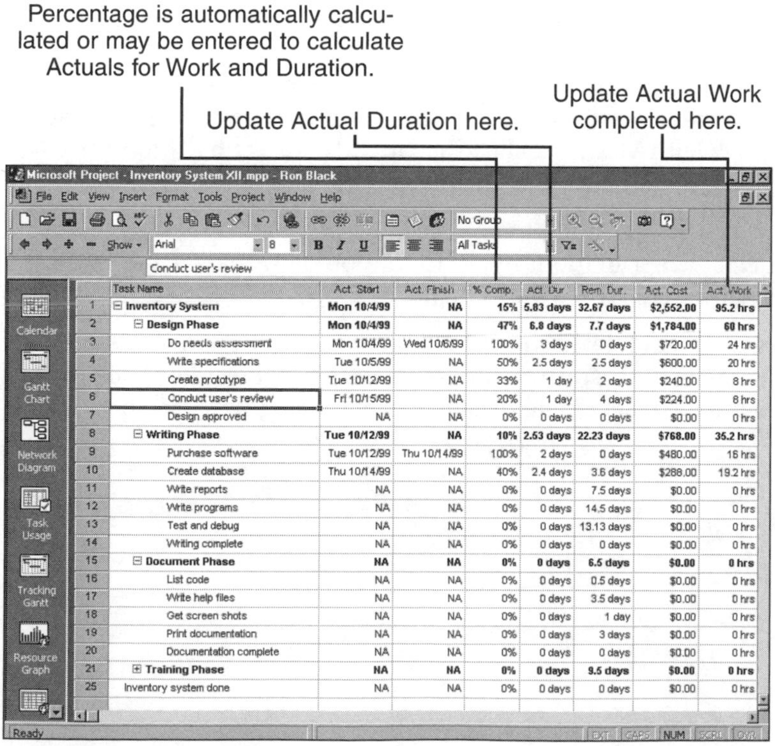

Percentage is automatically calculated or may be entered to calculate Actuals for Work and Duration.

Update Actual Duration here.

Update Actual Work completed here.

**Figure 12.3**

*The Tracking table in the Task Sheet view makes fast work of entering Actual Work, Actual Durations, or Percentage of Completion.*

151

When you enter a percentage of completion, Project 2000 calculates Actual Work and Remaining Work. First it calculates Actual Work as Work times the Percentage Complete. Then Remaining Work is calculated as Work minus Actual Work.

Summary Task percentages of completion are calculated as the total Actual Work of the related subtasks divided by the total Work of the subtasks. In other words, subtasks are rolled up to calculate their summary task's percentage of completion. You can manually change the summary task's percentage of completion also. However, the subtasks are set as complete according to their listing order, not their actual completion. It looks nice, but don't rely too heavily on the information!

Another method of updating tasks is available directly from the toolbar. Place your pointer on the toolbar and right-click. Select the **Tracking** toolbar from the pop-up list as shown in Figure 12.4.

**Figure 12.4**

*Open the Tracking toolbar to quickly mark the percentage of completion for selected tasks in any view.*

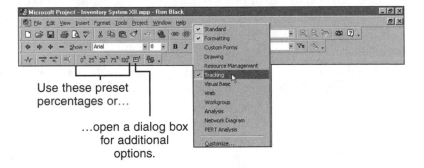

One of the great things about Project is that you can immediately see what effects your changes and updates make on the schedule. To view these effects when updating actuals, open the Tracking Gantt view and click the **Update Tasks** button on the Tracking toolbar. The Update Tasks button is shown in Figure 12.5.

The Update Tasks dialog box may be used to change Percentage of Work Complete, Actual Duration, and Remaining Duration. In addition, you may change a task's Actual Start and Finish dates here, as shown in Figure 12.5.

When you don't need this level of detail in your actuals, use the Update Project dialog box to track progress. Select the **Tools** menu as shown in Figure 12.6. Then, select **Tracking** and click **Update Project**. The Update Project dialog box shown in Figure 12.7 appears.

Sets a task's percentage of completion

Opens the Update Tasks dialog box

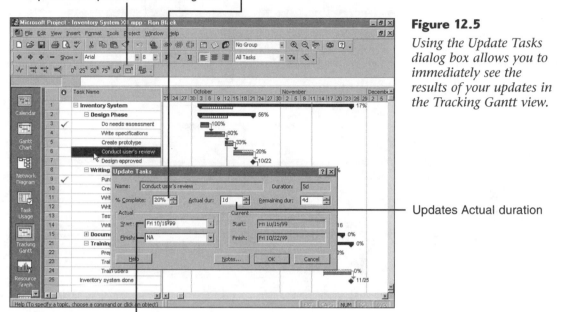

**Figure 12.5**

*Using the Update Tasks dialog box allows you to immediately see the results of your updates in the Tracking Gantt view.*

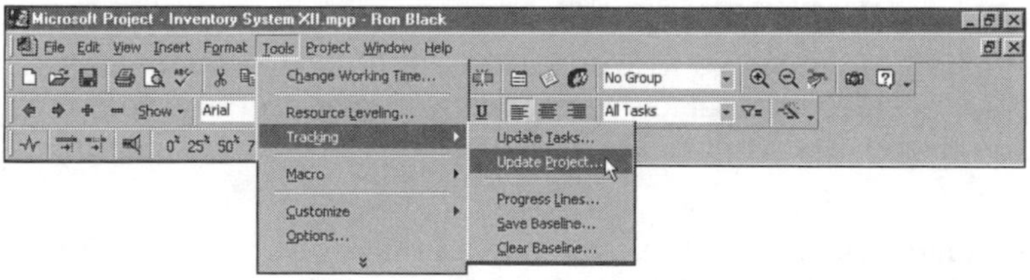

Updates Actual duration

Entering Start or Finish Dates takes precedence over other entries.

**Figure 12.6**

*Select **Update Project** from the **Tracking** menu.*

Work has been set as
complete through October 15.

**Figure 12.7**

*When your project is
being completed exactly as
planned, the fastest way
to update is with the
Update Project dialog box.*

Percentage complete is
calculated based on
planned start and
finish dates.

Tasks are shown only as
0% or 100% complete.

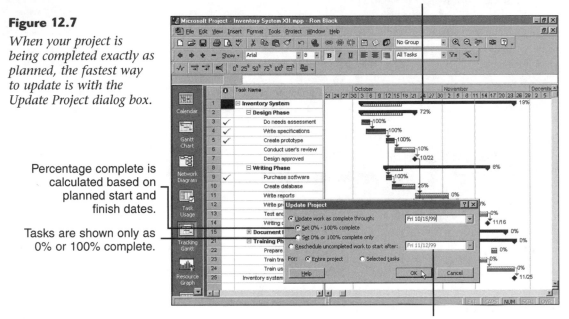

Remaining work is rescheduled after this date
with a Start No Earlier Than constraint.

# *Bringing Your Costs Incurred Up to Date*

By default, costs are automatically updated for you in Project 2000. As you update
duration or work, costs are accrued as a percentage of task completion times the sum
of the task's resource and fixed costs. This makes updating costs easy (and sometimes
overly simplistic)!

It is rare that costs are actually incurred at the same rate as a task's completion. For
example, consider the task of roofing a large building. The materials would probably
be delivered (and the costs incurred) long before labor on the task begins. In this
case, Project 2000 would accrue material costs, incorrectly, throughout their application (or at the beginning or end) rather than upon their delivery. Worse yet, if installation of the roofing was delayed, actual costs on this task would be understated for
quite some time.

Although the costing method employed by Project is rudimentary, it provides adequate tracking capability for many projects.

If you decide to override the default cost accrual methods (and this is often wise), and
enter your own actual cost information, the procedure is straightforward. First, stop
Project 2000 from automatically calculating costs on an accrual basis. To do this,
choose **Options** from the **Tools** menu to open the Options dialog box. Then click
the **Calculation** tab and clear the check mark from the **Actual costs are always
calculated by Microsoft Project** check box, as shown in Figure 12.8.

## 154

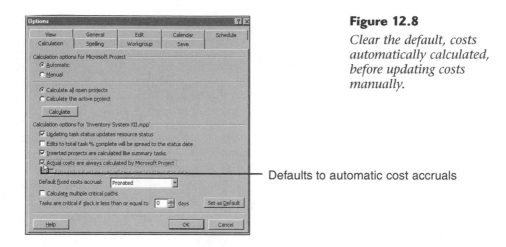

**Figure 12.8**

*Clear the default, costs automatically calculated, before updating costs manually.*

— Defaults to automatic cost accruals

The easiest method to update costs depends on the type of cost involved. Methods for updating actuals for accrued resource assignment costs, per-use resource costs, and fixed task costs are described next.

### Updating Actuals for Accrued Resource Costs

Accrued resource assignment costs are those costs that result from resource assignments. This includes labor, rent, or other costs that accrue as a function of the amount of work or duration the task requires. To enter actuals for these costs, select **Task Usage** from the **View** menu. Select **Table Tracking** from the **View** menu, and then select **Tracking** from the submenu that appears (see Figure 12.9).

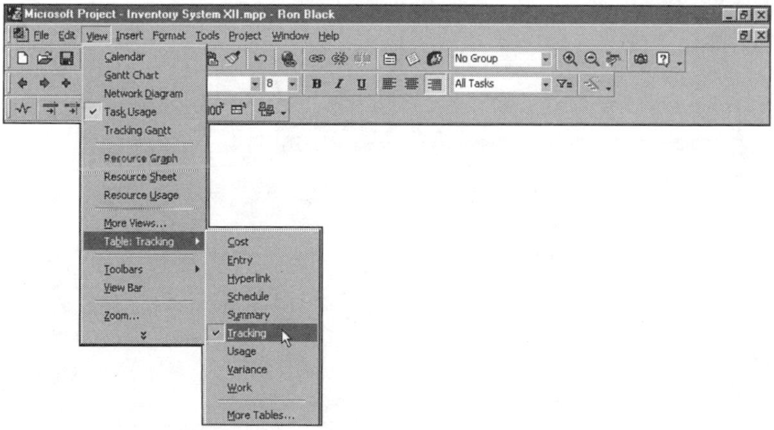

**Figure 12.9**

*Using the Table Tracking and Task Usage options allows easy updates to actual costs for resources.*

To update actual costs for the resource up to the current date, click the **Act. Cost** field and enter the total costs (see Figure 12.10).

**155**

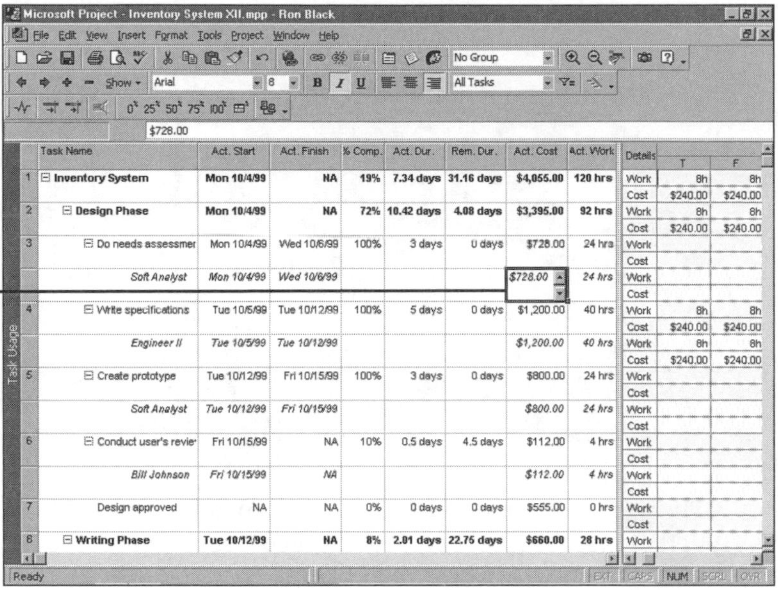

**Figure 12.10**

*To update an accrued resource assignment cost, use the Task Usage view.*

Enter the actual cost
for the resource.

To update the costs for a resource on a day-by-day basis, use the Task Usage pane. Drag open the pane until the dates are revealed. Right-click in the Task Usage table and add **Actual Cost** to the table from the pop-up menu, as shown in Figure 12.11.

Scroll to the dates and tasks you want to update and enter the actuals. Notice that the Act. Cost field changes as you enter the actuals. If the wrong timescale is showing (perhaps weeks rather than days), right-click the Task Usage table column heads and select **Timescale**. Change the scale to match your actuals data. Return to the Task usage table and enter the actuals.

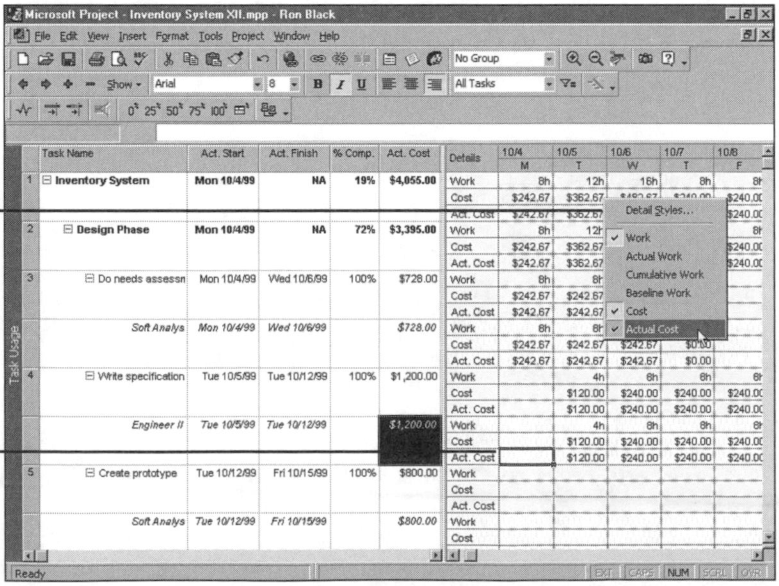

**Figure 12.11**

*To enter actual costs by resource and period, use the Task Usage table.*

Right-click in the Task
Usage table to add Actual
Costs to the fields shown.

Enter actuals for each
resource by period.

## *Updating Actual Per-Use Resource Costs*

Per-use resource cost actuals are entered in the Resource Sheet. In the **View** menu select **Resource Sheet**, point to **Table** and then click **Entry**. Go to the Cost/Use field and enter the actual for the resources you want to change, as shown in Figure 12.12. The change is updated to all tasks that resource is assigned to as well as the project's total scheduled costs.

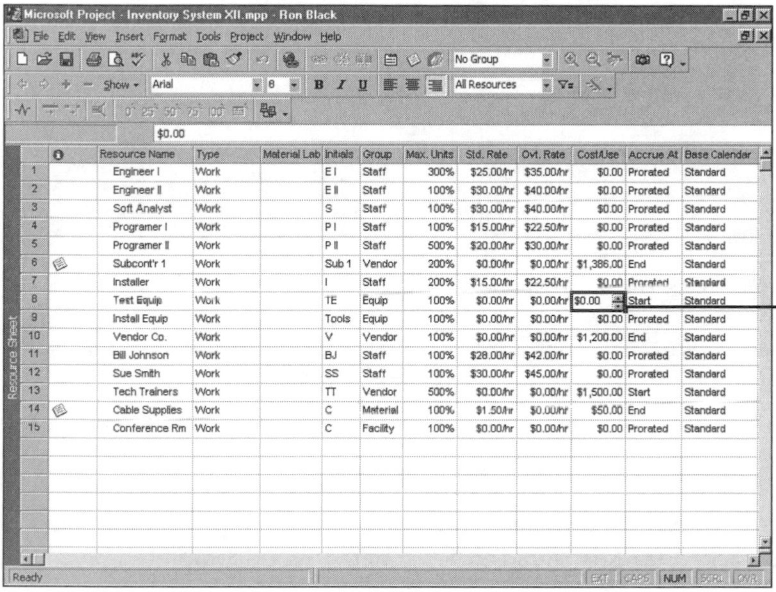

**Figure 12.12**

*Use the Resource Sheet Entry table to update per-use actuals. Costs for all tasks using this resource are recalculated.*

Enter actuals for per-use costs here.

## *Updating Actual Fixed Task Costs*

To update actuals for fixed task costs, use the Task Sheet. From the **View** menu, select **More Views**, and then apply the **Task Sheet**. Then point to **Table Tracking** from the **View** menu and select **Cost**. You're ready to enter fixed costs. Click in the **Fixed Cost** field and enter the actual value, as shown in Figure 12.13. Project recalculates the project's scheduled costs whenever the Fixed Cost is changed.

Congratulations! You've just mastered updating the project plan with actuals. In the next chapter, you'll learn how to turn all this new data into information you can use with Project's powerful analysis tools.

157

**Figure 12.13**

*The Task Sheet cost table provides the easiest way to update Fixed Cost actuals.*

Change Fixed Cost
actuals here.

| | Task Name | Fixed Cost | Fixed Cost Accrual | Total Cost | Baseline | Variance | Actual | Remaining |
|---|---|---|---|---|---|---|---|---|
| 1 | ⊟ **Inventory System** | **$0.00** | **Prorated** | **$16,002.00** | **$0.00** | **$16,002.00** | **$3,500.00** | **$12,502.00** |
| 2 | ⊟ **Design Phase** | **$0.00** | **Prorated** | **$3,848.00** | **$0.00** | **$3,848.00** | **$2,840.00** | **$1,008.00** |
| 3 | Do needs assessment | $0.00 | Prorated | $728.00 | $900.00 | ($172.00) | $728.00 | $0.00 |
| 4 | Write specifications | $0.00 | Prorated | $1,200.00 | $1,400.00 | ($200.00) | $1,200.00 | $0.00 |
| 5 | Create prototype | $0.00 | Prorated | $800.00 | $750.00 | $50.00 | $800.00 | $0.00 |
| 6 | Conduct user's review | $0.00 | Prorated | $1,120.00 | $2,000.00 | ($880.00) | $112.00 | $1,000.00 |
| 7 | Design approved | $0.00 | Prorated | $0.00 | $0.00 | $0.00 | $0.00 | $0.00 |
| 8 | ⊟ **Writing Phase** | **$0.00** | **Prorated** | **$6,766.00** | **$0.00** | **$6,766.00** | **$660.00** | **$6,106.00** |
| 9 | Purchase software | $1,200.00 | Prorated | $480.00 | $1,800.00 | ($1,320.00) | $480.00 | $0.00 |
| 10 | Create database | $0.00 | Prorated | $720.00 | $750.00 | ($30.00) | $180.00 | $540.00 |
| 11 | Write reports | $0.00 | Prorated | $1,200.00 | $1,500.00 | ($300.00) | $0.00 | $1,200.00 |
| 12 | Write programs | $0.00 | Prorated | $1,740.00 | $3,000.00 | ($1,260.00) | $0.00 | $1,740.00 |
| 13 | Test and debug | $0.00 | Prorated | $2,626.00 | $3,100.00 | ($474.00) | $0.00 | $2,626.00 |
| 14 | Writing complete | $0.00 | Prorated | $0.00 | $0.00 | $0.00 | $0.00 | $0.00 |
| 15 | ⊞ **Document Phase** | **$0.00** | **Prorated** | **$4,238.00** | **$0.00** | **$4,238.00** | **$0.00** | **$4,238.00** |
| 21 | ⊟ **Training Phase** | **$0.00** | **Prorated** | **$1,150.00** | **$0.00** | **$1,150.00** | **$0.00** | **$1,150.00** |
| 22 | Prepare materials | $400.00 | Prorated | $400.00 | $400.00 | $0.00 | $0.00 | $400.00 |
| 23 | Train trainers | $250.00 | Prorated | $250.00 | $250.00 | $0.00 | $0.00 | $250.00 |
| 24 | Train users | $500.00 | Prorated | $500.00 | $500.00 | $0.00 | $0.00 | $500.00 |
| 25 | Inventory system done | $0.00 | Prorated | $0.00 | $0.00 | $0.00 | $0.00 | $0.00 |

## The Least You Need to Know

➤ Project actuals provide the information you need to keep a project on track. Actuals can be tracked for task start and finish dates, work completed, and costs incurred.

➤ Baselines can be set for the project to provide a comparison of actuals to the plan.

➤ At minimum, closely watch task start and finish dates on the critical path. When these tasks slip, the entire project may be at risk of not finishing on time.

➤ In turbulent project environments, milestones should be carefully selected and managed. Trying to stay abreast of the minutiae can take your attention away from true achievement.

➤ Not all the information you need to complete your project successfully can be tracked with the project plan. To gather other essential information, be observant, ask open-ended questions, and maintain high levels of communication with your team.

# Chapter 13

# Managing Progress

## In This Chapter

➤ Analyzing project progress with charts, tables, views and reports

➤ Keeping your team informed of commitments, schedules, and deadlines

➤ Identifying project bottlenecks and problems before they occur

➤ Developing strategies to get a project back on track

The entire project management body of knowledge was created around the notion that a picture is worth a thousand words. Understanding workflow, time, resources, and costs requires a lot of data. Unfortunately, data isn't information. It's just detail: facts, figures, amounts, costs, dates, relationships, tasks,...well, you get the point. In most projects there is enough data to get lost in. And that's exactly what some project managers do. They're stuck in their offices until late at night, sorting through reams of meaningless data, trying to sort the good news from the bad. And while they're lost in all that data, the project is unmanaged, possibly wandering off course or, worse yet, grinding to a complete halt.

You, on the other hand, made the good decision to bring order and control to this chaos. You invested in Microsoft Project 2000 and this book. And now you get to cash in on all your work thus far. In this chapter you get to turn all the data you've so meticulously created into the stuff success is made of: information! Get ready to be amazed. You're about to experience the primary benefits of Project 2000. You're about to take a quantum leap and turn data into information. You'll be able to monitor progress, analyze options, communicate with your team, and keep your boss smiling. You may even be able to make it home in time for dinner!

# Analyzing Project Progress

Good project managers know exactly where their project stands every step of the way. Their fingers are on the project's pulse, monitoring progress, catching problems early, anticipating needs, and effectively using every resource at their disposal. Most of their information comes from the views, charts, and reports that are ready to use right out of the Project 2000 box.

If you need to emphasize key information, filter out unnecessary data, or highlight elements with special formatting, Project won't disappoint you. In fact, there are so many options that they can get in the way if you let them. Just remember, the idea is to make your job faster and easier, not more difficult. Learn to use the basics expertly, and leave the fancy window dressing to the rookies. You're seeking project success, not an award for best-dressed network diagram!

## Project Statistics at a Glance

For a quick overview of your project, use the Project Statistics dialog box, as shown in Figure 13.1. This quick look describes the project in broad brushstrokes—start dates, finish dates, variances, duration, work, and cost. It is a good way for department heads or division managers to stay abreast of multiple projects within their areas of responsibility.

For example, if all project plans are accessible from the manager's computer (perhaps in one directory of a local area network), the manager can easily pop open this screen for each project and monitor progress. To view the Project Statistics dialog box, select **Project Information** from the **Project** menu and click **Statistics**.

This is a trick you may or may not want to teach to your boss!

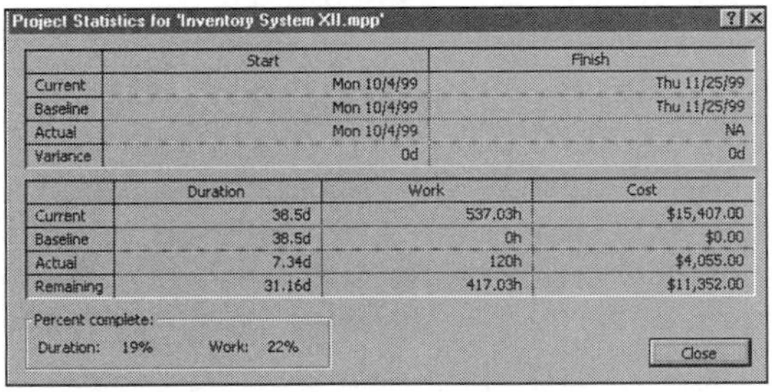

**Figure 13.1**

*The Project Statistics dialog box provides a quick look at project status.*

## Gantt Charts

The Gantt chart may be the most useful project management document ever developed. It has been around since the beginning of the 20th century, and it's still going strong! (We should all be so lucky.) Its popularity is no doubt due to its power to communicate and its inherit ease to understand. With little instruction, even the most bone-headed member of your team (just kidding) can understand a Gantt chart. This is one useful, easy to read project document!

### Thanks, Henry!

The Gantt chart was developed around the turn of the century (one hundred years ago, that is) by industrial engineer Henry Gantt. America was in the middle of the industrial revolution (the revolution just before the information revolution, that is). Complex manufacturing and construction projects abounded—skyscrapers, battleships, and new assembly lines were common projects. Mr. Gantt added greatly to the project management body of knowledge by developing his graphical representation of a project's tasks, duration, and sequence of work. His simple bar chart is so useful and easy to understand that I'll bet it'll be around for another hundred years! Thanks, Henry!

### The Critical Path

The *critical path* determines how long the project will take to complete. Tasks on the critical path are called critical tasks, not because they are more important to the project's success, but because they are more important to the project finishing on time. If a task on the critical path finishes late, the project will finish late. On time-sensitive projects, manage the critical path carefully.

The Gantt chart is great because it shows task start and stop times, durations, and workflow sequences, all on a timeline. And if you hang a little more information on it, you can communicate resources, costs, completion, and other detailed information clearly. With the right formatting, the critical path is visible and kept in the forefront of your thinking. When time is of the essence (and it usually is), a Gantt chart is good to have around.

## The Gantt Chart View

This is the default view for Project 2000, and for good reason. This view uses both text and graphics to communicate tasks, durations, and workflow sequence, as shown in Figure 13.2. The graphical depiction is created on a timescale where each task is represented as a bar whose length indicates the task's duration.

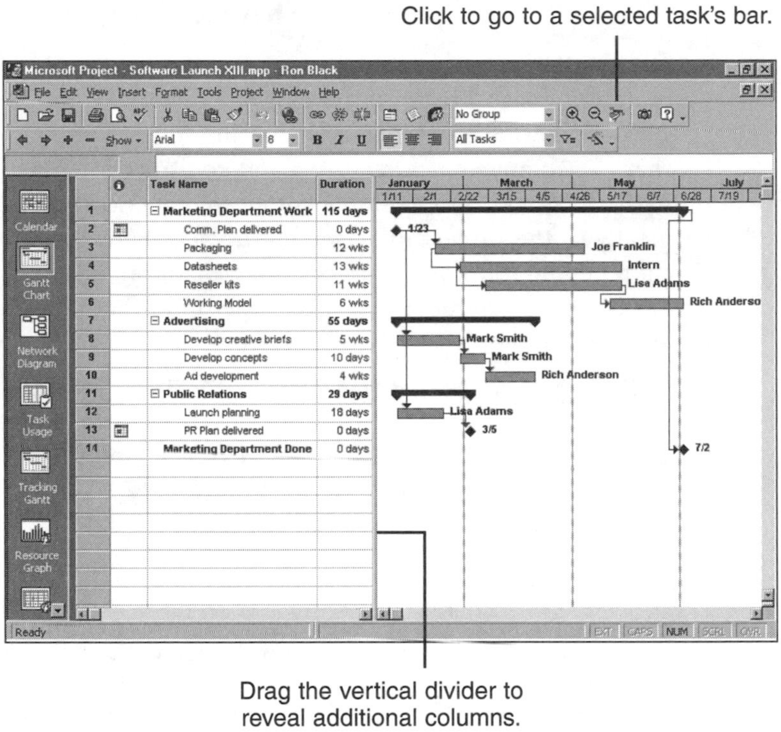

Click to go to a selected task's bar.

**Figure 13.2**

*The Gantt Chart view is the default view. Use it to set up your project's basic information and to communicate workflow to team members and stakeholders.*

Drag the vertical divider to reveal additional columns.

The right side of this view is displayed as a Gantt chart and the left side as a sheet. The sheet provides detailed information, such as start and finish dates, duration, predecessors, and resources assigned to the task. Columns may be hidden or inserted by right-clicking the column header and selecting **Insert Column** or **Hide Column**. Column widths may be adjusted by clicking and dragging the column head divider lines. The vertical divider between the sheet and the chart may be dragged to the left or right, providing additional space for the information you are interested in.

The Gantt view is good for

➤ Entering the work breakdown structure and establishing tasks, summary tasks, and milestone tasks.

➤ Creating the initial workflow sequence by establishing task dependencies either in the predecessor column or by linking tasks in the Gantt Chart view.

➤ Entering estimated durations, and with the PERT Analysis toolbar activated, entering weighted average durations with PERT estimates.

➤ Establishing a project schedule and total project duration.

➤ Assigning personnel and other resources to the project, task by task.

➤ Communicating to project personnel when they will need to start and finish the tasks they are responsible for.

➤ Communicating an overview of the project's workflow and total duration to stakeholders.

Wow! No wonder this chart has been so popular all these years! To open the Gantt Chart view, click **Gantt Chart** from the **View** menu or from the View bar.

## The Detail Gantt View

The Detail Gantt view is an important view for managing your project's scheduled completion dates. Slack and slippage is graphically displayed, alerting you to potential deadline problems. In Figure 13.3, the task "Reseller kits" was completed 10 days late. This caused the task "Working Model" to start 10 days late, which in turn has pushed out the originally planned project completion date by the same 10 days.

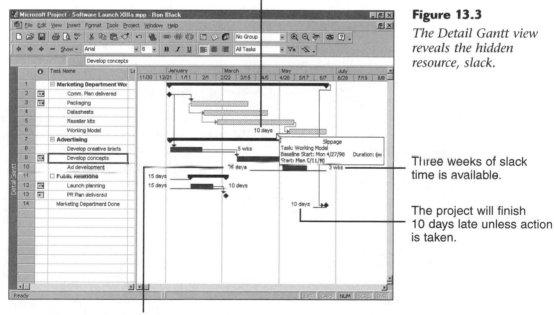

A critical task has started 10 days late.

**Figure 13.3**

*The Detail Gantt view reveals the hidden resource, slack.*

Three weeks of slack time is available.

The project will finish 10 days late unless action is taken.

Slippage of 25 days has occurred.

The alert project manager may be able to bring additional resources to this critical task and expedite its completion. If she can trim 10 days or more out of the task, the project can still be completed on time. The problem is, where is the project manager going to get the additional resources?

The Detail Gantt sometimes come to the rescue as well as to the alert! Assuming that the resources assigned to "Ad development" are qualified, they may be able to help out. According to the Detail Gantt, although "Ad development" has already slipped 25 days, it isn't yet in danger of being late. In fact, it has slack time of 3 weeks available. In other words, this task can be delayed up to 3 more weeks and not impact the project's deadline. Pulling the resources off "Ad development" and using them on the "Working model" task should do the trick!

Now that's putting the power of information to work—this time saving the project manager's reputation!

The Detail Gantt view is good for

➤ Everything the Gantt chart is good for, but because of the additional information it depicts, the Detail Gantt may confuse team members who do not understand the concepts of critical paths, slack, and slippage.

➤ Identifying task slack time and task slippage.

➤ Evaluating resource use options.

### The Leveling Gantt View

When you have a limited supply of resources to cover all the work in a project, your favorite view is bound to be the Leveling Gantt. This view is used in conjunction with the robust leveling features of Project 2000. When a resource is scheduled for two or more tasks at the same time, leveling reschedules the tasks. That way, you don't have to clone people!

To open the Leveling Gantt view, select **More Views** from the **View** menu and apply the **Leveling Gantt**. As shown in Figure 13.4, the right side of the view is just like a Detail Gantt except for one thing: The task bars are split horizontally to indicate the before and after effects of leveling. In Figure 13.4, the effect of leveling workloads on the limited resources was to extend the project's duration one week. To learn more about leveling, refer to Chapter 11, "Leveling Workloads."

The Leveling Gantt view is good for

➤ Viewing the before and after effects of leveling resources.

➤ Understanding which tasks were leveled, the amount of delay used, and how those changes impacted the rest of the schedule.

➤ Reassigning resources to tasks in response to overallocations.

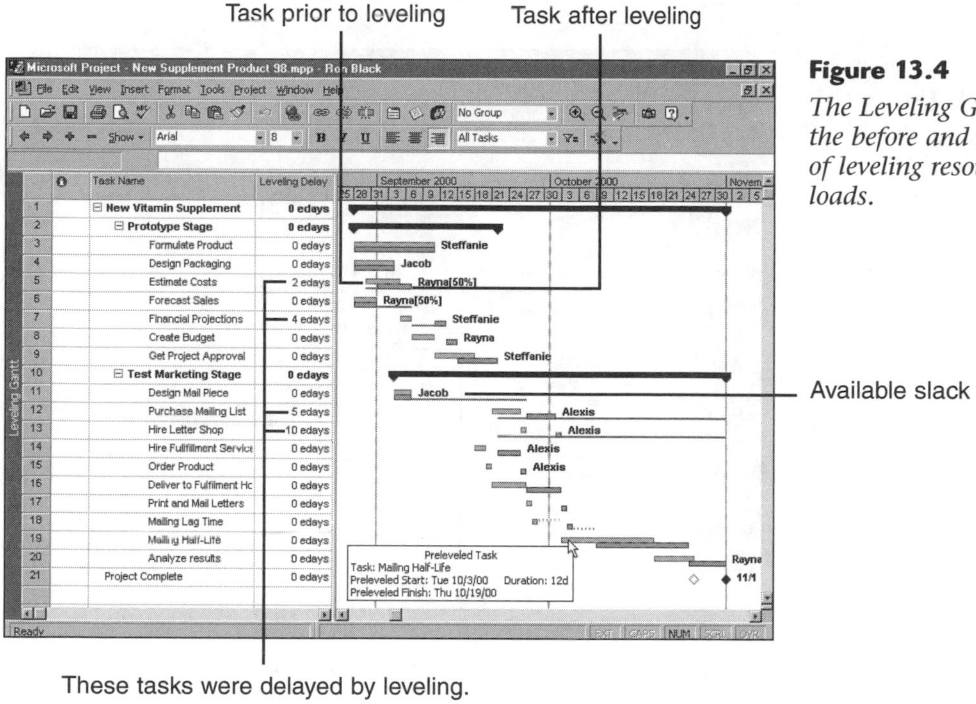

Task prior to leveling    Task after leveling

**Figure 13.4**
*The Leveling Gantt shows the before and after effects of leveling resource workloads.*

Available slack

These tasks were delayed by leveling.

## The Tracking Gantt View

There should be a drum roll playing as this view opens! With one look at the Tracking Gantt view, you can tell whether your project is behind or ahead of schedule. The Tracking Gantt chart displays two bars, similar to the Leveling Gantt. However, this time the lower bar is the plan you originally saved as the baseline. As you update progress, the actuals are shown as the top bar, giving you a task by task view of where you're ahead and where you're behind.

To open the Tracking Gantt, click on it in the View Bar or select it from the **View** menu. As shown in Figure 13.5, task completion is indicated by a solid dark bar and a percentage. As you can see in the figure, this project's difficulties are immediately visible. The "Create database" task has been rescheduled, requiring twice or more its original duration. The resulting delay will extend the project's completion by two weeks.

**Figure 13.5**

*Use the Tracking Gantt view to compare actual progress to the project's baseline.*

Partially completed task

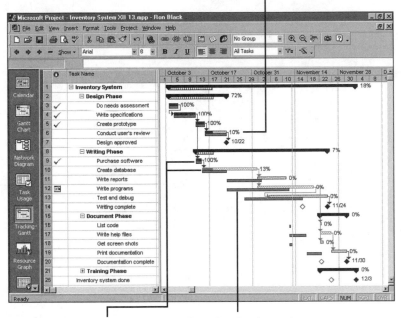

The critical path is recalculated as the project progresses.

Baseline for the task

The Tracking Gantt view is good for

➤ Viewing actual progress compared to the project's baseline.

➤ Viewing actual start and finish dates and their impact on the reminder of the schedule.

➤ Managing the achievement of project milestones.

### Enhancing Your View with Baselines and Progress Lines

You may enhance the communication capability of any Gantt view by adding a baseline or progress line. These enhancements use the project's planned data and actuals to make a visual comparison of progress.

#### Baselines

To use any of the features for comparing actuals to the baseline plan, as you saw in Figure 13.5, you first must set a baseline for your project. Do this when your plan is complete, just before you start the project. If you change the plan, you can always update the baseline. To set a baseline, select the **Tools** menu and point to **Tracking**. Then choose **Save baseline**, and select **Entire project**.

The baseline information that is stored for later comparisons includes

➤ **Task information**—Start and finish dates, duration, work, costs, and splits.

➤ **Resource information**—Work and costs.

➤ **Assignment information**—Start and finish dates, work, cost.

### Progress Lines

Progress lines provide a graphical representation of actuals to the plan as of a given date. Project 2000 draws a vertical line in the Gantt chart. As you can see in Figure 13.6, when it runs over task bars the line stretches to the left or right, connecting at the percentage of completion as of the progress date. For tasks behind schedule the line stretches to the left, and for tasks ahead of schedule, to the right.

Click to add progress lines.

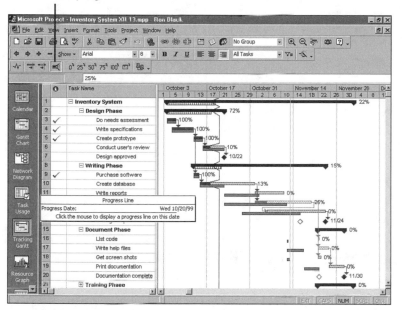

**Figure 13.6**

*Progress lines add a graphic comparison of actuals to a given progress date on any Gantt chart.*

Multiple progress lines may be set to indicate key dates. To add a progress line to your Gantt chart, right-click on the Toolbar and select **Tracking**. Then, click the **Add Progress Line** button on the Tracking toolbar, as shown previously in Figure 13.6. Place the pointer on the Gantt chart where you want to insert a progress line and click.

You may use the actual plan or baseline plan as the comparison point. To change how progress lines are displayed or to remove unwanted lines, select **Tracking** from the **Tools** menu and then click **Progress Lines**.

## The Network Diagram View

Close behind the Gantt chart in popularity is the activity on node diagram. Project calls this diagram by its generic name, the Network Diagram. The name helps to explain its popularity. Network Diagrams clearly display the sequence of workflow and task dependencies as a network of boxes and arrows. (Users of earlier versions of Project will recall that activity on node diagrams were called PERT charts.) See the example in Figure 13.7. Each task is represented as a node (a box), and the dependencies are shown with connecting arrows. To open a Network Diagram view, select **Network Diagram** from the **View** menu or from the menu bar.

**Figure 13.7**

*The Network Diagram provides a good visual representation of the workflow sequence.*

Completed tasks are crossed out.

Tasks in progress are marked with a diagonal line.

Hover your pointer over a node to expand it.

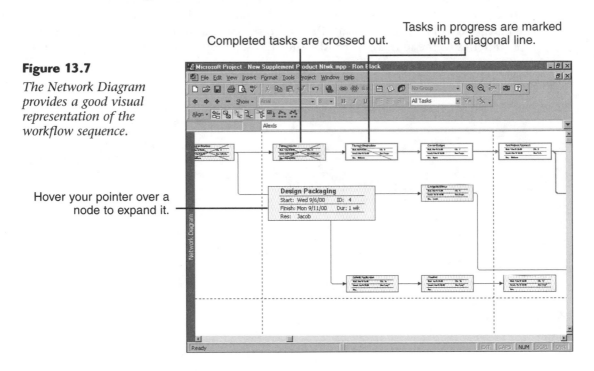

The Network Diagram view is good for

➤ Understanding complex workflow sequences.

➤ Graphically communicating how a task relates to the rest of the project.

➤ Locating strategically important tasks, such as those that must be accomplished before several other paths of work can begin (these are known as work bursts).

## Communicating with Your Team

Don't expect your team to automatically be able to decipher your project documents. Gantt charts and network diagrams can be confusing to the uninitiated. Rather, take some time and discuss each document with those who will be using it. Your project will do better if everyone understands how to use project information to his or her advantage.

There are numerous conventions and vocabulary words that project managers use to mean special things. These include *critical path*, *critical task*, *slack*, *float*, *lead*, *lag*, and *delay*, to name a few. Once again, those who don't understand the special project management meanings of these words will not be as well informed about the project as they should be. Make it a habit to establish an appropriate team vocabulary. The "Speak Like a Geek" glossary can serve as an excellent reference.

## The Calendar View

If you have to communicate a project schedule to anyone who isn't familiar with basic project management documentation, the Calendar view is just what you need! As shown in Figure 13.8, the Calendar view displays tasks as a bar spanning the days it is scheduled on. Everyone knows how to read a calendar, so communicating task responsibilities to even the least informed teammate can be quick and mistake-free.

To display the Calendar view, select **Calendar** from the **View** menu or the View bar.

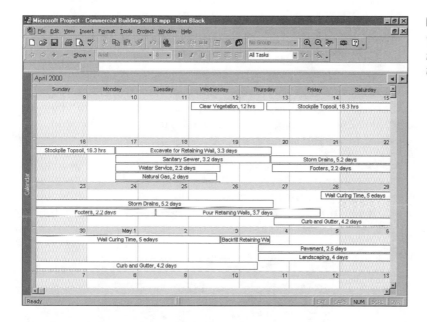

**Figure 13.8**

*The Calendar view makes it easy to communicate the project's schedule.*

## Filtering Information

Information overload is a real possibility in project management. Sometimes it's important to be able to screen out unwanted information so you can focus on the important items. Whenever you find yourself in that situation, you can put project 2000's filters to work and hold back the tide of information overload! Figure 13.9 shows figures in action.

Activate an autofilter by
clicking the **Autofilter** icon
and choosing from this list.

Select standard filters
from this pull-down list.

Turn on the autofilters
by clicking here.

**Figure 13.9**

*Filters limit the information in your sheet, table, or chart.*

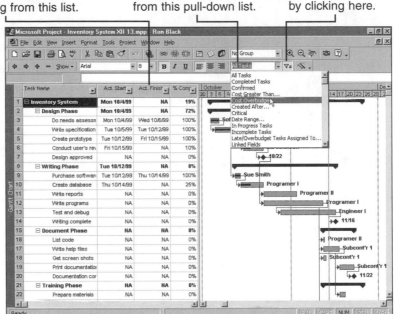

## Project Reports

Project reports may not look as exciting as a Tracking Gantt or Network Diagram, but they serve up information by the page-full. There are 29 predefined reports in Project 2000, so you won't have any trouble finding what you need. However if you must, you can create new reports or modify existing ones.

To print or view a report, open the Reports dialog box by selecting **Reports** in the **View** menu. The dialog box is shown in Figure 13.10. The most frequently used reports are accessed by selecting one of the categories and choosing a report from those graphically depicted. If you don't see what you need there, click **Custom** and browse all 29 reports.

**Figure 13.10**

*Access all reports from the Report dialog box.*

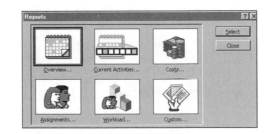

The Project Summary report is found in the Overview section. It lists key date, duration, work, cost, and status information on one sheet. When a report is selected, Project automatically takes you to a print preview screen, as shown in Figure 13.11. From there you can verify that the report is what you want before you print it.

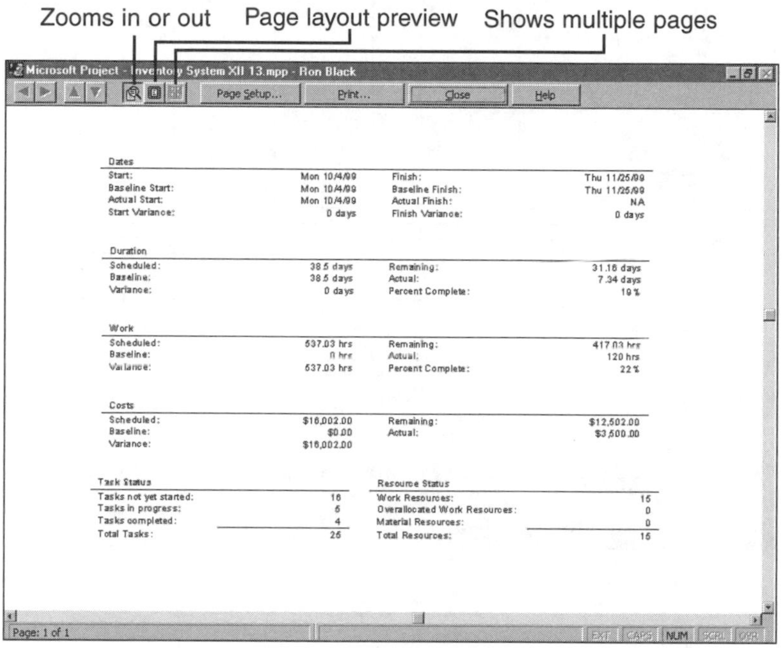

Zooms in or out    Page layout preview    Shows multiple pages

**Figure 13.11**

*The Project Summary Overview report is one of 29 standard reports.*

The first page of the Who Does What When report is shown in Figure 13.12. This report demonstrates the power of Project's crosstab capability. Resources are listed by task and the number of hours they are assigned per day to each task. This is a perfect report to show how fairly you distributed the workload!

The Earned Value report is commonly required by a project's contract documentation. In many instances progress payments are based on the earned value calculations. And if you've ever created this document by hand, you know what a chore that can be! Fortunately, an earned value report is ready and waiting for you. You can find the Earned Value report by choosing **Reports** from the **View** menu and then selecting the **Costs** reports category in the Reports dialog box. The first page of the report appears in Figure 13.13. The report is useful even when it isn't required by the project's contract documentation. It shows you how much of the planned expenditures should have been spent at this point of completion.

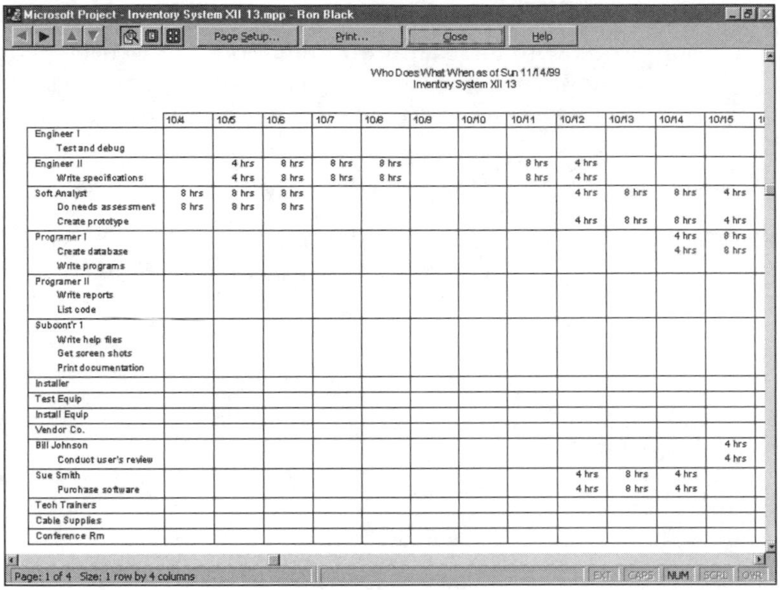


Who Does What When as of Sun 11/14/99
Inventory System XII 13

| | 10/4 | 10/5 | 10/6 | 10/7 | 10/8 | 10/9 | 10/10 | 10/11 | 10/12 | 10/13 | 10/14 | 10/15 |
|---|---|---|---|---|---|---|---|---|---|---|---|---|
| Engineer I | | | | | | | | | | | | |
| Test and debug | | | | | | | | | | | | |
| Engineer II | | 4 hrs | 8 hrs | 8 hrs | 8 hrs | | | 8 hrs | 4 hrs | | | |
| Write specifications | | 4 hrs | 8 hrs | 8 hrs | 8 hrs | | | 8 hrs | 4 hrs | | | |
| Soft Analyst | 8 hrs | 8 hrs | 8 hrs | | | | | | 4 hrs | 8 hrs | 8 hrs | 4 hrs |
| Do needs assessment | 8 hrs | 8 hrs | 8 hrs | | | | | | | | | |
| Create prototype | | | | | | | | | 4 hrs | 8 hrs | 8 hrs | 4 hrs |
| Programer I | | | | | | | | | | | 4 hrs | 8 hrs |
| Create database | | | | | | | | | | | 4 hrs | 8 hrs |
| Write programs | | | | | | | | | | | | |
| Programer II | | | | | | | | | | | | |
| Write reports | | | | | | | | | | | | |
| List code | | | | | | | | | | | | |
| Subcont'r 1 | | | | | | | | | | | | |
| Write help files | | | | | | | | | | | | |
| Get screen shots | | | | | | | | | | | | |
| Print documentation | | | | | | | | | | | | |
| Installer | | | | | | | | | | | | |
| Test Equip | | | | | | | | | | | | |
| Install Equip | | | | | | | | | | | | |
| Vendor Co. | | | | | | | | | | | | |
| Bill Johnson | | | | | | | | | | | | 4 hrs |
| Conduct user's review | | | | | | | | | | | | 4 hrs |
| Sue Smith | | | | | | | | | 4 hrs | 8 hrs | 4 hrs | |
| Purchase software | | | | | | | | | 4 hrs | 8 hrs | 4 hrs | |
| Tech Trainers | | | | | | | | | | | | |
| Cable Supplies | | | | | | | | | | | | |
| Conference Rm | | | | | | | | | | | | |

**Figure 13.12**

*Resource use is clearly reported with the Who Does What When report.*

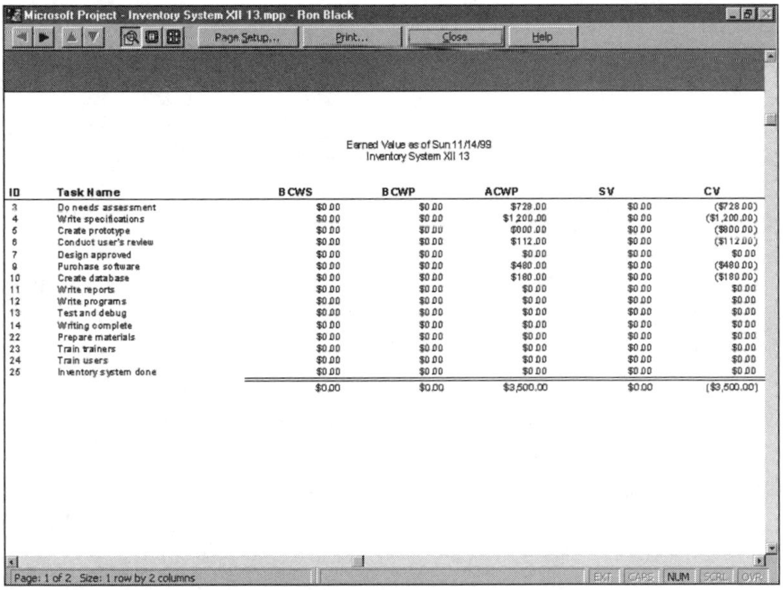


Earned Value as of Sun 11/14/99
Inventory System XII 13

| ID | Task Name | BCWS | BCWP | ACWP | SV | CV |
|---|---|---|---|---|---|---|
| 3 | Do needs assessment | $0.00 | $0.00 | $728.00 | $0.00 | ($728.00) |
| 4 | Write specifications | $0.00 | $0.00 | $1,200.00 | $0.00 | ($1,200.00) |
| 5 | Create prototype | $0.00 | $0.00 | $800.00 | $0.00 | ($800.00) |
| 6 | Conduct user's review | $0.00 | $0.00 | $112.00 | $0.00 | ($112.00) |
| 7 | Design approved | $0.00 | $0.00 | $0.00 | $0.00 | $0.00 |
| 9 | Purchase software | $0.00 | $0.00 | $480.00 | $0.00 | ($480.00) |
| 10 | Create database | $0.00 | $0.00 | $180.00 | $0.00 | ($180.00) |
| 11 | Write reports | $0.00 | $0.00 | $0.00 | $0.00 | $0.00 |
| 12 | Write programs | $0.00 | $0.00 | $0.00 | $0.00 | $0.00 |
| 13 | Test and debug | $0.00 | $0.00 | $0.00 | $0.00 | $0.00 |
| 14 | Writing complete | $0.00 | $0.00 | $0.00 | $0.00 | $0.00 |
| 22 | Prepare materials | $0.00 | $0.00 | $0.00 | $0.00 | $0.00 |
| 23 | Train trainers | $0.00 | $0.00 | $0.00 | $0.00 | $0.00 |
| 24 | Train users | $0.00 | $0.00 | $0.00 | $0.00 | $0.00 |
| 25 | Inventory system done | $0.00 | $0.00 | $0.00 | $0.00 | $0.00 |
| | | $0.00 | $0.00 | $3,500.00 | $0.00 | ($3,500.00) |

**Figure 13.13**

*Earned value reports are a snap with this ready-to-go report.*

The earned value report uses three basic values for each task:

| | |
|---|---|
| BCWS | Budgeted Cost of Work Scheduled—The amount that is planned to be spent between the task's start date and the date of the report. |

BCWP      Budgeted Cost of Work Performed—The percentage of the budget that should have been spent getting to this completion point.

ACWP      Actual Cost of Work Performed—The actual expenditures incurred over a given period.

Using these three measures, cost variance (CV), scheduled variance (SV), cost performance index (CPI), and scheduled performance index (SPI) are derived. If your project requires any of these measures, you'll be happy to know the hard work is already done! Just update your actuals and print the report.

# Printing Project Documentation

To print any of the project views, select **Print** from the **File** menu and click **Preview.** You can see a Gantt chart ready to be printed in Figure 13.14.

### Handy Printing Tips

To print the entire Gantt chart on one page, right-click on the time scale. When the pop-up menu appears, select **Zoom**, and then select **Entire project**. The width of the time scale can also be adjusted slightly without modifying the units shown. To do this, right-click on the time scale, select **Timescale**, and then choose the **Timescale** tab. In the lower-left corner of the dialog box, adjust the **Size** as required. You can also hide or display columns by right-clicking the column header and selecting **Hide Column** or **Insert Column**. In any view with a chart and table area, double-clicking on the separator line between the table and chart automatically adjusts it to the closest column edge. Double-click the right edge of a column header in the Gantt chart view to adjust the column width to the best fit. Always preview before printing to ensure that your print results will be what you intended.

**Figure 13.14**

*Printing Gantt charts, sheets, and tables is as easy as clicking **Print**.*

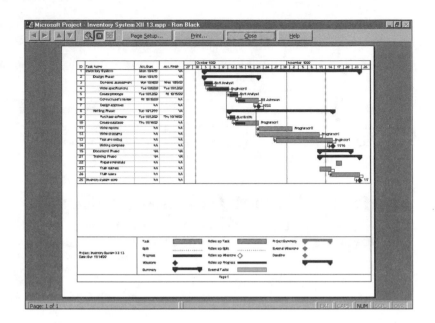

---

### The Least You Need to Know

➤ Project data isn't information until it's in a format you can understand and use. Project 2000 provides a robust set of views, sheets, tables, reports, diagrams, and filters to provide all the information you need to complete your project successfully.

➤ One of the essential duties of the project manager is to keep the project team informed. Be sure everyone who relies on your project documentation thoroughly understands it. Use project management terms correctly, and make sure your team does as well.

➤ There is always more than one strategy to get a project back on track. Understanding how to read Gantt charts and Network Diagrams is fundamental to finding options and evaluating their effectiveness.

# Part 5

# Dealing with Problems and Staying on Track

*Congratulations! You've been selected to be the first project manager in history who doesn't have any problems. All right, so you caught me exaggerating a little. A guy can wish, can't he?*

*Although you can avoid many problems with careful planning, you'll probably have to deal with some problems on all your projects. Part 5 shows you how to distinguish the little problems from the big ones. It helps you identify possible solutions, choose a course of action, adjust your plan accordingly, and monitor your implementation. This part is about breaking rules (don't worry—your mom will approve) to bring your project in successfully.*

# When the Going Gets Tough, the Tough Get Creative

## In This Chapter

➤ Using Project to identify and solve problems before they arise

➤ What to do when unexpected problems appear

➤ Decision making methods you can use to prioritize options and keep your project on the road to success

➤ The problem solving checklist

➤ Using the triple constraints to protect your project's success

Every once in a while, a project is initiated, implemented, and completed without its success being threatened. Problem-free projects, although rare, do exist. However, for the most part, you'll have to deal with problems on almost every project. Problems are an integral part of accomplishing that which has not been done before.

In some projects, you'll spend most of your time dealing with problems. Occasionally, you'll run into a project that makes you want to reconsider your career choice! You know the one...the project where Murphy is calling all the plays. I have a colleague who jokingly describes projects like these as vampire projects—they live forever and drain the lifeblood out of you! Indeed, I think we've all experienced projects like that.

Fortunately, good planning and an experienced team can help you avoid most of the serious problems. (And keep you working safely in the daylight or the dark.)

# Identifying Potential Problems

You can identify potential problems either in the planning stage or while you're implementing the plan. The earlier you spot a problem, the more options you have to do something about it. The earlier you deal with a problem, the less likely it will have a negative impact on your project's success. Therefore, the best time to avoid problems is always in the planning stage.

## *Spotting Problems During Planning*

The first opportunity to prevent potential problems is usually the best opportunity. Many problems can be foreseen long before the project even begins. And that's the best time to deal with them—before they cause any serious trouble! It's then that you have the best choices to solve or avoid the problem.

In this early phase of the project, watch for the killer problems—those that could prevent the project from achieving success. Many of the major risks your project faces are not unknowns. When trying to decide what could go wrong in a project, you and your project team's collective experience is your most important asset.

When you first start planning the project—thinking through implementation options, creating the work breakdown structure, and establishing the initial schedule—be alert for potential problems. It's impossible to avoid or even detect all the problems, but that's okay. You're looking for the big ones. The problems that could turn your project (and possibly your reputation) into toast. To uncover potential problems in the planning phase, ask yourself the following questions:

➤ **Of all that could go wrong, what do you fear most?**—Trust your experience and intuition. No one is in a better position than you to assess threats to your project's success. Guard against everything your hunches tell you are potentially large problems.

➤ **How do the triple constraints stack up?**—Are all of them highly important, or are one or two of them flexible? Be especially alert for anything that might impact the driving constraint. If the driving constraint is not met, the project is a failure. Having at least one constraint that is flexible greatly reduces project risk. Where there is flexibility, there are alternatives. Moreover, when you have alternatives, your risk is reduced. (For more information on the triple constraints, see Chapter 2, "The Project Management Process.")

➤ **Is the project goal overly optimistic?**—Is the time available adequate? Are all the resources you need readily available? Do you have access to all the people, money, equipment, facilities, materials, information, and technology required by the project? Of all the mistakes project teams make, over optimism is not only the most common, it's also the most deadly. Too many project managers base their assumptions on how they want their project's operational environment to be, rather than on how it actually is. In the early stages of planning, you should tend toward pessimism rather than optimism. The goals you set now are the goals you'll be judged by later. Make it as easy as possible to be successful! Bosses never care how difficult the project is, they just care about how successful it is.

### Assess Resource Needs Early

There's a growing trend in many industries toward a shortage of trained workers. Don't assume that all the resources you will need will automatically be available. Rather, assess your resource needs with Microsoft Project as early in the planning stage as possible. Create a preliminary schedule and load it with resources as described in Chapter 8, "The Resourceful Use of Resources." The preliminary schedule can help you identify the areas that are understaffed and therefore at risk. The following section describes how to identify resource shortages.

## Using Microsoft Project to Deal with Potential Problems

Microsoft Project can be a valuable tool for assessing potential problem areas. Whenever a proposed project appears difficult, complex, or time-sensitive, create a preliminary project plan. Even a roughly estimated plan greatly improves your understanding of the required tasks, sequence of work, and resource requirements. Creating the preliminary plan is a learning process. It often reveals many of the challenges that lie ahead.

### Workflow Considerations

Experienced project managers are alert to potential problems in the workflow sequence. As discussed in Chapter 4, "Thinking of Everything, Even If You Don't Know What You're Doing", every task in the project is important. Every task must be accomplished for the project to be a success. The sequence of workflow is also important. Many tasks depend on the completion of others before they can begin. In some cases, if a task is delayed many others will be adversely affected. Some tasks have no flexibility as to when they may be accomplished—they have no slack. Others lie on the critical path and, if delayed, the entire project will be delayed. For all these reasons, it is important to understand the workflow sequence and how to identify potential trouble spots.

## Work Bursts and Work Merges

Network diagrams make it possible to identify points that are strategically important to the workflow. Tasks that have many successor tasks are called *work bursts*—
many new paths of work burst open when these are accomplished. Conversely,
any delay on or before a work burst will block the start of many tasks. Tasks that
have many predecessor tasks are *work merges*—before they can begin, several tasks
must be accomplished within the same time frame. To accomplish a work merge,
many predecessor tasks must be undertaken in unison. To keep your project in a
high state of forwardness, manage work bursts and merges carefully.

The best way to understand the workflow sequence is with Microsoft Project's
Network Diagram view, as shown in figure 14.1. To open this view, click on **Network
Diagram** from the **View** menu. For an overview of the project, zoom out by
clicking on **Zoom** from the **View** menu, check **Entire project**, and click **OK**. The
maximum reduction is 25%, so you may have to drag the View bar and scroll in order
to view large projects.

**Figure 14.1**

*For a strategic under-
standing of the project's
workflow, use the Network
Diagram view.*

A long critical path
exposes the project to
many potential delays.

Work burst delays block
the start of many tasks.

Work merges require many
tasks to be accomplished
before progress can
continue.

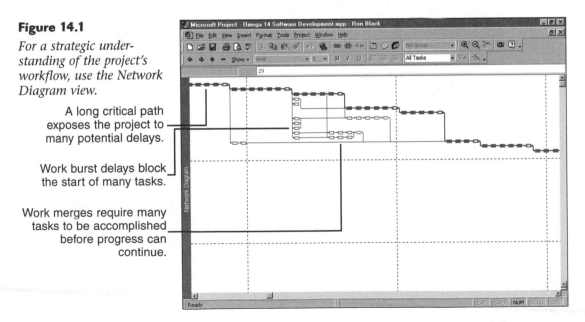

Every project has an optimum sequence of work, depending on the available time, resources, and desired level of risk. The Network Diagram view helps you understand the strategic importance of each task and its relationship to the whole project. For example, after viewing the network diagram for the project in figure 14.1, the project manager might decide the project's completion date is overly optimistic. The project has a very long critical path, and if anything delays any of these tasks, the due date may be in jeopardy. A cushion of additional resources or a time extension may be in order.

### Resources Versus Time Considerations

Generally speaking, the faster a project must be accomplished, the more resources are required. Conversely, the fewer resources available for a project, the longer the project will take. It is therefore important to assess the intended duration of the project in conjunction with resource availability. Once again, the best way to do this is with a preliminary plan.

When time and resources are both in short supply, create the plan with the **Schedule from: Project Finish Date** option selected in the Project information dialog box. You may want to review the section entitled "Start Date or Finish Date Scheduling" in Chapter 9 for more information. Create a resource list as described in Chapter 7, "Getting a Handle on Your Resources, Costs, and Budgets." Next, assign resources to the tasks as described in Chapter 8, "The Resourceful Use of Resources." The final step is to level resource allocations with the option **Level only within available slack** selected in the Resource Leveling dialog box. If resource overallocation warnings appear as Microsoft Project levels the project, select **Skip All**. Bingo! You now have a schedule that finishes within the given time and exposes any resource shortages as overallocations.

To find the resources shortages, select the **Resource Sheet View** from the View menu. As shown in figure 14.2, overallocations that remain after leveling are tagged with a yellow exclamation point icon in the indicator column. These are the resources your project is lacking. To quantify the shortage, increase the **Max. Units** for each overallocated resource until the warning icon is gone. (After each change, click outside of the field to make Project recalculate.) Although this process is not exact, it is a good preliminary method to estimate the number of required resources.

If resources are only 10% or 20% off, small adjustments in the schedule may compensate for the shortages. On the other hand, if the required resources fall short by 100% or 200%, serious problems are likely to occur. Proceeding without substantial changes in resources, time, or project scope would be foolish.

To determine exactly where your resource shortages are and how they relate to the workflow, the combination view shown in figure 14.3 is a powerful tool. With it you can find each overallocation and drill down to the detail on a task, resource, or time-period basis.

**Figure 14.2**

*Locate resource shortages by allocating available resources and leveling within available slack.*

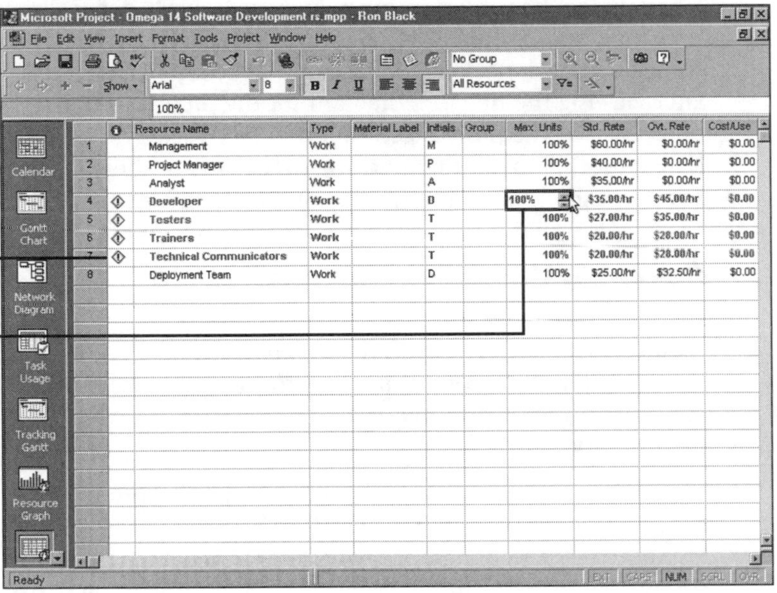

The exclamation point icon warns of resource overallocations.

Adjust the units available to estimate required staffing levels.

To create this view, select **Network Diagram** from the View menu. Next, open the lower pane by clicking on the pane bar (found just below the vertical scroll bar) and dragging it up. Now make the lower pane current by clicking in it, and then select **Resource Usage** from the View menu. Right-click on the right side of the Resource Usage sheet, and from the pop-up menu select **Detail Styles**. Choose the **Usage Details** tab and select **Work**, **Overallocation**, and **Percent Allocation** from Available fields and add them to **Show these fields**. Click **OK**—your crystal ball, er, combination view, is complete.

**Figure 14.3**

*Scroll through the network diagram with the arrow keys to find potential problems.*

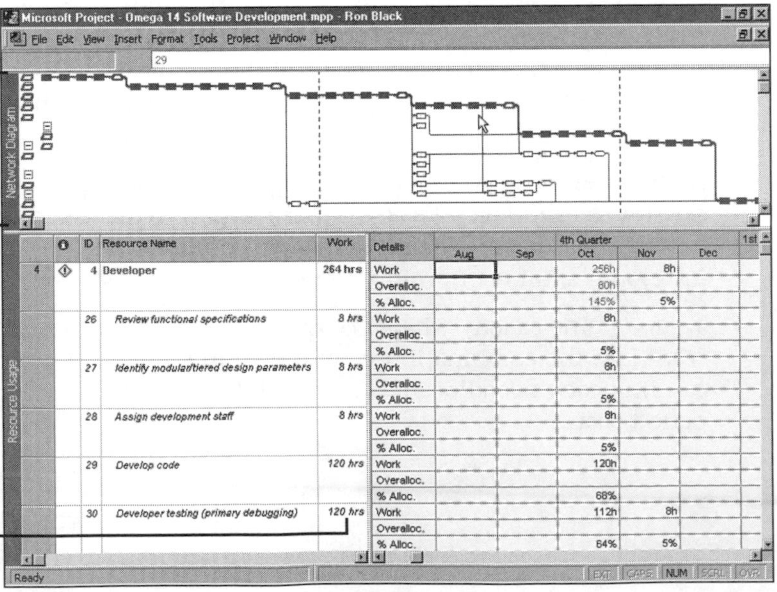

The combined effects of critical path, work burst, and resource shortage reveal a potential disaster.

After finding potential problems, adjust the time scale to reveal greater detail.

A good preliminary plan coupled with this combination view is the closest thing there is to predicting the future! When the stakes are high, use this technique to minimize your risk.

Now that you've spotted a few problems, let's see what you can do about them.

# Problem Analysis

At the first sign of trouble, don't panic. In fact, don't do anything yet. Problems will undoubtedly arise in your project, but not all of them are worthy of your attention, time, or resources. Remember, you're seeking success, not perfection. To stay on the path to success, save your limited resources for the serious problems. Sometimes you just have to ignore the little problems and save all your energy for the big ones!

To decide which problems to ignore and which to address, use the following problem analysis checklist:

➤ **Will it impact the critical path?**—Problems that threaten the start or finish of any task on the critical path will threaten the project's scheduled completion date. Time is usually very important, and if it happens to be the driver of your project, the project's success is seriously threatened. When a problem is "on the path," move quickly and forcefully to resolve the issues. These problems need your immediate and full attention.

### Getting Critical About Paths

Tasks that have no flexibility in time without adversely affecting the completion of the project are called *critical tasks*. The critical path is determined by finding all full paths (those continuos sequences of tasks that stretch from the beginning to the end of the project) and adding up the durations for each task on the path. The longest path determines the shortest time in which the project can be completed. Being on "the" path means the task is on the critical path and cannot be delayed without delaying completion of the project. Reserve your use of the word *critical* to describe those tasks that lie on the critical path. For more information see Chapter 10, "Shortening the Schedule."

➤ **Will it impact the driver?**—The driving constraint must be protected at all costs. If the driving constraint is not achieved, the project is a failure. Don't do anything your mom wouldn't approve of; but otherwise, do whatever you have to do! Your project, your team, and your reputation are at stake. When the driver is at risk, take decisive action immediately.

### The Driving Constraint

Every project can be described in terms of time, resources, and outcomes. These three categories are described frequently as the triple constraints. The least flexible of the three is the project's driving constraint. In order for the project to be a success, the driving constraint must be met. Always protect the driver. When hard decisions must be made, protect the project's driving constraint at the expense of a more flexible constraint. For additional information on this important concept, see the section entitled "Understanding the Physics of Project Management" in Chapter 2, "The Project Management Process."

➤ **Who will be affected?**—When problems arise, people can get hurt. One of the responsibilities project managers have is to make sure no one gets hurt on their projects. Never blindside a teammate, never hurt the project's customer, and never surprise your boss (negatively, of course). As soon as you realize the potential for harm is present, advise all parties who may be affected. There is another reason besides "It's the right thing to do." When you've found and informed all the stakeholders who could be negatively affected, you've just populated and motivated a problem solution team! These individuals are most likely to help you solve the problem.

## You've Got a Problem—Now What?

When problems that require your attention arise, don't try to solve them alone. You have a team, and now is the time to rely on it. Also, solicit help from everyone who is likely to be affected by the problem. Those who are in harm's way, even though they are not official members of your team, will be motivated to help solve the problem!

Brief this problem solution team on the importance of the problem. Now is not the time to be diplomatic. State the nature of the risk frankly and honestly. Don't underplay or overplay the significance of the situation.

Next, define the apparent problem. Take nothing for granted. Don't assume you completely understand the problem. You want to have a good definition of the problem, because with the definition lies the solution strategies you're seeking. State the apparent problem from your team's points of view as well as your own.

## Creative Thinking When Your Job Depends on It

The ability to be creative is a function of how willing one is to take a risk. When you have an organizational climate of risk aversion, creativity is stifled. Always strive to maintain a nurturing, rather than criticizing climate in your project team. That way, when you need creativity to solve a problem, you're halfway home!

The best way to get a good idea is to get a lot of ideas. There is always more than one solution to every problem. Our job is to find the best one for now. The goal when seeking solutions is to create as many ideas as possible. Project managers often use brainstorming techniques to find solutions.

Finding solutions can be difficult, so the tendency is to stop at the first idea that comes along. Don't do that, because you need options! In fact, don't even consider the first idea. Just make a note of it and continue the search. Tell your team to turn their creativity throttle up and their evaluation throttle down. Create as many new ideas as possible. When some are truly ridiculous, that's good. You know the team is comfortable enough with one another to be playful, take a risk, and be genuinely creative.

### Breaking the Right Rules

Some of the most creative people I know arc playful, incorrigible rule breakers. They probably spent most of their school days in the principal's office, explaining why their idea was better than the teacher's. When you're faced with a tough problem (and they're all tough until you find a solution) ask your team this question: "What rules can we break?" Now is not the time to be compliant! Hopefully that unruly student has grown up and is now on your team. So long as you protect the driving constraint and achieve the project's ultimate goal, break any rule you must. It's best if you don't bend or break any of the triple constraints, but when necessary, break the weak constraint first. This way, the project can still be a success. What rules can you break? All of them, as long as your mother approves.

Even with creative people who work well together, you'll usually find a long gap between the first idea and the second. And usually there is an equally long gap between the second and third. However, somewhere along the line, the flow of ideas picks up noticeably. When that happens, it's a good sign that the team is focused on the task at hand, not on their last phone call or yesterday's meatloaf. Collect all the ideas you can and then begin the evaluation process.

### Try It Before You Buy It

If your proposed solutions involve schedule, resource, or scope changes, be sure to check out the effects in Microsoft Project before implementing the changes. Make sure your plan is current, save it, and then make the proposed changes in a copy of your plan. Carefully explore the effects of your changes and be alert for any unwanted ripple effects.

The team should also evaluate the ideas. What may seem like an impassable road-block to one person may be easily solved by another. After you've considered the options and examined their effects on your schedule, seek consensus from the group. Although everyone may not agree that any given solution is the best choice from their point of view, they can agree to support the idea.

### Gaining Consensus

Consistently use the same phrase to gain consensus in collaborative work groups. This helps everyone understand that you're trying to gain group support for a decision. Use these words: "Is there anyone who cannot support this solution (idea, approach, method...)?" When you use these words, even those who never speak up in a meeting must actively voice their disapproval or agree to support the decision.

Now it's time to implement the solution. This may be done by the team as a whole, or (more likely) by one or two individuals. And when the solution is being implemented by a few for the good of the whole, it is important to remember that they are part of the team. Should things not work out as planned, don't allow them to take the heat for the team. On the other hand, when the implementation is successful, don't allow them to bask in all the praise, either. (If your organization is like most, very little praise basking is done. You probably won't have to worry about that one!) Good teams hold themselves equally and mutually accountable in all situations.

### Using the Language of a Team

It's not *my* idea or *your* idea, it's *our* idea or *the* idea. Leave all the personal, singular, possessive pronouns out of your language and out of your thinking. To remind yourself to use good team language and thinking, before you enter team meetings, leave all your personal possessions in the hallway—your personal possessive pronouns, that is. You'll see an immediate effect in your team's attitude and behavior.

And while you're leaving things in the hallway, leave all your *buts* out there too. Replace them with *and*. Which is better, "Yes I heard what you said, and..." or, "Yes I heard what you said, but..."? Using *but* negates everything that comes before it. When you replace *but* with *and*, trust and respect is higher because the other person's point of view is accepted as valid, not rejected out of hand. These simple changes (with genuine trust and respect) dramatically improve a team's communication effectiveness.

Follow up on the implementation of all solutions carefully! You've already determined the problem is an important one to solve, so make sure the intended solution is rapidly put into effect. The only thing worse than getting bitten by something you didn't see is being bitten by something your could see coming. Monitor implementation closely and make sure the team's solution is rapidly implemented.

## Bright Ideas for Dark Times

Your best insurance against success-threatening problems is flexibility. Knowing how to adapt, how to move fast, and how to bend without breaking are essential skills if you want to build a reputation as a successful project manager.

Paradoxically, flexibility comes from tight control—an accurate schedule and close monitoring of actuals versus planned durations, costs, start and finish times—and milestone achievements. Knowing where you can slow down or let tasks slip out in time (using slack), thereby releasing resources for other work (resource leveling), is also determined only with an accurate plan. In fact, flexibility is revealed only with an accurate plan as your guide.

### Slack Is Your Friend!

The biggest hidden resource in every project is slack—the amount of time a task can slip without affecting the project's completion. Knowing where slack is hiding is knowing where there's flexibility. To learn more about this hidden resource, see the section entitled "Identifying Slack or Float" in Chapter 10, "Shortening the Schedule."

Most problems we deal with have to do with not meeting the project's time, cost, or performance requirements. One or all three are in jeopardy. It's increasingly more difficult to save a troubled project if all three constraints are threatened. When you're behind schedule, over budget, and the deliverable isn't deliverable...it may be time to dust off your resume or add a helmet and flak jacket to your wardrobe!

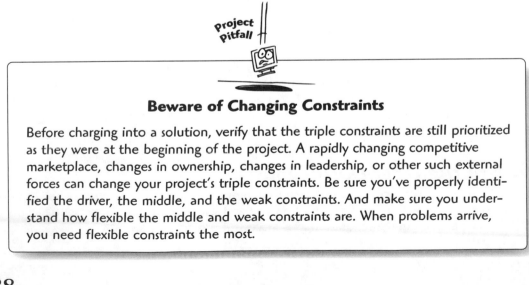

### Beware of Changing Constraints

Before charging into a solution, verify that the triple constraints are still prioritized as they were at the beginning of the project. A rapidly changing competitive marketplace, changes in ownership, changes in leadership, or other such external forces can change your project's triple constraints. Be sure you've properly identified the driver, the middle, and the weak constraints. And make sure you understand how flexible the middle and weak constraints are. When problems arrive, you need flexible constraints the most.

Projects facing trouble on three fronts are suffering from many issues, not just one or two. And the genesis of these problems was probably in the definition stage of the project. Goals were overly optimistic. Assumptions were incorrect. Stakeholders were never truly committed. Resources weren't forthcoming. Information was lacking. Alas, the vampire project was born!

When you find yourself in a situation like this, the first job of a team leader is to save the people. All too often the team takes the heat for management's overly optimistic (or overly simplistic) view of the world. The second job is to save as much of the project as possible, knowing that you've likely missed the only real opportunities for success long ago. Focus all energies on salvaging the driving constraint and the people. It's all you can do.

Fortunately, you now have this book to guide you through the danger-wrought early stages of project management. So from here on out, the problems will be fewer and less pervasive. And for problems that aren't killer bugs, there are three basic strategies: What can I slow? What can I cut? Where do I spend?

The following list describes these strategies as they apply to most projects. Use this as a checklist of possible solutions.

➤ **Parallel more tasks or paths**—When you're finishing too late, a good solution to consider is to parallel more tasks. Of course, you must first shorten the critical path to use this strategy. One way of doing this is to examine every task on the critical path and see if any of them could be split off into a parallel path. You may also be able to use one of the following suggestions on a critical task to split off several others for the new path.

➤ **Add resources**—Managers often resort to piling on more resources. But unless the resources are taken from tasks that might be delayed (using their slack time), and the resources were assigned for the duration of the project, this option may get expensive quickly. In some cases, you may be able to spend the same amount of money in a shorter time, and that's great. But all too often, you reach a point of diminishing returns—overtime, double-time, or just-too-tired-to-think-time—and costs go up.

➤ **Make or buy considerations**—In some situations, you may be able to buy or hire out work segments you originally planned on doing with your own resources. Sometimes you can save both time and money by doing this. Other times you may have to spend more or wait longer. Don't decide to reject this option until you've researched the situation. Send out a request for proposals and see what rises to the opportunity! You may be surprised that someone is willing and able to do the task better, faster, and cheaper than your own work force.

➤ **Use incentives and disincentives**—These can be a powerful way to motivate vendors and subcontractors to prioritize the use of their resources in your project's favor. When all else is equal, limited resources will be loaded onto those tasks (or projects) where there is the largest penalty for late completion or the greatest reward for early completion. Be sure all rewards or disincentives are agreed to before the project begins.

➤ **Substitute alternatives**—As a reminder, Adam Smith is on your team. And besides working against us from time to time with the notion of unlimited needs and limited resources, he also keeps the spirit of competition alive and well. Chances are, there is a second source for almost everything you need on your project. Shop around. Make Adam proud.

➤ **Go for substantial completion**—If the project's main goal can be achieved without finishing all tasks, focus on those tasks that produce a usable, although not complete, project. Finish the non-essentials later.

➤ **Narrow the scope**—Once in a while you can or must narrow the scope of a project. Perhaps needed resources weren't available, the weather was unusually unruly, or you just didn't realize how difficult the project would turn out to be. In the face of major changes in project assumptions, it's wise to return to the definition stage and narrow your project's scope. Salvage as much progress (not work, but progress) as possible, and set a new, more realistic goal.

➤ **Renegotiate**—When worse comes to worst, beg for mercy. Call in favors, beg for forgiveness, or just plan grovel. If you have something you can negotiate with, which is thrown-in for reconsideration of the agreement, now's the time to do it. This is not always a pleasant task, but renegotiating beats failing. Use this option as a last resort.

➤ **Expedite**—If the project is running over schedule and the budget is not the driver, consider expediting the project. This is also called crashing the schedule. (I've found owners and originators get a little nervous when project managers use the word *crash*, so save yourself some trouble and always refer to crashing as expediting.) This is a formal technique in which you consider how to shorten the duration of each task and at what cost. The resulting information can be considered in conjunction with the workflow sequence diagram (your network diagram or Gantt chart), and you can see how much it would cost to shorten a task, path, or series of parallel paths. This is an important tool to understand, so Chapter 15, "Expediting (Crashing) a Project," is devoted to it.

Murphy reminds us that things always look darkest just before they turn totally black. But that's okay. With your new problem analysis and solution tools, you'll never have to be afraid of the dark, or vampire projects, again.

## The Least You Need to Know

➤ An understanding of the triple constraints provides you with the information you need to prioritize solution options. The constraint's priority sometimes changes during the project, so be careful to reassess them before implementing solutions.

➤ Solutions come from options that are only spotted with a thorough understanding of the project's goal, its constraints, and its workflow sequence. An accurate plan and tight monitoring provides the impetus and the alternatives you need to solve difficult problems successfully.

➤ Microsoft Project can be used to identify potential problems early in the planning stages. During implementation, it is a powerful tool for testing proposed solutions.

➤ Not all problems are worthy of your attention. If they do not affect the critical path or the project's goal, ignore them. Save your attention, energy, and resources for the important problems.

➤ When seeking solutions to project problems, protect the project's goal and its driving constraint at all costs. Take whatever action is required, break whatever rules you must, so long as your mother would approve.

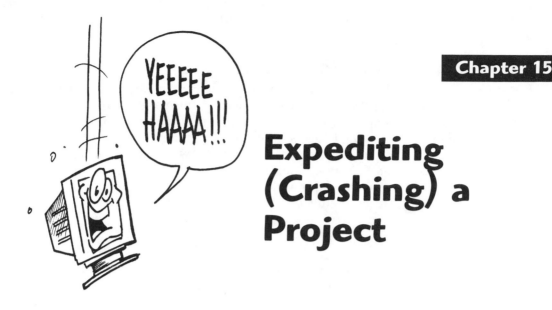

# Chapter 15

# Expediting (Crashing) a Project

## In This Chapter

➤ Determine the cost of shortening a project's overall duration by reducing the duration of the remaining tasks

➤ Choose which tasks to expedite and which ones not to based on the project's workflow sequence and each task's expedite costs

Expediting a project is a technique used to determine the cost of compressing a project's schedule. The old saying "time is money," goes a long way in describing the importance of expedite analysis. Knowing how to analyze a project's time/cost relationship serves two important purposes.

First, if you ever have to squeeze a schedule into a seemingly impossible timeframe, expedite analysis can make you look like a hero. You can identify exactly how much it will cost to speed the project's completion without spending more than is absolutely essential. On a task-by-task basis, you can select which tasks to expedite to get an effective return on each additional dollar spent.

Second, understanding the principles of expediting gives you solid business footing when making project decisions. You'll be better able to discuss or negotiate changes that affect the amount of time a task may be completed in and the resulting changes in the budget or contract.

# When Crashing Is a Good Thing

Expediting is commonly referred to as *crashing the project* or *crashing the timeline* in the project management profession. And like many of the terms project managers use freely, your customers, project originators, and team members won't always understand what you mean. Crashing is a good thing when you need to speed up the completion of a project. It is however, the rare customer who wants to have anything they care about crashed. Save yourself some trouble. Refer to crashing the project as expediting. Everyone knows that expediting makes things happen faster. Moreover, everyone understands that expediting usually comes at a premium price.

# Buying Time

Essentially, expedite analysis reveals what additional costs will be incurred to shorten the duration of a task. When the task was originally planned, certain assumptions were made. We call these the normal assumptions. Under normal conditions, what costs would be incurred and what duration is required? This is your preferred method of completing this task.

For some reason, however, it may become necessary to complete the task in a shorter timeframe. In project management terms, the priority of the triple constraints has changed. For whatever reason, time has become a driving constraint, performance remains unchanged, and cost has become the most flexible.

### The Safe Choice: Crashing or Fast Tracking?

Two popular methods of shortening a schedule are expediting (commonly known as crashing) and fast tracking. Crashing compresses the schedule by applying more resources to tasks in order to shorten their durations. Crashing typically increases the project's costs but produces reliable results. Fast tracking alters the workflow logic by running tasks in parallel that would normally be run in finish-to-start sequence. Examples of this include writing software before the needs analysis is complete, and building a payload module before the launch vehicle's lifting capacity has been verified. Fast tracking therefore compresses the schedule by assuming additional risks—cost, time, quality, and results may all be adversely affected (or not). When compressing a schedule, choose your method carefully. The crash course is probably safer than the fast track!

To expedite completion you may need to work overtime, hire temporary employees, or buy rather than make certain work components. A commonly used expedite method is the purchase of overnight air delivery. If you had the time, ground shipping would be much cheaper. However, the situation justifies additional expenditures. Usually these options are more expensive. To understand exactly how much more expensive expediting a task is, project managers use expedite analysis.

I was once asked to expedite the installation of a series of telecommunication relay sites across a remote stretch of the Rocky Mountains. A tax law had been changed that made it desirable for the investors of the project to have the construction complete before year-end. Rather than waiting for spring and better weather to construct these remote sites (when the cost and durations had been planned), the owners were motivated to build them in the middle of winter.

The remoteness of the sites required over-snow vehicles to transport crews, materials, and equipment. The cold weather slowed crews as they fought just to stay warm and safe. Sites that would normally be worked with standard excavating equipment and techniques had to be blasted into submission with high explosives. Concrete had to be prepared, poured, and cured in subzero temperatures with small onsite mixing systems. It was obvious that every step of the process would be more costly, but how much more costly was the question. The owners of the project performed an expedite analysis to understand how much should be spent in the process of expediting the project.

**Project Pitfall**

**The Short and Long of Overtime**

When projects don't have adequate staffing, many organizations rely on their salaried employees to make up the difference. Hiring temps, working hourly employees overtime, and hiring additional people add to the cost of a project. On the other hand, the more a fixed salary employee is worked, the lower their effective hourly rate becomes! This tactic can be effective for resolving short-term situations or problems. However, working salaried staff excessively over the long term will probably result in lowered productivity, bad decisions, poor morale, and a loss of your most capable team members. Don't let short-term tactics become long-term problems.

## Expedite Analysis

Fortunately, half the work of every expedite analysis is already done, as long as you've already estimated your project's duration and costs. All you need to do is re-estimate each task remaining on the project, and compare the crashed duration and costs with the original durations and costs. This process of comparison yields the difference (known as the *slope* to project managers) between the normal and expedited costs and durations. This process can be done by hand or on a spreadsheet program.

After the slope has been identified for each of the remaining tasks, you'll want to transfer it into Microsoft Project 2000. You can then display the slope on the Gantt Chart and have a better understanding of the expedite options available.

# Putting Expedite Analysis to Work—An Example

Consider the Telemetry System project shown in Figure 15.1. As originally planned, the project was expected to cost $97,800 and require 49 days to complete. The project originator requested an expedite analysis to consider what a shorter project duration would cost.

**Figure 15.1**

*The project is planned to be completed under normal conditions in 49 days at a total cost of $97,800.*

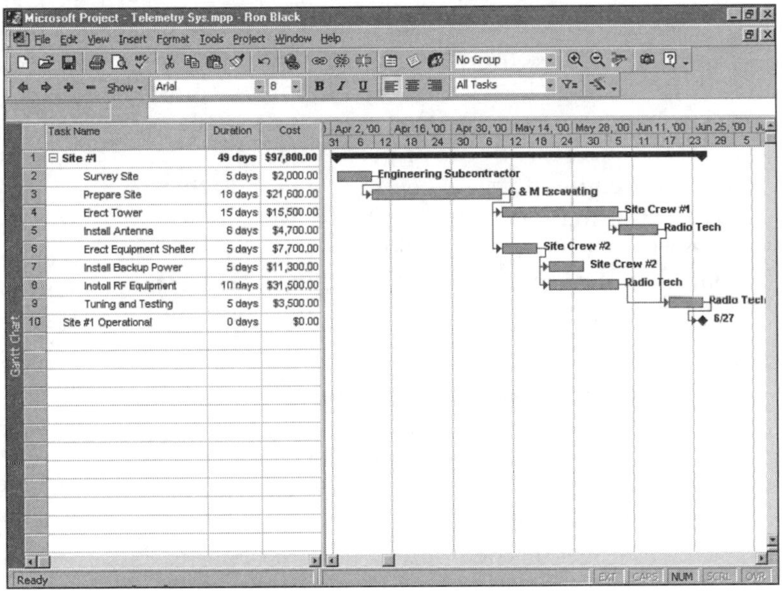

The project manager needed to analyze how much it would cost to expedite each task in the project. The easiest way to do that is in a spreadsheet such as Excel. The result is shown in Figure 15.2.

When creating an expedite analysis, ask yourself this question: "If money were no object, how could I shorten the duration of this task?" Although there are usually limits to the money, asking this is a good way to begin creatively shortening the project's schedule.

Applying every option available to the project manager shortens the duration of each task. This may include working overtime, adding additional resources, requiring subcontractors to complete their assignments earlier (which often involves a bonus or other incentive), using faster equipment, purchasing rather than making deliverables, and any other strategy the project manager can come up with. After the expedited durations and costs are estimated, they can be compared to the original durations and costs for each task. The difference is the slope.

Duration and cost of each task as originally planned

Duration and cost of each task when shortened by all available means

The reduction in duration and corresponding increase in cost is called the slope.

**Figure 15.2**

*A spreadsheet was used to determine the slope for each task.*

| ID | Name | Normal Duration | Normal Cost | Expedited Duration | Expedited Cost | Slope Duration | Slope Cost |
|----|------|-----------------|-------------|--------------------|-----------------|-----------------|------------|
| 1 | Site #1 | 49 | $97,800 | | | | |
| 2 | Survey Site | 5 | $2,000 | 2 | $2,000 | -3 | $0 |
| 3 | Prepare Site | 18 | $21,600 | 9 | $25,700 | -9 | $4,100 |
| 4 | Erect Tower | 15 | $15,500 | 8 | $17,750 | -7 | $2,250 |
| 5 | Install Antenna | 6 | $4,700 | 4 | $4,700 | -2 | $0 |
| 6 | Erect Equipment Shelter | 5 | $7,700 | 4 | $8,300 | -1 | $600 |
| 7 | Install Backup Power | 5 | $11,300 | 4 | $11,900 | -1 | $600 |
| 8 | Install RF Equipment | 10 | $31,500 | 5 | $31,500 | -5 | $0 |
| 9 | Tuning and Testing | 5 | $3,500 | 4 | $3,900 | -1 | $400 |
| 10 | Site #1 Operational | | | | | | |

Speak Like a Geek

## Don't Slip Up Using Slope

*Slope* is a word project managers borrow from mathematics and (shame on us) we abuse! In mathematics, slope is a ratio of the vertical distance to the horizontal distance of a straight line. It implies that for any incremental change in one factor, the other factor is directly and proportionally changed. In project management, slope describes the difference in the two points, not the ratio. Project managers aren't always able to make the smooth, incremental changes that the word *slope* implies. The choices may be all or nothing, whole units only, or for other reasons, unrealistic. For example, if expedited shipping cuts three days out of a task but only one extra day is needed, paying for only the day needed is not an option—it's all or nothing.

Notice that the term *slope* is not used in its traditional, mathematical format indicating a linear set of choices along a line. In project management, the slope is closer to a step function. If you decided to add resources to the project, you could add only full units, not half or two-thirds of a machine. You could choose to work overtime at time and a half or not. You could ship by ground or air. In this regard, a reduction of ten days at a cost of $10,000 does not indicate that an additional reduction of a day would cost $1000.

# Comparing Options and Paths

After the slope for each of the individual tasks has been established, it is necessary to use the Gantt Chart view to understand how each of the changes in costs and duration will actually affect the overall project. If all tasks were in a finish to start sequence without parallel paths, the project manager could simply select which tasks to expedite to get the intended results. More frequently, the project manager will want to see how each of these proposed changes is integrated into the workflow sequence.

The best way to facilitate this is to add the slope to the Gantt Chart view. From the Gantt Chart view shown in Figure 15.3, right-click the column head entitled Start and select **Insert Column** from the pop-up menu. Scroll down to **Text1** and highlight it. Rename this text column by entering Slope into the **Title** field and click **OK**.

**Figure 15.3**

*Insert a text column into the Gantt Chart entry table for your expedite analysis slope results.*

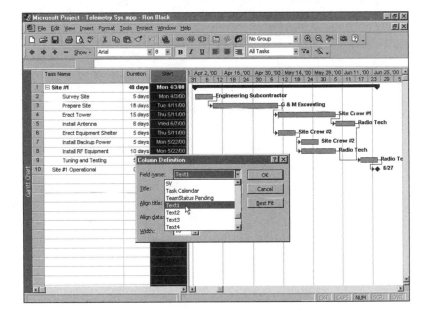

After the column has been inserted, enter the duration and cost for each task from your expedite analysis. Traditionally, the slope is noted within parenthesis as the change in duration and change in cost separated by a comma. Now right-click in the Gantt Chart view and select **Bar Styles** from the pop-up menu. As shown in Figure 15.4, select the **Text** tab and select **Text1 (Slope)** from the list of available fields for placement to the left of each bar.

The resulting view enables the project manager to fully understand the costs associated with expediting any task or group of tasks. This view is shown in Figure 15.5. For example, by choosing to expedite those tasks with zero increases in costs, the project manager could reduce overall project duration by a total of 5 days. By choosing to expedite task number four, Erect Tower, the project could be shortened to 37 days at an additional expense of $2,250.

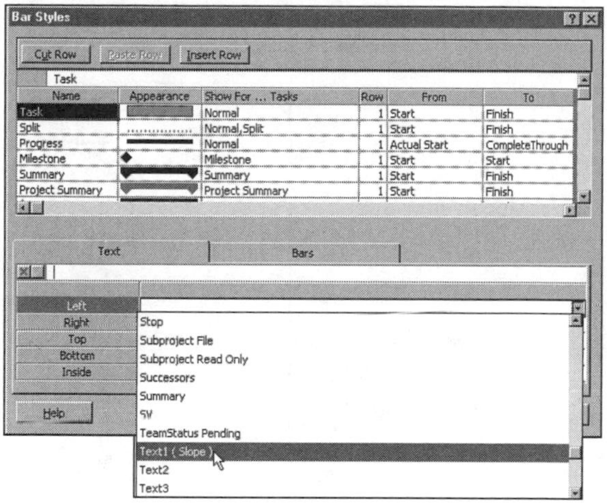

**Figure 15.4**

*Place the results of your expedite analysis on the Gantt Chart by adding a text field to be displayed to the left of each task's bar.*

### Finding the Optimum Solution

To get the most time for your money, shorten tasks with zero costs first. Next, shorten tasks on the critical path, beginning with the least expensive. (For additional information on the critical path, see Chapter 10, "Shortening the Schedule.") Continue altering durations and watching for changes in the critical path until the best combination of costs and durations are achieved. As you can see, finding the optimum solution is a trial-and-error process. Fortunately, Project 2000's automatic redrawing of the schedule makes it easy to test alternate solutions rapidly.

With the Gantt Chart and the slope data clearly visible, it is apparent that expediting the Erect the Equipment Shelter or Install Backup Power would be not beneficial. Incurring these expedite costs could therefore be avoided. However, an additional schedule compression of 10 days could occur by expediting the Prepare Site task for an additional $4,100 and Tuning and Testing for $400. This would bring the total project duration down to 27 days for a total additional expense of $6,750.

**Figure 15.5**

*The cost of expediting a project can be carefully analyzed by posting the slope next to each task.*

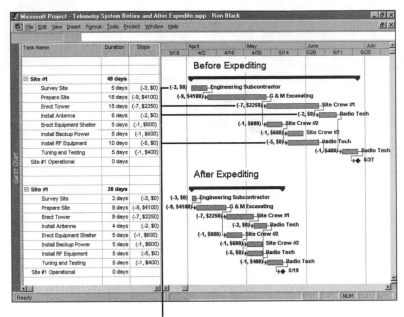

Expedited tasks

---

## The Least You Need to Know

➤ Expedite analysis provides the project manager with the information needed to make sound decisions on how to shorten a project's duration with the least additional expense.

➤ Alternate methods of schedule compression can be compared for cost and time effectiveness.

# Whew! Wrapping Up the Project

"Are we there yet?" Anyone who has ever managed a substantial project (or a road trip with children) is familiar with this mantra. Some projects seem like a journey that lasts forever. The anticipated destination is always just around the corner, within sight but out of reach. Eventually, even the longest journey comes to an end. Sometimes projects end with elation and celebration. Other times projects just roll over and sink below the surface with little more than an oil slick marking their demise.

Hopefully you took the advice of this book when planning your project. If you did, chances are good that your project has steadily picked up speed on its journey to completion. Rather than grinding to a lurching, stumbling halt, project completion has arrived as expected—on time and in good order by all accounts.

In any case, the project manager has several closing responsibilities to the project and the stakeholders of the project. No matter if the project falls short, meets, or even exceeds expectations, it's best to bring professional closure to the endeavor.

## Save the People

When all else is lost on an unsuccessful project, do everything you can to save the people. Many organizations like to oversimplify difficult situations and fix blame on an individual or group. More likely, the project failed because of many issues, and no one person or team was responsible for its demise. If there are lessons to be learned, these are the individuals who are most aware of them and most able to help the organization improve its performance. Save the people—their experience is the organization's most important asset.

# Gaining Project Acceptance

Your first goal (and responsibility) in project closure is to make sure that the project is accepted as complete. The project must meet its specified goals and objectives.

Oddly enough, the most important step you'll ever take toward the completion of the project is in the initial stages of the project—in the definition stage. That's when you set the rules that your project's success will be judged by. That's when you set the expectations that must be met for the project to reach a successful conclusion. It is here that the specific, measurable project outcomes are documented and agreed upon by all stakeholders. Trying to negotiate a completion agreement at the end of a project is at best frustrating and at worst suicidal.

Many organizations have a formal procedure for documenting project acceptance. If you do not have a formal procedure or if the project documentation does not specify a procedure, use Table 16.1 as a guide.

## Table 16.1   Project Acceptance Checklist

| Procedure | Description |
| --- | --- |
| Notice to Complete Project | At the 80–90% completion point, send a notice that you are about to complete the project. This alerts the project's end users to be ready for the deliverables. It alerts the project's originator that this stage is about to conclude and accordingly, to prepare for completion. It also puts the team on notice that the final push is on and to prepare for the transition to other duties. |
| Substantial Completion | Hopefully, communication between the stakeholders has continued throughout the project. In any case, the focus of one formal communication should be to review the project's progress against the plan. First identify and list all work that has been successfully completed to date. Then identify and list all the remaining work items. The original definition of the project and any agreements made during the project should be used as the baseline for this review. |

| Procedure | Description |
|---|---|
| Remaining Work Identified | Any remaining work needs to be explicitly identified. If possible, gain stakeholder signatures at this point. In this way, work that does not appear on the list will not be expected at some indeterminate point in the future. Frequently called a punch list, the identification of remaining work can help to successfully bring even troubled projects to a satisfying close for all parties. |
| Final Completion Plan | The final push to completion can be facilitated with a good completion plan. This important, time sensitive stage of the project must be closely managed. Don't let down your guard at this point. Too many things can derail your project's success if you ignore this step. Team members may lose focus, owners may be overly anxious to accept the deliverables, and many people's lives will change as they move on in their professional endeavors and personal relationships. Stay alert and stay in close contact with all stakeholders. Make sure you have the personal commitment to the final completion plan from each responsible party. |
| Formal Notice of Completion | After the final items have been delivered and the project has been completed according to the documentation, send a written notice of project completion to the stakeholders. Contractual responsibilities, ownership, and authority may dramatically change at this point. Check with your legal and financial team to make sure all your i's are dotted and your t's are crossed. |
| Formal Acceptance | This may come as a legal document, a letter of acceptance, or a thank you note. If a legal document is required by the project's documentation or your organization's policies, don't ignore this final task. The job isn't done until the paperwork is signed, sealed, and delivered. And as always, the project manager is ultimately the person who accepts the responsibility. |

# Final Project Reports

If required, a project's final reports will probably be outlined in the project's documentation. These may include quality assurance audits, specification compliance test results, engineering documentation, training manuals, or as-built drawings. It's not unusual for project documentation to include union, state, or federal labor-compliance reports as well.

Some project managers create a wrap-up report for their management. This is a perfect opportunity to communicate to your principals the project's accomplishments, challenges, and lessons learned. It is also a good time to formally thank key contributors, team players, and others who made your job a little easier or more successful.

## Writing the Final Report

The wrap-up report may be as brief as an interoffice memo or as lengthy as a total project review. Regardless of the size, write the report with a professional, objective tone. Keep your report as brief as possible. The longer the report, the less likely it will be read! Focus on the reader's point of view, and make sure the report is appropriate for everyone who will have access to it—upper management's report is probably not appropriate for the project team or the customer. It's the project manager's responsibility to handle all sensitive information carefully.

## Report Content

At a minimum, include the following five sections in every final report. This format sets the stage for objective, positive, and professional renderings of your projects. Each section's length and exact content can be altered depending on your audience.

> ➤ **Executive Summary**—A short, written overview of the project's goals and achievements, a summary of the project's implementation process, and an overview of how well the project met the performance, time, and cost constraints. The Project Summary report shown in Figure 13.11 of Chapter 13, "Managing Progress," is an excellent report to include in this section. The project's baseline, actual, and variance is reported for start and finish dates, duration, work, and costs in an easy-to-read format. Wow! Write a couple of paragraphs, and you've got a great executive summary.

> ➤ **Achievements**—A complete listing and analysis of the project's goals and objectives. Refer to the project initiation document, statement of scope, and any amendments made to these during the project. For larger projects, add the required test, audit, or inspection documents.

> ➤ **Implementation Analysis**—A detailed analysis of how well the project met performance, time, and cost objectives; and how well the project used resources, met financial objectives, and attained quality objectives. The Tracking Gantt chart and two Task Usage combination views can add communication punch to this section of your report. One Task Chart shows the Work table and the other shows the Cost table. These views are described in the next section, "Key Final Reports."

> ➤ **Recommendations**—Report any new issues or tasks that need future consideration. Recommend changes to methodology, staffing, administrative procedures, technology, resources, and any other issues that can make the organization more productive or cost effective.

➤ **Special Acknowledgments**—You didn't do it alone, so give credit to those who made the project a reality.

### View Formatting Tips

To display text on multiple lines in the Gantt Chart view, click and drag open a dividing line between any two row numbers in the row header. To automatically adjust the width of a column to best fit the entries, double-click the column dividing line in the column header. To adjust the vertical pane divider to the nearest column edge, double-click the vertical divider. To quickly hide a column from view, click the column's right edge and drag the column edge to the left until the column is hidden. To reveal the column, place the cursor slightly to the right of the line where the column was, click, and drag it open. Alternatively, right-click in the column header and select **Insert Column** or **Hide Column**.

## Key Final Reports

An excellent overview of the project's planned and actual progress is provided by the Tracking Gantt chart. Figure 16.1 provides an example. To access and print this report, choose **Tracking Gantt** from the View menu. Click and drag the vertical divider until only the Gantt Chart and the Task Name column is shown. Select **Print Preview** from the File menu. To adjust how the page will print, click **Page Setup**. If this is the first time you've used Page Setup, select each of the tabs in the Page Setup dialog box and investigate the available options. When you're satisfied with the look of your page, click **Print.** The Tracking Gantt is ready to include in your final report.

The Task Chart compares baseline versus actual work (or costs) by task. Figure 16.2 shows the Task Usage view using the Work table, and Figure 16.3 shows the Task Usage view with the Cost table. To print these reports, click on **Task Usage** from the View menu, **Table** from the View menu, and then select either the **Work** or **Cost** table. Then select **Print Preview**, and if you like what you see, click **Print.**

**Figure 16.1**

*The Tracking Gantt provides an excellent comparison of the project's actual versus baseline progress.*

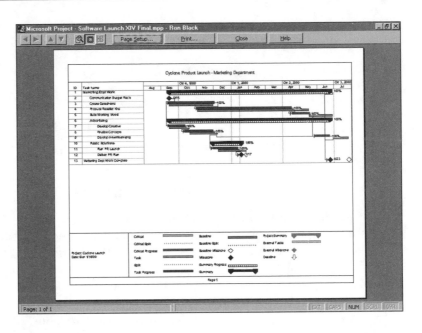

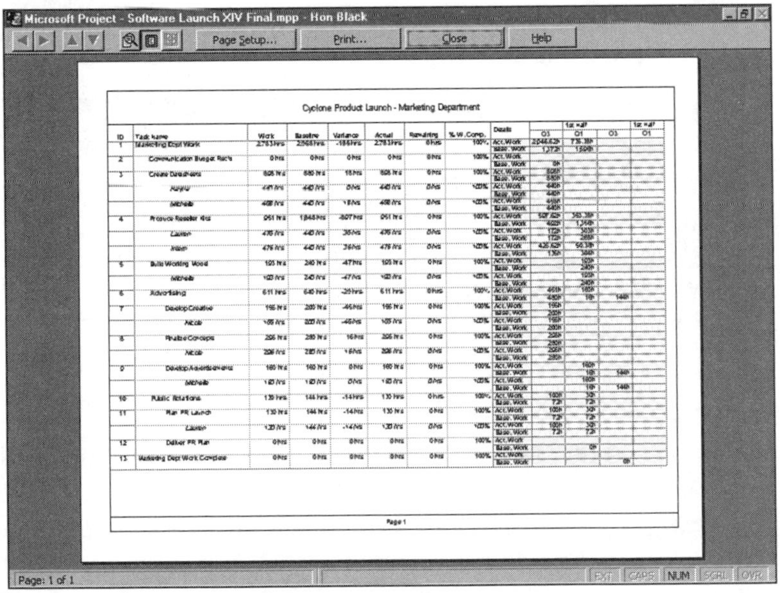

**Figure 16.2**

*The Task Usage view with the Work table selected provides a comparison of baseline vs. actual work data for each task by resource and date.*

**Figure 16.3**

*The Task Usage view used with the Cost table provides a comparison of baseline versus actual cost data for each task by resource and date.*

# Creating a Project Archive

Every project is a learning experience; to make the most of it, create a project archive. To borrow a few words from the poet, you never know when you may pass this way again!

Some of the most important bits of information to collect before it's thrown out by the cleaning crew are all time cards and records of time spent on tasks. As you have seen, accurate duration estimating is the key to creating an accurate schedule. And an accurate schedule is the project manager's best (and sometimes only) friend! It exposes the project's hidden resources, slack time, and flexibility. It provides the primary baseline for successful monitoring and control of the project. It allows you to gain meaningful commitments by and for stakeholders. And the single best source of accurate duration estimating is from your own history file.

**Continuous Improvement**

The difference between good project managers and excellent project managers is often surprisingly small. Take some time at the end of the project to survey your team. Ask them what went well, what they learned, and what they would do differently next time. Ask them how you could help them be more successful on the next project. Small lessons can turn into big wins on the next project.

So, even if you have to dig through the trash to get them, save all the time records for every project you work on. You don't have to compile or evaluate the data right now. Just save it. If a similar project is in your future, you'll be glad you turned into a time-card collector!

If you've tracked actuals against your baseline plan in Project 2000, you're way ahead of the game. The time card information has already been applied to each task. The information you need to evaluate the actual versus estimated durations is ready and waiting in Project 2000! All you need to do is make an archival copy of the project data file and store it in a safe place. Simply save your project onto a floppy or other removable media and place it with the hard copies of your project documentation. If and when it's needed, you'll be ready!

It's also a good idea to maintain a complete set of project communication documents. On rare occasions I've been asked to explain what happened or who did what several years after a project has been completed. It's amazing how much you can recall with a few dated meeting notes, memos, or archived email messages to jog your memory.

Okay, call me a pack rat, but I would rather have it and not need it than need it and not have it!

# Reassigning Project Personnel

Some projects grind to a halt as they approach completion. Most of the time these problems are a direct result of poor definitions or lack of stakeholder buy-in during the crucial, early stage of the project. However, other times the resistance to completion comes from within the team. For many reasons, some teams just don't want to finish up and move on. If you find yourself (or your team) trapped in a self-imposed never-ending project, you need to be ready to provide some nurturing leadership.

Personnel problems come disguised in excuses and ambiguity, so they can be hard to identify. When nearing the completion of a project, be on the alert for these people problems.

## *Woe Is Me—The End Is Near!*

You can expect two kinds of personnel problems when nearing the end of a project. In one case, team members are abandoning the project like it was a ship on fire. They're doing just enough to get by and the bulk of their energies are spent finding their next landing spot. You can expect a few of these nervous types on every project. It's easy to understand their point of view. Perhaps they've worked long and hard, and now, as they realize the end is near, they're panic stricken!

"What next? How am I going to make my mortgage?" Their fears are understandable. Whether or not they're justifiable fears is another question. In any case, it becomes a major challenge to keep these folks on task and achieving at acceptable rates.

The best course of action with these nervous types is one of reassuring leadership. Stay with them emotionally. Let them know they've done a good job, they've been noticed, and that you'll hate to see them go. A little honest respect goes a long way in reassuring these folks that it will all work out in their best interest. Your confidence in their abilities is a powerful stabilizing force. Keep them focused and informed. Help them understand the situation, the wrap-up process, and the time line involved. These folks need to be in control of their own destinies, so the more forthcoming you are with the facts, the better off you'll both be.

On the other extreme are the people who don't want the project to end, no matter what! They like it here (or perhaps anything is better than the unknown future). From these types of team members, stretching the job out or downright sabotage can be a real threat to your project's success. Be on the alert for work slowdowns. Don't wait for the first sign of trouble. Just expect it and take action. You see, the folks who are afraid to move on need exactly the same reassurance and leadership as the group that is already running for cover. They have the same fears; they're just acting them out in a different way.

**If You Can't Say Something Nice...**

When the project is over, refrain from complaining about a team member's behavior. Little can be improved after the fact, and no one responds to whining. What has been done is done, so drop the past and focus on the future. What's important now is to spend your energy celebrating the success of those who contributed to the success of the project. Make sure they understand that you recognize and appreciate their contribution.

Both of these troublesome sets of team members will respond to your genuine caring and honest support. Their fears are real and they are, of course, entitled to them. Now is the time to dial up your skills of nurturing leadership. Let your team know you genuinely care about them, the work they've done, and their future success. Most of your team will respond positively as professionals.

Moreover, if you can help them find a new project, write a sparkling letter of recommendation, or put in a good word to a colleague, all the better. Your team took care of you; now it's time to take care of the team. What goes around comes around!

# Following Your Mother's Advice (Again)

It seems like moms are getting a lot of good press in this book! You have to admit, they've usually got some pretty good advice. Earlier, we took Mom's advice by scheduling every task as soon as possible—never putting off until later what we could do now.

Well, there is at least one more great piece of Mom's advice every project manager should remember: Don't forget to say thank you! These are probably the most powerful words in a project manager's vocabulary (and on some projects, the least frequently heard). Not only do these simple words make people feel good, they also send a powerful message. Recipients know that you understand the contribution, risk, hard work, and sometimes sacrifices they've made for the good of the project.

### Gift, Card, or Bonus Check?

Some organizations maintain a budget for bonuses, incentives, and rewards. If yours does, use it! But take care. In some industries (such as defense contracting), there are strict rules of what is and is not permissible. There's another problem with gifts and bonuses—if there's one secret that's impossible to keep in any organization, it's who got the biggest bonus (or no bonus at all)! Team parties or victory celebrations often have a better team-building effect. And if you don't have a budget for such festivities, get creative! Have a pot-luck lunch in the conference room or order in pizzas. Make certificates of appreciation on your computer. Whatever you do, the important thing is to say something positive about every team member's contribution. No matter how modest the embellishments may be, it's the thank you and recognition that counts the most.

And as an added bonus, saying thank you even makes you feel good! Seriously, the next time a project rolls around and you want to staff it with high achievers, those who know you appreciate their contribution will be on the list of volunteers. If there is one thing I've learned leading project teams, personal recognition is a powerful commodity. Put it to work; it's effective. Moreover, I guarantee your mother will approve!

## The Least You Need to Know

➤ The best way to close a project is determined in the initial planning stages by carefully defining the project's goals and objectives in measurable terms.

➤ Ideally, the project progress continually picks up speed from planning to execution to completion. When projects falter in late stages it is symptomatic of inadequacies in the definition or planning stage.

➤ Your success and the success of your project depends on how well the stakeholder's expectations are met. It is difficult, if not impossible, to change stakeholder expectations late in the project.

➤ Personnel issues frequently arise in the late stages of a project. Some team members lose focus in anticipation of their eminent departure while others may tend to hang on beyond their usefulness. Astute project managers are aware of these problems and actively smoothe job transitions for the team.

211

# Part 6

# Other Neat Things Microsoft Project 2000 Can Do For You

*Fasten your seatbelt. In Parts 1–5 you learned how to use planning skills with Microsoft Project 2000 to fly a project on the straight and level. In Part 6, you'll learn how to do a few really cool, high-speed aerobatic maneuvers. (I hope you aren't a white-knuckle flyer.)*

*You'll learn how to control and manage multiple projects, how to import and export information, how to publish your plan to the Web, and how to keep a virtual team in perfect sync with email. In short, this is where you become a project ace!*

# Chapter 17

# Too Many Projects, Too Little Time

---

**In This Chapter**

➤ Use master projects and subprojects to make large projects more manageable

➤ Create a common resource pool to facilitate resource sharing and leveling between projects

➤ Consolidate project files for reports, scheduling, or coordination purposes

---

One of the benefits of being a capable project manager is that the projects never stop coming—well, it's nice to know you're appreciated, isn't it? Moreover, it's likely that your boss doesn't have a clue of how resource leveling works, at least not when it comes to you! So more often than not, you're probably managing several projects at a time.

## Managing Multiple Projects

There's one fundamental problem with managing multiple projects—it's hard! You just can't do two projects at a time as well as you can do one. And, you certainly can't do three as well as you can do two. And you...well, you get the point. The more projects you manage at one time, the more difficult it is to manage any of them successfully. In short, your risk as a project manager goes up in direct proportion to your project management workload. Those are the facts of life at work.

In addition to the issues of time and effectiveness, two other key problems make managing multiple projects far more difficult than managing one. In a multiproject environment there is almost always a question of which project should take priority when conflicts occur. Deciding which project has the right-of-way is not a job that should be left to the project manager. These issues must be decided at a higher level in the organization. Otherwise, the organization sets competing groups at odds with one another. Eventually, the organization as a whole suffers.

The other important issue facing project managers in a multiproject environment is one of resource utilization. Thanks to our invisible teammate Adam Smith, there's never an abundance of resources. Scarcity is the rule. Consequently, it's important to carefully manage a given set of resources across several projects. As you'll soon see, Project 2000 comes to your rescue in a big way here!

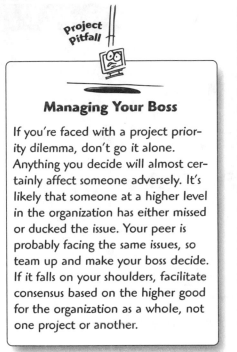

### Managing Your Boss

If you're faced with a project priority dilemma, don't go it alone. Anything you decide will almost certainly affect someone adversely. It's likely that someone at a higher level in the organization has either missed or ducked the issue. Your peer is probably facing the same issues, so team up and make your boss decide. If it falls on your shoulders, facilitate consensus based on the higher good for the organization as a whole, not one project or another.

### Managing Multiple Projects

The first step in learning how to manage several projects at a time is to learn how to manage one project effectively. As described in Chapter 2, "The Project Management Process," begin by creating a solid project definition. After that is done, create the plan. With an accurate plan you can implement and control the project much easier. Moreover, if you've achieved success in each of these steps, successful project closure is the natural outcome. Don't skip any of the steps just because you're busy. There's an old saying that's appropriate in the multiproject environment: "If you don't have time to do it right, when will you have time to do it over?"

# Consolidating Project Files

Project 2000 allows you to create a master project and insert subprojects. This greatly simplifies managing large projects. Each subproject can be broken down by project manager, phase of work, budget, responsible team, or any other division your organization needs. In addition, the master project can be expanded or contracted just like any project file to limit what is shown on the screen. This allows you to coordinate an entire set of projects from an overview perspective and still drill down for complete detail at any time. Now, that's living!

To create a master project, open the file you want to be the master project. This may be an existing project or a new file. On the **View** menu, choose the **Gantt Chart** view. Now click the row below where you want to insert the subproject, and choose **Project** from the **Insert** menu. Figures 17.1 and 17.2 illustrate this process.

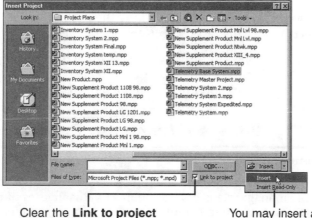

**Figure 17.1**

*Open the file you want to be the master project and click* **Project** *in the* **Insert** *menu.*

**Figure 17.2**

*Choose the project you want to insert into the master project and click* **Insert**.

Clear the **Link to project** check box to prevent changes in the master project from changing this file.

You may insert a project as read only.

### On the Level with Linking Subprojects

When working with master projects, carefully consider the effects of linking inserted projects. Subprojects inserted with **Link to project** checked (found at the lower right of the Insert dialog box) will be leveled as an integral part of the master project. On the other hand, when **Link to project** isn't checked, leveling the master project has no affect on the inserted subproject. In a like manner, changes made to linked subprojects are reflected in the master project even when the modifications are made outside of the master project. Subprojects that are not linked may be opened and modified without changing the master project in any way.

After the projects have been added to the master project, you can work with them just like they were still separate projects. Unless you inserted them as read-only, all changes made to these files will be saved in the individual project files as well. If you don't want to update the subproject files from the master file, clear the **Link to project** check box before inserting the project file.

Subprojects are treated like summary tasks in the master project so you can indent or outdent tasks. Be careful, however; these changes will be shown in the original project file as well. For this reason, it is usually best to refrain from changing the task hierarchy in the master project file.

By clicking the plus or minus signs next to the tasks, you can hide or show the subproject's tasks. You can also link tasks just as you would normally. The easiest way to do this in the master project is to click the predecessor task and drag the new link to the successor task. As you link tasks between subprojects, the new critical path is calculated and the project's schedule automatically adjusts, as shown in the Detail Gantt Chart view in Figure 17.3.

A master project with four subprojects is shown in Figure 17.4. Clicking the outline symbol reveals all the tasks within the subproject.

Using a master project file to coordinate your projects is helpful for several reasons. Some of the most important ones are described in Table 17.1.

## Table 17.1   When to Use Master Projects

| Situation | Comments |
| --- | --- |
| Complex Projects | Breaking a large project down into smaller subprojects that are more manageable is one of the most valuable uses of master projects. Simplifying complex projects makes them easier to understand, monitor, and control. |
| Multiple Projects | When you or your organization has multiple projects, it can be helpful to combine them into a master file even if they are not directly related to one another. Viewing all the subprojects, their start dates, and completion dates on one screen provides an important perspective for top level management. Project priority can be shown in the master project file. In addition, organization-wide reports can be created from the master file. |

| Situation | Comments |
|---|---|
| Multiple Stakeholders | One project file can be used to create several master project files. Each master file can then be set up to meet the needs of the various stakeholders. Modification to project data in any of the master files is captured in the subproject file. |
| Shared Resources | One of the most important benefits for combining files into a master file is the ability to use a common resource pool. Resource information can be stored in a central location, and master projects or subprojects can draw on this pool for resources. Resource leveling, resource allocation, and resource priority problems can be effectively dealt with using a common resource pool. |

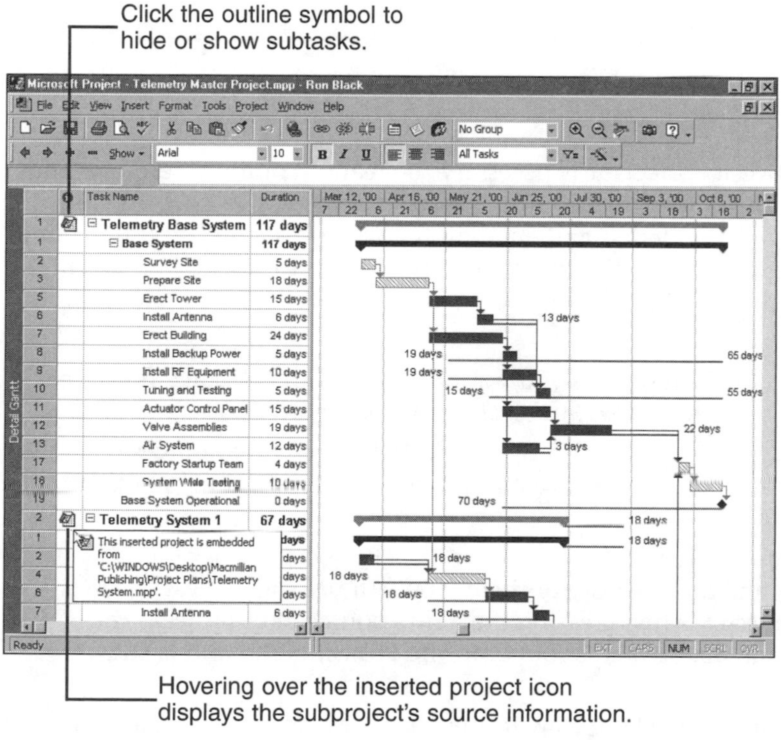

Click the outline symbol to
hide or show subtasks.

Hovering over the inserted project icon
displays the subproject's source information.

**Figure 17.3**

*The critical path, slack, and delay are automatically calculated for the master project when you modify task dependencies.*

**Figure 17.4**

*Each subproject is shown as a summary task in the master project.*

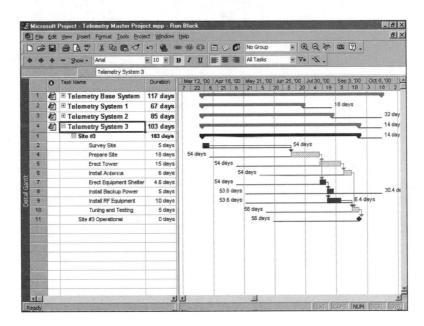

## Sharing Resource Pools

To share resources between projects it is necessary to create a common resource pool. The easiest way to do this is to set up a project without any tasks to hold all your resources. You can start from scratch and enter all the resources, costs, and pay rates as you would for any new project. However, there is no need to work that hard if you already have the resources you want in the pool in another project. Here's what you do:

1. Open the files that have resources you want to place in the resource pool. On the **View** menu, select **Resource Sheet**, as shown in Figure 17.5.

2. In the resource sheet view of each project, check that no two resources have the same name and that no one resource has different names. Edit any conflicts before continuing.

3. In the Project Information dialog box, check the project start or end dates for each project, and make a note of them. You will use the earliest or latest of these dates in step 5 when creating the new resource pool project. The Project Information dialog box is found on the Project menu and is shown in Figure 17.6.

4. Create a new project by clicking **New** in the **File** menu and selecting a **New Blank Project** from the New dialog box.

5. In the Project Information dialog box, type a start or finish date that is early enough or late enough to make the resources available for all open projects. Now save the project with a representative name such as ResourcePool.

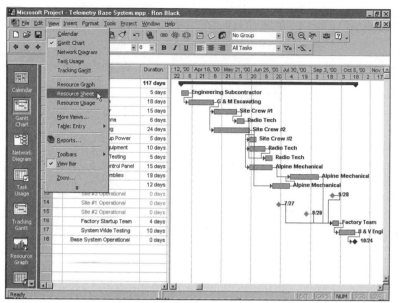

**Figure 17.5**

*Open each file that has resources you want to add to the resource pool and select the **Resource Sheet** view.*

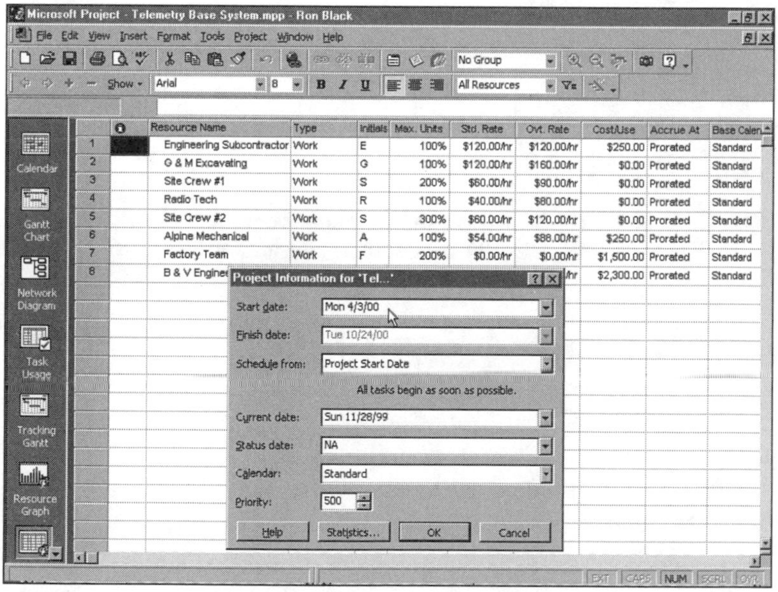

**Figure 17.6**

*Make a note of each project's start or end date before creating the new project that will be used as a resource pool.*

6. In the **Window** menu, select the first project whose resources you want to add to the resource pool. In the **Tools** menu, choose **Resources**, and then select **Shared Resources** as shown in Figure 17.7.

**Figure 17.7**

*Select the project whose resources you want to add to the resource pool and click* **Shared Resources**.

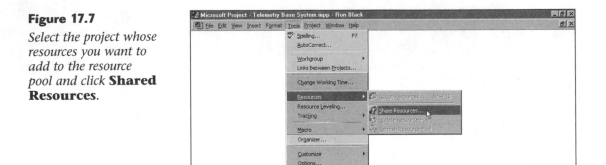

7. When the Shared Resources dialog box appears, check the **Use resources** box and then choose the resource pool file in the **From** box. This process is illustrated in Figure 17.8. In this way, add each project file you want to connect to the resource pool. Save each of the files before closing them.

**Figure 17.8**

*Choose the resource pool file name from the list in the* **From** *field.*

Pool file overwrites sharing file on conflicts of calendars or resource information.

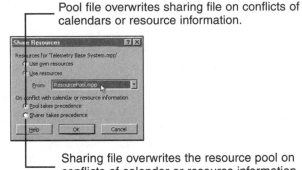

Sharing file overwrites the resource pool on conflicts of calendar or resource information.

# Getting Speedy with Project Templates

If you do many similar projects, you can save much time and effort by creating and using project templates. Any and all of the information stored in a project file can become a project template. This can include your work breakdown structure, task durations, workflow sequence, resource names and rates, views, baselines, or any other information you want.

The best way to set up a project template is to use an existing project file as the basis. Review the file you want to use as a template for its usefulness. Remember, it's always easier to edit than to create, so when in doubt, keep the data! When you're satisfied with the file, click **Save As** on the **File** menu. Type a name for your template in the **File name** field and select the drive and folder where you want to store it. Choose **Template** from the **Save as type** field and then click **Save**, as shown in Figure 17.9.

### Too Busy to Plan? Use Templates!

If many of your projects are similar, use templates to speed planning. A well thought out template can save hours of project planning and data entry. Wouldn't it be nice not to have to start from scratch on the work breakdown structure, duration estimates, task dependencies, cost information, and resource assignments? Even if your next project isn't exactly like the template, you could still be hours ahead of the game. Templates serve two other important functions: First, they help prevent leaving out essential items. Second, templates can help transfer knowledge throughout your organization by helping others replicate proven project methodologies. When you're too busy to plan, you need to be planning more—with templates!

**Figure 17.9**

*Save common project files as templates for the next time you do a similar project.*

When the Save As Template dialog box appears, check each item you do *not* want to save, as shown in Figure 17.10. That's it!

**Figure 17.10**

*You may choose to save all or part of a project file as a template.*

The next time a project like this one comes along, you'll be ahead of the game! To use your new template (or any of those that come with Project), select **New** from the File menu. In the New dialog box, select the **Template** tab and double-click the desired template. Voila! You're off to a running start! If a short note is better than a long memory, I wonder how much better a whole template is!

---

### The Least You Need to Know

➤ Projects can be combined into master project files to facilitate resource sharing, project prioritization, and management reports, and to improve the control of project responsibilities.

➤ Successful project managers resist the temptation to skip the definition and planning stages of a project when pressed for time. When managing multiple projects, it's more important than ever to carefully plan each project.

➤ Resource pools may be established to ease the burden of resource allocation and overallocation. Common resource pools also help an organization more effectively use scarce resources.

# Chapter 18

---

TA DA!!

# Publishing Projects on the Web

---

## In This Chapter

➤ Export Microsoft Project 2000 text data in HTML format to create tables for publishing information on the Web

➤ Save charts as GIF picture files for publishing on the Web or pasting into other programs

➤ Using Microsoft Project Central to broaden project team involvement and productivity

---

Some projects go so well that you just want to tell the whole world! And to do that, there's no place like the Web. With the growing importance of the Internet and intranets, project managers are frequently turning to the Web as a distribution point for their project's information. The Web is a good place to make project information available to a wide audience.

You can prepare information to be published on the Web in two formats: text and images. Both of these methods are static—as your project changes, the published information stays the same.

## Exporting Text Information to HTML Format

To publish text information on the Web, one good method is to export data in an HTML (Hypertext Markup Language) format. The data can then be incorporated into pages that can be published on the Web by your Web administrator. This information can then be viewed by anyone accessing the Web site with a browser program. To export a project's data, click **Save as Web Page** on the **File** menu, as shown in Figure 18.1.

**Figure 18.1**

*Project data may be exported in an HTML format by using Save As.*

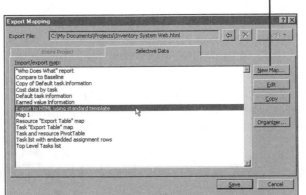

In the Export Mapping dialog box, choose **Export to HTML using standard template** as shown in Figure 18.2. This selection exports task names, ID, duration, start date, finish date, resource names, and percent complete; resource names, group, max units, and peak; and assignments task ID, task name, resource name, work, start date, finish date, and percent complete. These HTML documents are shown in Figures 18.3, 18.4, and 18.5.

**Figure 18.2**

*You may select the data you want to export in the Export Mapping dialog box.*

Select **New Map** to limit data exported.

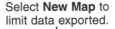

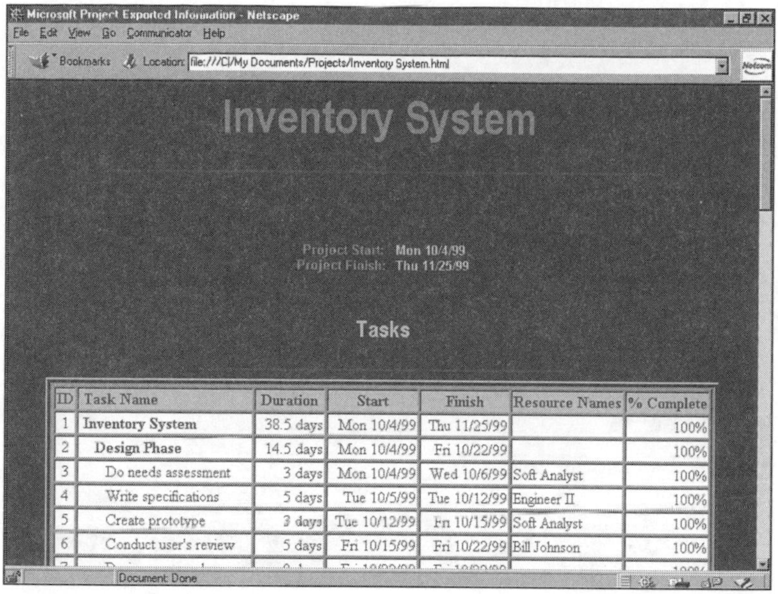

**Figure 18.3**

*A sample of the project's task data as it appears when exported to an HTML format.*

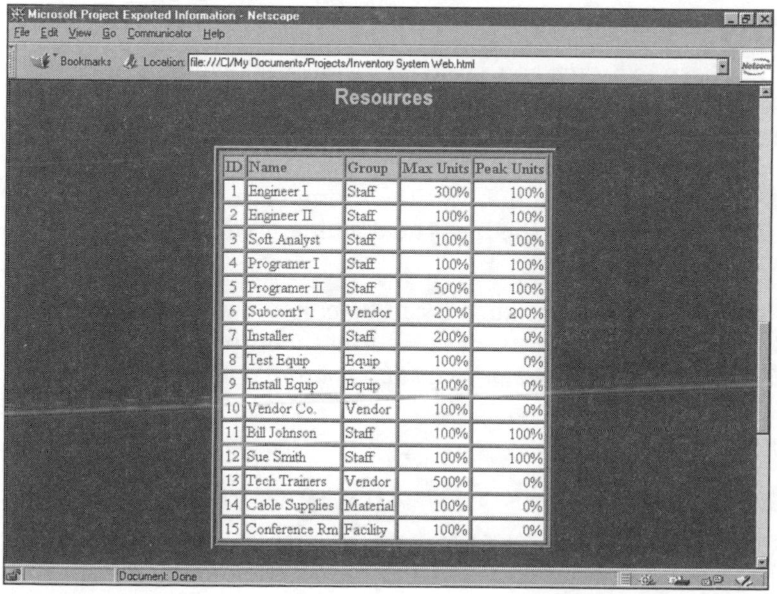

**Figure 18.4**

*The resource information as exported in an HTML format.*

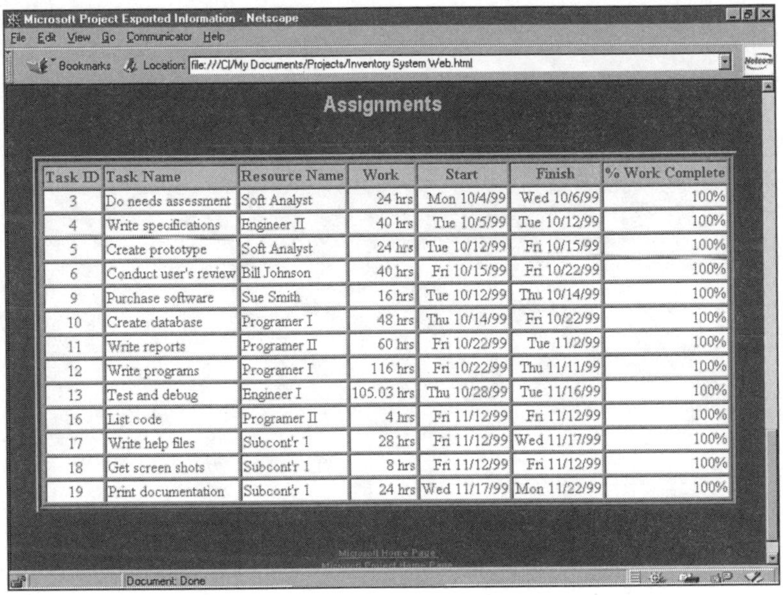


| Task ID | Task Name | Resource Name | Work | Start | Finish | % Work Complete |
|---|---|---|---|---|---|---|
| 3 | Do needs assessment | Soft Analyst | 24 hrs | Mon 10/4/99 | Wed 10/6/99 | 100% |
| 4 | Write specifications | Engineer II | 40 hrs | Tue 10/5/99 | Tue 10/12/99 | 100% |
| 5 | Create prototype | Soft Analyst | 24 hrs | Tue 10/12/99 | Fri 10/15/99 | 100% |
| 6 | Conduct user's review | Bill Johnson | 40 hrs | Fri 10/15/99 | Fri 10/22/99 | 100% |
| 9 | Purchase software | Sue Smith | 16 hrs | Tue 10/12/99 | Thu 10/14/99 | 100% |
| 10 | Create database | Programer I | 48 hrs | Thu 10/14/99 | Fri 10/22/99 | 100% |
| 11 | Write reports | Programer II | 60 hrs | Fri 10/22/99 | Tue 11/2/99 | 100% |
| 12 | Write programs | Programer I | 116 hrs | Fri 10/22/99 | Thu 11/11/99 | 100% |
| 13 | Test and debug | Engineer I | 105.03 hrs | Thu 10/28/99 | Tue 11/16/99 | 100% |
| 16 | List code | Programer II | 4 hrs | Fri 11/12/99 | Fri 11/12/99 | 100% |
| 17 | Write help files | Subcont'r 1 | 28 hrs | Fri 11/12/99 | Wed 11/17/99 | 100% |
| 18 | Get screen shots | Subcont'r 1 | 8 hrs | Fri 11/12/99 | Fri 11/12/99 | 100% |
| 19 | Print documentation | Subcont'r 1 | 24 hrs | Wed 11/17/99 | Mon 11/22/99 | 100% |

**Figure 18.5**
*The assignment information as exported in an HTML format.*

## *Opening an HTML Document*

After the information has been exported and saved as an HTML document, it can be uploaded to a Web site or viewed and edited like any other HTML document. To view HTML files before they are posted to a Web site, start your Internet browser, such as Microsoft Internet Explorer (or Netscape), and select **Open** (or **Open Page**). Go to the folder where the file is stored and follow the prompts in your browser's Open (or Open Page) dialog box to open the file. The document will appear on your screen.

If the information isn't formatted to your liking, it can be edited. For more information on creating or editing HTML documents, or uploading them to a Web site, an excellent reference is *The Complete Idiot's Guide to HTML, Fourth Edition,* by Paul McFedries.

# Saving Charts and Views As GIF Image Files

Project 2000 also makes it easy to save a picture for Web publishing. You can copy any information from a Project view and save it in a format used in Web publishing. You can also paste the picture into programs that support this format. To capture a view of your plan as a picture file, click the **camera** icon on the toolbar as shown in Figure 18.6.

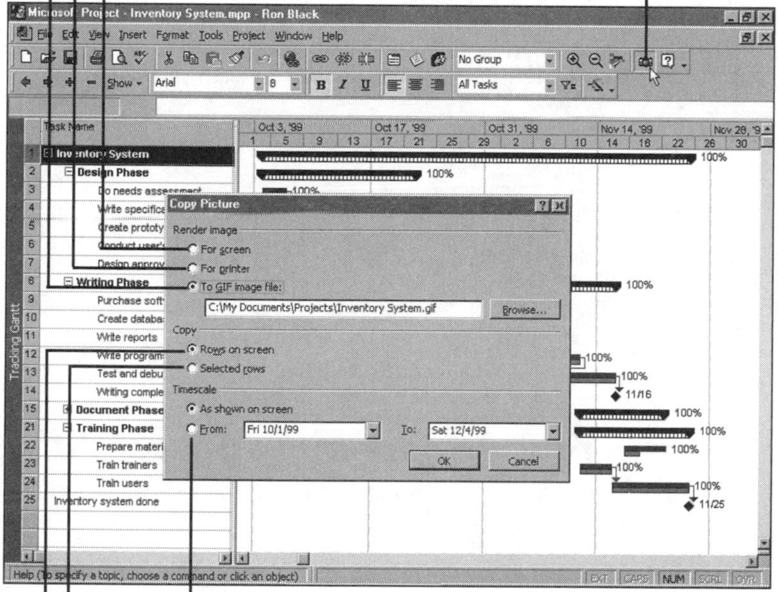

**To GIF image flle** copies and saves the picture in an image format widely used on the Internet.

**For printer** copies a picture as it would look when printed by your currently selected printer.

**For screen** copies a picture for pasting into another program.

Click here to capture a picture of the current view.

**Figure 18.6**

*A wide range of image copying options are available on the Copy Picture dialog box.*

Limits information copied to a date range

Limits picture to those rows that are highlighted

Limits picture to those rows showing on the screen

# Improving Teamwork with Project Central

Successful project managers engage the minds and expertise of everyone on the project team. Throughout the five phases of project management (see Chapter 2, "The Project Management Process"), the project is best served when everyone is able to communicate actively and effectively. To facilitate these high levels of collaboration, Microsoft has created Project Central, a companion product that ships with Project 2000.

## Using the Web to Collaborate

Project Central is actually a separate database of a Project 2000 schedule that is published on the Internet or a corporate intranet. Project team members, stakeholders, and any others who have permission may access the Web site to view, update, or act on project data. The project manager controls what each person is able to do and whether or not certain actions can automatically be accepted into the schedule. All updates and proposed changes are sent to and from users in the form of messages.

Team members access the information by logging onto the site with a Web browser. The project manager or administrator updates Project Central data on the Web site from Project 2000. This operation can set up to automatically occur each time the project file is saved. It can also be done manually from the Tools menu, as shown in Figure 18.7.

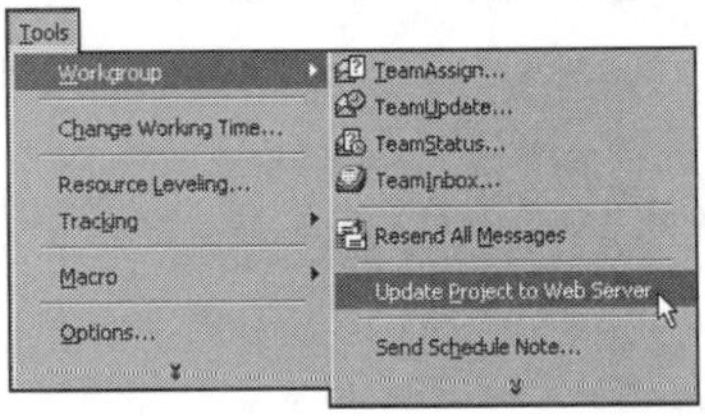

**Figure 18.7**

*Keeping project information current on Project Central's Web server is a simple task from Project 2000.*

## Features That Can Make Your Project More Successful

There's something for everyone in Project Central, and it's all designed to make your project more successful.

### For the Project Manager

Project managers can improve the accuracy of their schedules by involving more people in the development and use of project information. Depending on the rules set by the project manager, Project Central can solicit input regarding tasks, durations, and status directly from resources. This information can be accepted automatically into the project plan or reviewed and included selectively by the project manager. Project Central automates many time-consuming project management tasks, such as accepting project updates, sending schedule reminders, and compiling status reports.

### For Project Team Members

Team members can be more involved in the project management process with Project Central. Depending on the amount of control and information the project manager grants to the team, resources can become more active in creating and maintaining the project's schedule. They may add new tasks to the schedule, delegate tasks to others, enter actuals and time sheet data, and view a Gantt Chart of their personal task commitments. They can even import their schedule data from Microsoft Outlook calendars to inform the project manager of their availability.

### For Upper Management

With Project Central, upper management can stay better informed. Ease of access to a project's up-to-date information may improve management's ability to make quality decisions. And in a multiproject environment, Project Central can provide summaries of all projects across the organization. Managers can zoom to as much detail as desired.

The net result of Project Central is the ability to create, control, and distribute a project's schedule with a higher level of accuracy and timeliness.

## An Overview of Project Central's System Requirements

Unfortunately, not every project manager will be able (or want) to use Project Central. Using Project Central adds a layer of complexity, technical support, and system requirements that may not be appropriate for smaller organizations. A detailed listing of Project Central's system requirements is provided in Chapter 19, "Communicating with Teams via Email," in Table 19.2.

In general, Project Central Server must be installed on an Internet or intranet computer that runs Windows NT or Windows 2000. The project manager must have Project 2000 installed. Project 2000 isn't required for team members; however, they must have a licensed copy of Project Central client. Those using Microsoft Internet Explorer 4.01 or later will be prompted to install other necessary client components the first time they access Project Central. Clients who don't have Internet Explorer must manually install the Browser Module supplied with Project 2000.

Before installing or using Project Central, check with your system administrator. Information on complete Project Central requirements can be obtained at http://www.microsoft.com/office/project/default.htm or on your Project 2000 CD in the file svrsetup.htm.

---

### The Least You Need to Know

➤ Both text and pictures can be exported for publishing on intranets and the Internet. The information doesn't change after it has been exported, so it may get out of date quickly.

➤ Any view on the screen can be copied as an image file. This includes charts, tables, and sheet views. The information can be published on the Web or pasted into any program that can display GIF images.

➤ Project Central is a companion product that comes with Project 2000. It enables a project manager to involve more team members in planning and updating schedules. In addition, it facilitates the distribution of up-to-date project information to all project stakeholders.

---

# Chapter 19

# Communicating with Teams via Email

---

## In This Chapter

➤ Using email effectively in the project team environment

➤ Using workgroup email or Web messaging to assign tasks, monitor project progress, and stay informed

➤ Updating the project's progress using TeamStatus

➤ Routing a project file for review and comment

---

It's ten o'clock. Do you know where your teammates are? In a world of distributed work forces, international companies, telecommuting, and multiple project responsibilities, communicating with your team can prove to be difficult. Moreover, your project's success depends on maintaining effective communication throughout the team. In today's project environment, that's frequently much farther than down the hall or across the conference room. Indeed, you may have to communicate with people whose 10:00 a.m. is your 10:00 p.m.!

In addition to keeping others informed, it's also essential that they keep you informed. On even the best planned project, schedules change, problems arise, and the unexpected occurs. To make good, fast decisions, you need a steady stream of good, fast information. And that's where Microsoft Project 2000 really helps.

### Virtual Team or Virtually a Team?

In the age of email, cellular phones, teleconferences, faxes, Net meetings, and the Internet, virtual teams are becoming commonplace. Unfortunately, the lack of social contact in these distributed workgroups makes it difficult to build interpersonal rapport, trust, and mutual respect. Workgroups without these basics are virtually teams, not virtual teams. Make it a point to know your teammates as people, not just workers. Even small things like taking a few moments to discuss a book or movie helps build strength in team relationships. To be a team, people must stay connected emotionally, not just electronically.

## Email Etiquette for Project Teams

The thing I love most about having a computer is access to email. It's great to keep in touch with team members around the world (or across the building) with such speed and convenience.

On the other hand, if there is one thing I hate about my computer, it's also email! It seems the lure of cramming my electronic in-basket with junk is too much for some of my teammates to resist! I actually dread seeing some of their names appear as the sender, because I know how long it will take to sort through their clutter. I'm always afraid they've buried important information somewhere in all that trivia. It's the electronic version of finding a needle in a haystack!

## Here are a few tips to make email a more effective project communication tool:

➤ Limit the information you send to what is truly important. The "must-have" content should always outweigh the "nice-to-have" content. The "I-don't-know-if-you-need-it" content should be briefly described and sent only if requested.

➤ Don't bury important information at the end of a long message. The reader may hit the Delete button long before she finds your nugget of wisdom.

➤ Don't ask for more detail than you really need. Ask people to "net that out" for you or "send me the headlines and the bullets." Remember, you're seeking success, not perfection.

➤ Clean up your distribution lists frequently. Nothing destroys credibility faster than sending email to a person who has been gone for several months.

➤ Always place a brief description of the content in the subject area. Help the recipient prioritize their communication workload.

➤ Make your email reader-friendly by using appropriate grammar, capitalization, punctuation, and spelling.

➤ Avoid humorous content. Because email provides no immediate feedback in the way of body language or facial expressions, intended humor may easily become an unintended insult.

➤ Keep your messages professional in content. Inspirational quotes, promises of chain mail riches, and urban myths are best left to those with free email accounts.

# Workgroup Messaging Systems

To facilitate project communication via email or the Web, Project 2000 uses workgroup messaging. Anyone who has access to a MAPI-compliant email system or the Internet can participate in workgroup messaging as long as certain requirements are met. These requirements are shown in Table 19.1 for email-based messaging and later in Table 19.2 for Web-based messaging.

## Table 19.1  Email-Based Workgroup Messaging

| Requirement | Description |
| --- | --- |
| Microsoft Project 2000 | The workgroup manager must have Project installed on the computer used for workgroup messaging. |
| Access to email | All participating team members must have email access. This can be either through a LAN (local area network) or a dial-up networking system. |
| MAPI-compliant email system | Only MAPI-compliant, 32-bit email systems may be used. This is the most broadly supported electronic messaging standard. If you use Microsoft Outlook, Microsoft Exchange, or Microsoft Mail, your system is compliant. Check with your email system administrator if you use other email software. |
| WGsetup.exe | Each participating workgroup member must run this program on their own computer to enable sending and receiving email workgroup messages. The program is found on the CD included with Project 2000 and may be shared with the project team members with no additional licensing fees. Microsoft recommends that you place the entire Wgsetup folder on a drive accessible to the workgroup. If remote users are not on the LAN, they can connect using dial-up networking and Windows Explorer. |

To prepare a computer for workgroup email messaging that does not have Project 2000 installed, run WGsetup.exe. Open the Wgsetup folder in the Project CD or on the LAN where it is stored. Double-click **Wgsetup.exe**. A dialog box appears as shown in Figure 19.1. Follow the prompts to complete installation.

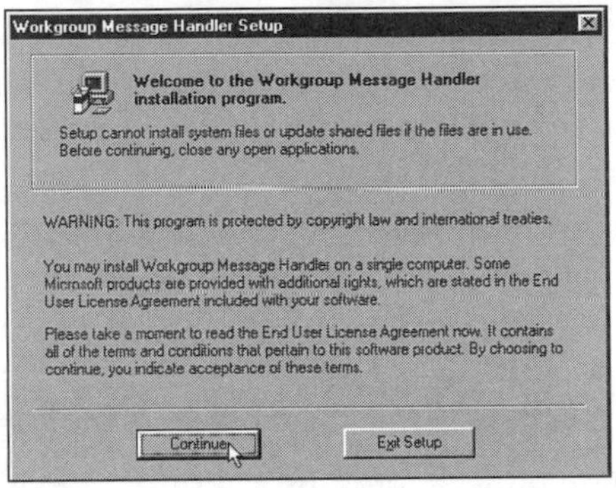

**Figure 19.1**

*To prepare computers for workgroup messaging with email, run wgsetup.exe on each workstation. The workgroup manager is the only one who must have an installed copy of Project 2000.*

Web-based workgroup messaging uses Microsoft Project Central. This program comes on the Project 2000 CD, but is not installed unless you choose that option. The requirements for workgroup messaging via the Web are shown in Table 19.2.

## Table 19.2   Web-Based Workgroup Messaging

| Requirement | Description |
| --- | --- |
| Microsoft Project | The workgroup manager must have Project installed on the computer used for workgroup messaging. |
| Microsoft Project Central | This program must be installed on an intranet or Internet server computer with Internet Information Server 4.0 or later, Windows NT Server service pack 4.0 or later, or Windows 2000 or later already installed. Contact your system administrator to set up Microsoft Project Central. Have the administrator provide you with the Web server's address (URL) used to access the site. Microsoft Project Central is located on the Project CD. |
| Required licenses and software | Each workgroup member needs a Microsoft Project Central license and a compatible Web browser. One Project Central license comes with Project 2000. Microsoft Internet Explorer 4.01 service pack 1 or later is also needed. When workgroup members access Microsoft Project Central with an incompatible browser, they will be prompted to download the browser that comes with Microsoft Project Central. Only the workgroup manager needs an installed copy of Project 2000. |
| Network considerations | All computers accessing Microsoft Project Central on an intranet must have a unique network identification. Check with your network administrator for this information. |

Some of your workgroup members may not have access to email or to the Web. But don't worry, Project 2000 allows you to use either or both email- and Web-based messaging on any one project. If both systems are used on your project, you must remember to check both places for your team's messages.

# Workgroup Messaging

Workgroup messaging via email or the Web makes it easy for team members to send and receive project information. The key areas of project communication usually revolve around resource assignments, task status, and project progress. Workgroup messaging uses three types of messages: TeamAssign, TeamUpdate, and TeamStatus.

## Using TeamAssign

You may use TeamAssign to notify workgroup members of task assignments. Of course, this presupposes that you've contacted the individuals regarding the project and their involvement on it. Receiving TeamAssign messages without prior notification is likely to conjure up feelings of electronic enslavement (remember "big brother" in Orwell's novel, *1984?*) for technophiles and technophobes alike! No one likes to be surprised with additional work.

It's always a good idea to save your project before starting a new procedure, so take a moment and save your file before continuing. A fast way to save your file is to press and hold the **Ctrl** key while pressing **S**. After your project file is safely backed up, select the Gantt Chart view by clicking **Gantt Chart** in the **View** menu.

Choose the task or tasks that you want to send assignment notifications to. Highlight the tasks you want by clicking one or by pressing **Ctrl** and clicking multiple tasks. The results are shown in Figure 19.2. To select a series of tasks, press and hold **Shift** while clicking the first and last tasks in the series. On some tasks there may be more than one resource assigned. In this case, each assigned resource is notified.

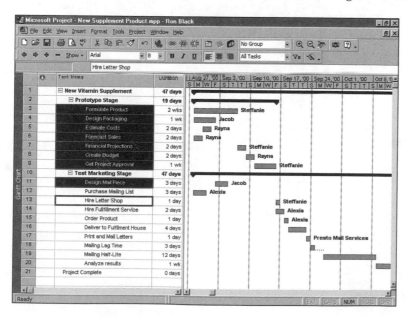

**Figure 19.2**

*Select the tasks you want to send resource notification messages to in the Gantt Chart view.*

237

After the tasks have been selected, select **Workgroup** from the **Tools** menu and then click **TeamAssign** as shown in Figure 19.3.

**Figure 19.3**

*Sending assignment notifications to resources is fast and easy with Project 2000.*

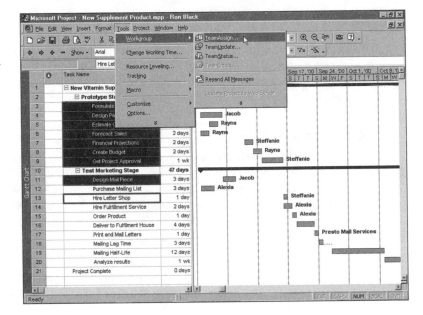

Modify the subject line and message as appropriate in the TeamAssign dialog box and click **Send**, as shown in Figure 19.4. Your workgroup will be notified of their respective tasks assignments just as soon as they receive their email.

**Figure 19.4**

*The TeamAssign message is ready to send to the workgroup.*

Type your message here or use the default message.

The manager or workgroup member may modify information in these fields. To change displayed fields choose Customize, and then Workgroup, from the Tools menu.

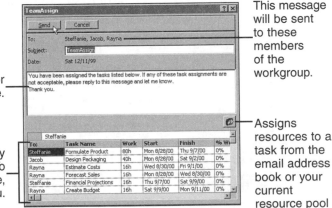

This message will be sent to these members of the workgroup.

Assigns resources to a task from the email address book or your current resource pool

When the workgroup members receive the message, they may accept or reject the assignment before replying. A TeamAssign message is shown in Figure 19.5.

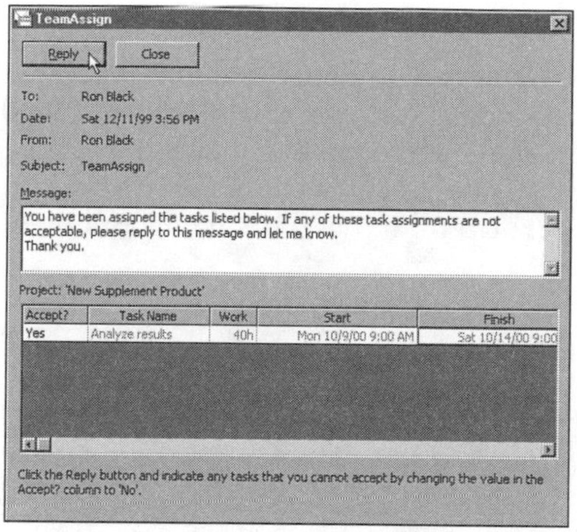

**Figure 19.5**
*Workgroup members receive TeamAssign messages in their email messaging system.*

When workgroup members reply to TeamAssign messages, the project manager can update the project as shown in Figure 19.6. The task assignment is marked as confirmed and task assignment information is updated.

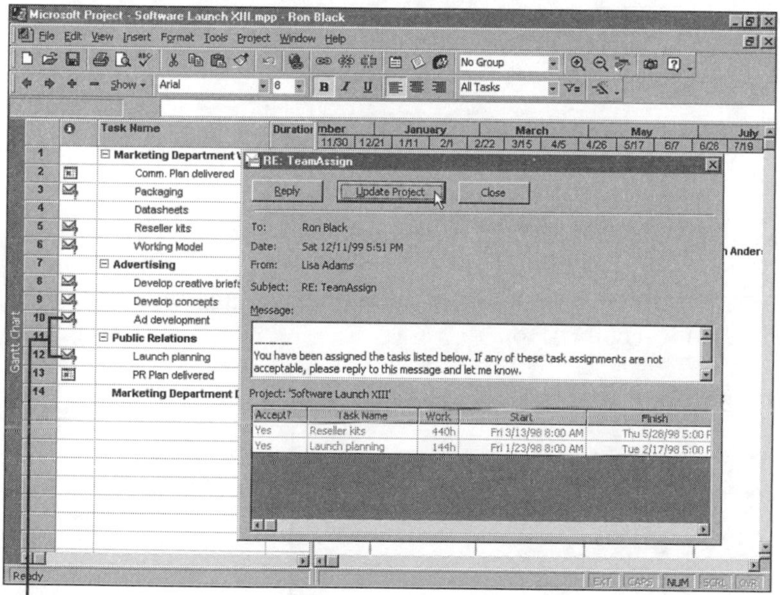

**Figure 19.6**
*Replies to TeamAssign messages can be applied to the project by clicking* **Update Project**.

The envelope and question mark icon indicate that not all resources have replied to the TeamAssign message.

239

### Using TeamUpdate

TeamUpdate messaging makes it fast and easy to notify resources who are affected by task slippage, changes in start or finish dates, or resources allocations. Sending, replying, and updating TeamUpdate messages follows an almost identical procedure, as described previously in the "Using TeamAssign" section. For example, to send a TeamUpdate message, select **Workgroup** from the **Tools** menu and then click **TeamUpdate** as shown in Figure 19.7.

**Figure 19.7**

*Sending a TeamUpdate is the fast and easy way to notify resources when dates slip or assignments change.*

The envelope and excla-mation point icon indicates that information for this task has changed and a TeamUpdate message should be sent.

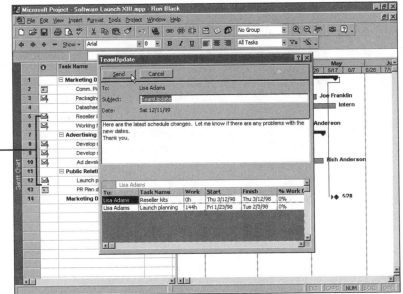

To update the project after the resource has replied, open the email message and click **Update Task List**, as shown in Figure 19.8.

**Figure 19.8**

*Entering accepted TeamUpdate information into your project schedule is as easy as opening the message and clicking* **Update Task List.**

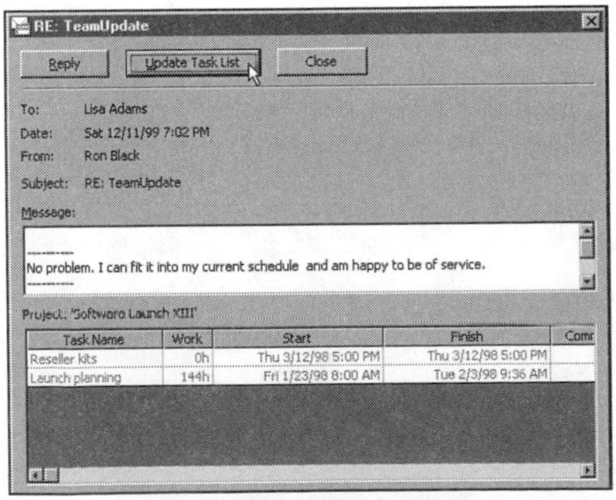

## Using TeamStatus

To request a status report from the resources on your project, select **Workgroup** from the **Tools** menu and then click **TeamStatus**. You may choose to request a TeamStatus from all resources or from a selection. The TeamStatus dialog box is shown in Figure 19.9.

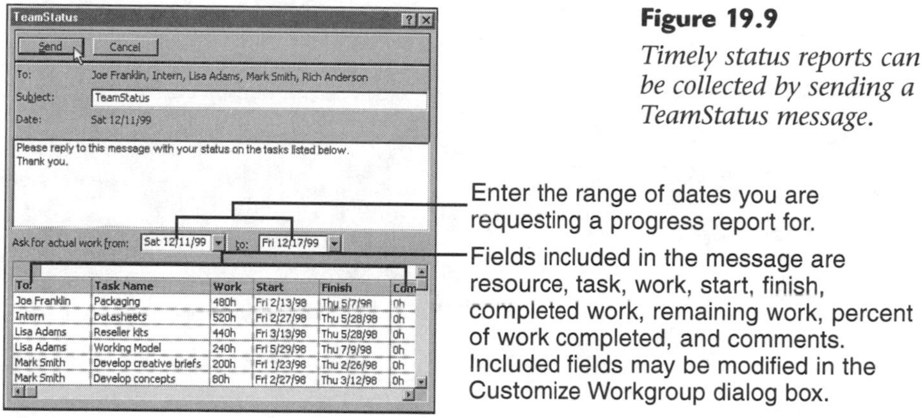

**Figure 19.9**

*Timely status reports can be collected by sending a TeamStatus message.*

Enter the range of dates you are requesting a progress report for.

Fields included in the message are resource, task, work, start, finish, completed work, remaining work, percent of work completed, and comments. Included fields may be modified in the Customize Workgroup dialog box.

The workgroup member enters their work for the period requested and sends the message back to the project manager. The TeamStatus message is shown in Figure 19.10.

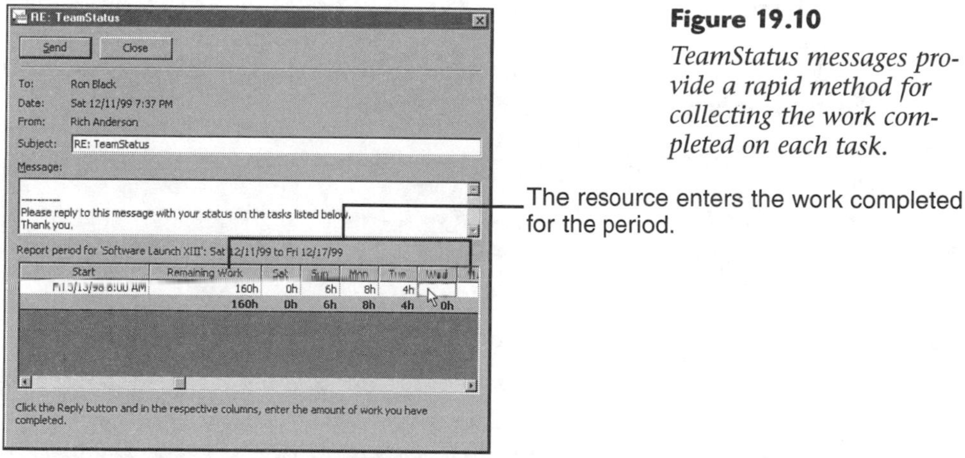

**Figure 19.10**

*TeamStatus messages provide a rapid method for collecting the work completed on each task.*

The resource enters the work completed for the period.

To update the project's status, open each workgroup TeamStatus message that has been returned and click **Update Project** as shown in Figure 19.11.

**Figure 19.11**

*Updating project status is quick and easy for the project manager after all resources have replied.*

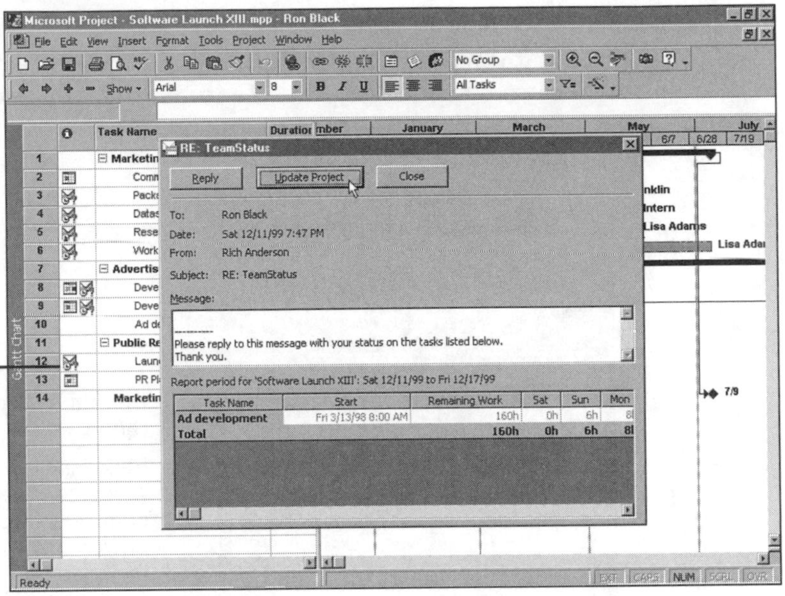

The envelope, clock, and question mark icon indicate that one or more resources on this task has not yet responded to the TeamStatus message.

## Sending a Note to the Project Team

There frequently are times when you want to send information to all or part of the project team. An easy way to do this is by sending a note using email directly from Project 2000. If you want to send information regarding a selection of tasks, highlight them, as described previously in the "Using TeamAssign" section, before proceeding. From the **Tools** menu, select **Workgroup** and click **Send Schedule Note** as shown in Figure 19.12.

**Figure 19.12**

*A fast way to send project information to all or part of the team is by sending an email note directly from Project 2000.*

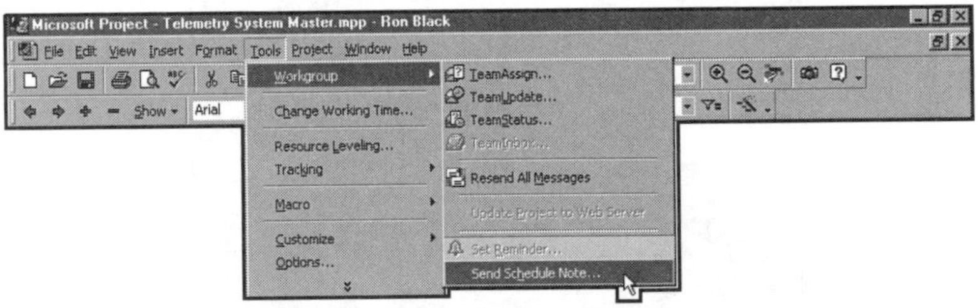

In the Send Schedule Note dialog box, select who you will send the message to and whether you want to attach a project file or a picture of the project schedule. Sending an entire project file can be overkill in some situations. And it's only useful if the message recipient has an installed copy of Project 2000. On the other hand, sending a picture of the project or the selected project tasks may be useful to limit the information sent or to allow those without project 2000 to see the project's schedule. The Send Schedule Note dialog box is shown in Figure 19.13.

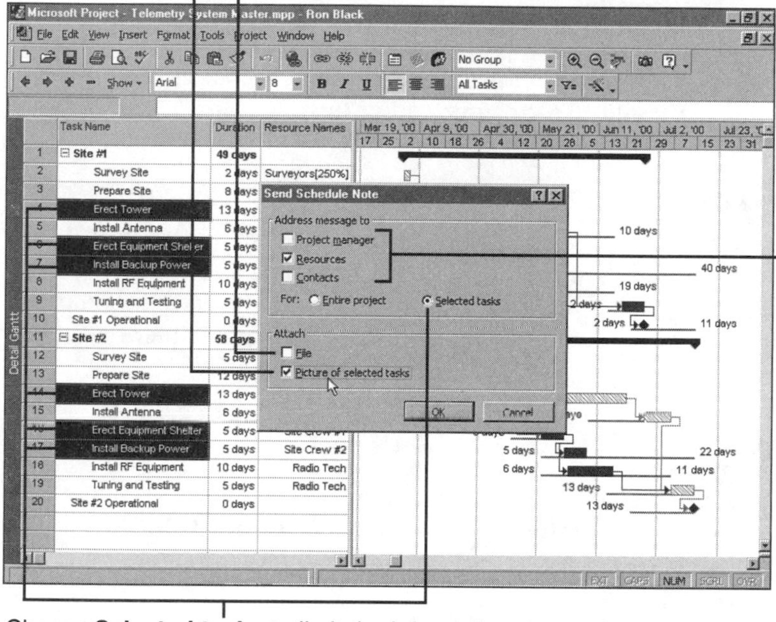

Check to attach a picture of the project schedule that can be viewed without Project 2000.

Check to attach a project file that can be opened in Project 2000.

**Figure 19.13**

*The Send Schedule Note dialog box allows you to choose how much and to whom project information will be sent.*

Check who will receive the Schedule Note.

Choose **Selected tasks** to limit the information sent to those tasks that are highlighted.

The resulting email message is shown in Figure 19.14 as received by the resources. Much of the power of the Send Schedule Note feature is its capability to send a project file or a picture of any current view.

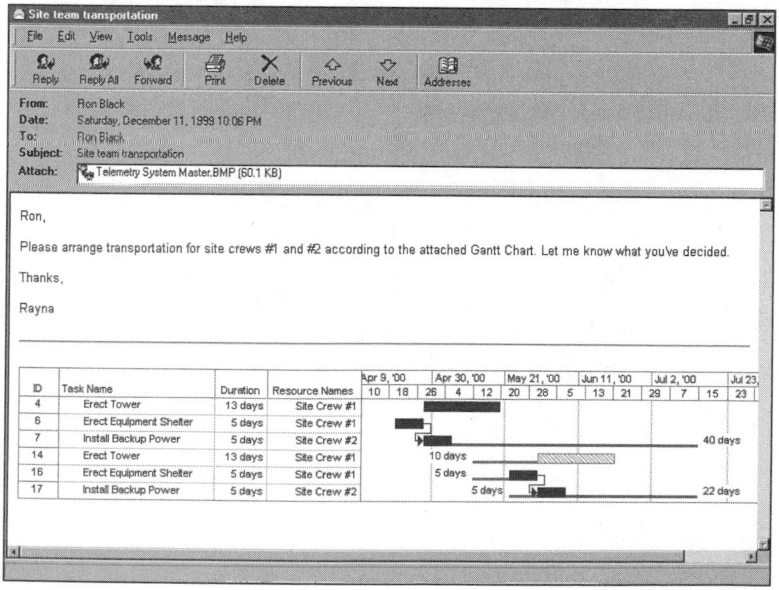

**Figure 19.14**

*Complex workflow relationships can be communicated with ease and accuracy by sending a schedule note.*

# Sending and Routing a Project File

Another important method of communicating project information with a workgroup is by routing or sending project files. This is useful when you want to send a project to one or more team members for comment or input. Also, you can route a file to a list of stakeholders for their review and comment. To send or route an entire project file, Project must be installed on all the recipients' computers.

## Sending Project Files

To send a project file, first open it in Project 2000. On the **File** menu select **Send To** and then click **Mail Recipient**. When the Email dialog box appears, choose the mail recipients as you would for any email message. Add a message if you like, and click **Send**. The entire project file is attached and may be opened by any recipient with Project 2000.

## Routing Project Files

To route a project file to a series of recipients, open the project file in Project 2000. On the **File** menu select **Send To** and then click **Routing Recipient**. In the Routing Slip dialog box, select the recipients and options as shown in Figure 19.15.

Adds the routing slip to the project file for sending or modifying at a later time

**Figure 19.15**

*Create a routing slip to send a project file to a series of stakeholders.*

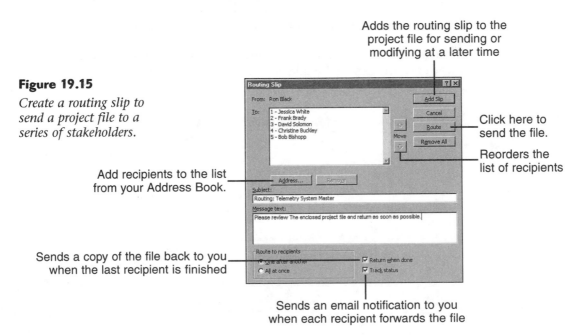

Click here to send the file.

Reorders the list of recipients

Add recipients to the list from your Address Book.

Sends a copy of the file back to you when the last recipient is finished

Sends an email notification to you when each recipient forwards the file

After selecting the recipients and options, send the file by clicking **Route**. If you aren't ready to send the file, click **Add Slip**. The routing slip is stored with the project file. You can then send the file or modify the routing slip later by choosing **Send To** from the **File** menu and clicking **Other Routing Recipient.**

---

## The Least You Need to Know

➤ Working with team members who are geographically separated provides additional communication and team building problems. Strive to establish trust, rapport, and mutual respect with all team members.

➤ Email is one of the project manager's most important communication tools. Beyond normal email, Project has provided workgroup messaging methods to assign tasks, monitor project progress, and keep all members of the project team informed of changes. These workgroup features are TeamAssign, TeamUpdate, and TeamStatus.

➤ TeamStatus allows each resource to reply to progress report requests. The returned information can be entered into the project file by clicking the **Update** button.

➤ Schedule Notes may be sent to any or all project resources directly from Project 2000. Pictures of the schedule or complete project files can be included.

➤ Project files can be sent or routed to a list of recipients for review or comment, and a notification can be sent back to the project manager each time the file is forwarded.

# Chapter 20

---

# Sharing Information with Other Programs

---

### In This Chapter

➤ Import and export information from Microsoft Project 2000 to word processor, spreadsheet, and database formats

➤ Insert documents and spreadsheets into your project file for viewing or editing from within Microsoft Project 2000

➤ Paste information, graphics, and pictures into note fields

---

The ability to create and maintain high levels of communication between all project stakeholders is an essential project management skill. No matter how unresponsive, incommunicative, or down right bone-headed some teammates may be, it's your responsibility to make sure everyone has the information they need. Whenever you hear that mournful whine coming from the rear of the conference room, "But nobody told me...," you know their need has not been met. Worse yet, you know your project's success may be threatened. You cannot afford anything less than complete, accurate communication throughout the project.

Communication is a two-way process. Not only do you have information the team needs, the team has information you need. It therefore benefits you to be receptive to their information in any format they are capable (or willing) of supplying it in. Whether a spreadsheet file, a word processing document, or written on the back of a 2×4 with a carpenter's pencil, gather every bit of information you can from the team. The more information you have, the more likely you'll be able to run a successful project.

### Who's Responsible for Effective Communications?

If a project team member doesn't understand your message, who's responsible? If you don't understand a team member's message, who's responsible? Communication is a two-sided proposition. It's best when both sender and receiver take on the responsibility for successful communication. However, if either party accepts the responsibility, neither one will be disappointed. You have it within your power to ensure communication success. Accept the responsibility for effective communication in all situations. Your project's success depends on it.

To help you collect, distribute, and analyze information, Project 2000 can import and export data in most popular formats. That doesn't include the carpenter's pencil format, however.

# Other Project Documentation Needs

A few important project management documents are not implemented in Project 2000. These include the expedite (crash) analysis (Chapter 15, "Expediting (Crashing) a Project"), project initiation documentation (Chapter 2, "The Project Management Process"), quotes, contracts, bills of material, payroll time sheets, specifications, and detailed cost estimates. In fact, this lack of coverage is just as well. Not all of these documents are needed or used in every organization. Furthermore, it would be difficult to provide a generic format of each of these that could be used across the many industries served by Project 2000. All these documents (if needed) should be custom created to ensure that your needs and your organization's policies and procedures are well served.

In addition, each of these documents is more useful if created in an appropriate program. For example, a project initiation document or specifications are best created in a word processor such as Microsoft Word. Quotes, cost estimates, and the like are best created in a spreadsheet program, such as Microsoft Excel. Detailed bills of material and time sheets are best created in a database such as Microsoft Access.

## Using the Web to Share Information

The Internet is a powerful tool for the distribution and collection of information. Microsoft Project 2000 has several features—ranging form the simple to the sophisticated—that help you tap into the power of the Internet. The easiest way to begin using the Web is to distribute project information. You can easily export both pictures of charts and fields of data into formats that can be posted onto existing Web sites. These snap-shots of information can then be viewed by anyone who has access to the Web. In addition, Project is shipped with a powerful new companion product called Microsoft Project Central. This software enables project managers to establish an interactive Web site exclusively for the project plan. Team members and stakeholders can view current project information, update work status, add or delegate tasks, and even view personalized Gantt charts of individual assignments. For more information about using the Web, see Chapter 18, "Publishing Projects on the Web."

## Don't Re-Create the Wheel!

Before you decide to create a specialized program, be sure you shop around. Project is the world's most popular project management program, and as such, many enhancements, program add-ins, and tools are designed specifically for Project. The best way to discover what's available is to do a little Web surfing. If you have access to the Internet, you can start right from Project. Select **Help** from the menu and choose **Office on the Web**. Your default browser will connect you to http://www.officeupdate.microsoft.com/welcome/project.asp. From there check out Downloads, 3rd Party Extras, and Other Links. The last one will connect you to many other companies that offer software, downloads, and user groups at www.officeupdate.microsoft.com/Articles/projassociates.htm.

Project 2000 is great for scheduling, tracking, resource loading and leveling, and communicating to the project team. Just don't try to use it for estimating, inventory control, cost accounting, or other tasks that it wasn't specifically designed for. You'll be working too hard! Rather, use the program best suited for those needs. But don't worry, Project facilitates all these other project management requirements by allowing you to easily import, export, and share data in all popular formats. These are described in "Sharing Large Amounts of Information" later in this chapter. They help you avoid the tedium of entering and re-entering information in several programs.

## Sharing Small Amounts of Information

The easiest way to transfer small amounts of information in and out of Project 2000 is with the copy and paste functions. This works well for a list of task names, durations, start or finish dates, or cost fields. For example, if your colleague has prepared a work breakdown structure in Excel, you can copy the information and paste it directly into Project 2000. Open the Excel file, select the area you want to copy. Right-click to open the pop-up menu and click **Copy**, as shown in Figure 20.1.

**Figure 20.1**

*Select the information you want and copy it to the Clipboard.*

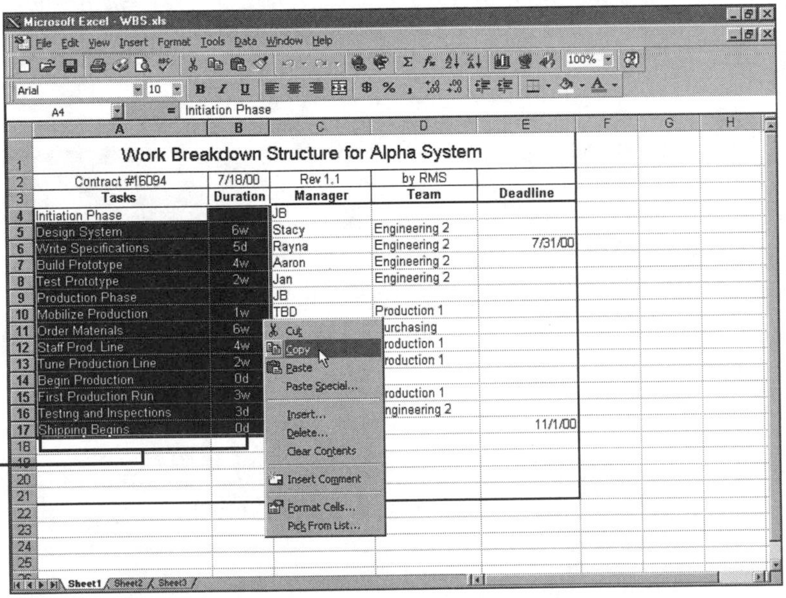

The format and layout of the information must be identical in the copied and pasted locations.

Now switch to Project and open the sheet view where you want to paste the information. In this case, open the **View** menu, select **More Views**, and then choose **Task Sheet.** Locate your cursor where you want the information to be pasted. Right-click to open the pop-up menu, and select **Paste** as shown in Figure 20.2. Presto! The information is transferred as shown in Figure 20.3.

## Jumping to Information with Hyperlinks

You can view any Microsoft Office document or a Web page with your Web browser by inserting a hyperlink. From any sheet view, select **Hyperlink** on the **Insert** menu and follow the instructions in the dialog box that appears. This is a fast and easy way to place supporting information at your fingertips. The information resides in its original location and format, ready for instant browser viewing. To access the information, click the **Hyperlink** icon (a small globe and chain link) displayed in the Indicators column. Your Web browser will automatically load the page for viewing.

**Figure 20.2**

*Place your cursor in the top-left corner of the area where you want to place the information from your clipboard.*

If you paste start or finish dates into Project 2000, they will be interpreted as constraints. As explained in Chapter 9, "What You Must Know About Microsoft Project 2000," constraints restrict the flexibility of your schedule. You should therefore avoid using constraints unless you specifically want to restrict the workflow sequence and the scheduling options available.

**Project Pitfall**

### Pasting Without a Mess

When copying and pasting information, be sure the source and recipient fields are in the same order and format. Also, be aware that pasting information into calculated fields may produce undesirable results.

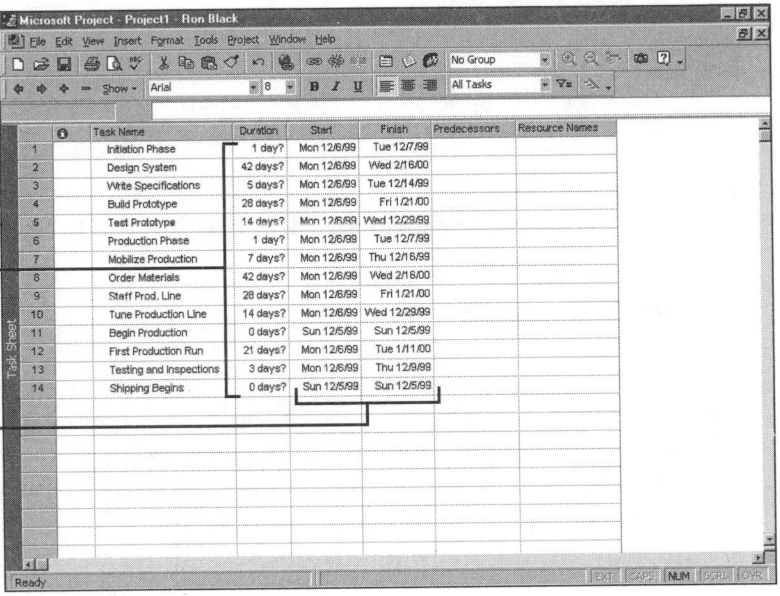

**Figure 20.3**

*Task and duration information from a spreadsheet can be quickly shaped into an effective work breakdown structure in Project 2000.*

Durations were converted to days when pasted.

Start and finish dates were automatically calculated.

## Sharing Large Amounts of Information

If the amount of information you want to share is large, it may be easier to use the import and export features of Project 2000. This method is used by saving or opening a file in one of the supported file formats. Table 20.1 describes these file formats.

### Table 20.1    Supported File Formats in Project 2000

| Name | Extension | Description |
|------|-----------|-------------|
| Microsoft Project | .mpp | The file format used by Project to store your project information. When saving Project 2000 files for use in Project 98, use **Save As** and change the **Save as type** to **Microsoft Project 98**. |
| Microsoft Project template | .mpt | Used to save common information for a given type of project. Several project templates come with Project 2000 and you may add others. |
| Microsoft Project exchange | .mpx | Used by older versions to exchange project information, Project 2000 can import field data from this format but cannot save to it. |
| Microsoft Project database | .mpd | The standard exchange format that has replaced the .mpx format. |

| Name | Extension | Description |
|------|-----------|-------------|
| Microsoft Access | .mdb | Used to save all or part of a project's data in the Access 2000 format. |
| Microsoft Excel | .xls | Project field data may be opened or saved in this file format for use in the Excel spreadsheet program. |
| Microsoft Excel PivotTable | .xls | A special format used to save field information in an Excel PivotTable. You can't import information into Project from a PivotTable. |
| HTML | .htm | Field data may be exported to this format for use in HTML documents used by browser programs on the World Wide Web and on intranets. You can't import data from this format into Project 2000. |
| Text or ASCII | .txt | A tab-delimited file of field data used to export or import information from programs not otherwise supported. |
| CSV | .csv | A comma-delimited file of field data used to export or import information from programs not otherwise supported. |

To use these file formats, select either **Open** or **Save As** from the **File** menu. When the dialog box appears, select the file type in the **Save as type** field and click on **Save** (or **Open**). This process is shown in Figure 20.4.

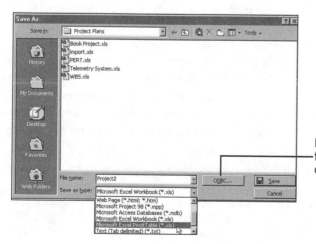

**Figure 20.4**

*You may import or export project information in several file formats by selecting the file type when using the **Open** or **Save As** commands.*

Data field information may be imported from or exported to ODBC-compliant databases by clicking here.

**253**

# Inserting Documents, Tables, Charts, and Other Items

Another helpful feature in Project 2000 allows you to insert information as an object into the project file. This can be done in several ways, allowing you to view or even edit another program's information from within Project 2000. Objects may be inserted into a Gantt Chart, and into task, resource, or assignment notes.

For example, you may embed or link an item, such as an Excel spreadsheet cost estimate or a Word project initiation document, into a task's note. The file can be displayed as an icon or as the actual information.

### Embedding Versus Linking Files

Don't confuse embedding and linking files. There are important differences in how the information is stored and updated. When a file is *linked* to a destination file, such as a project plan, the linked object is displayed in the destination file (the project plan) as a representation of the actual file. The actual data remains in its original location. If the data is changed, the change is automatically reflected in the destination file. This method keeps the destination file as small as possible and eliminates the risk of multiple file versions. It also allows you to dynamically link files that are not yet complete or that need to be changed throughout the duration of the project. On the other hand, *embedded* files become a part of the destination file. If you change the original file, no changes are reflected in the destination file. However, destination file users who don't have access to the original file can view the embedded version and even change it if they have a copy of the source program. Destination files sizes are larger and the embedded information is readily available to anyone with access to the project plan. To embed or link, the choice is yours.

To insert an object, you can first create and save it, or you can create it during the insertion process. For example, to place an object in a task's note field, right-click the task and select **Task Notes** in the pop-up menu. As shown in Figure 20.5, click the **Insert Object** icon. When the dialog box appears, choose the type of object you want to create or choose **Create from File**. In this case, you can **Browse** to the existing file and select it by clicking on it.

The types of information you can insert this way is almost endless. You can include documents, email messages, spreadsheets, sound files, pictures, presentations, video clips, and more. In this way, you can make every project file a powerful communication tool. You might even be able to prevent that whining from the back of the conference room, "But nobody told me..."!

## Two Great Picture Tricks

If your team has access to electronic cameras or scanners, try these tips on your next project. If your project team is spread out between buildings, or even around the world, they may never see the other members. Have each person take a self-portrait on an electronic camera and email the results to you. Insert each photo into the resource notes, and everyone accessing your project file can see who's on the team. Another great use of the electronic camera is to capture meeting notes taken on a white board or flip chart. Attach the pictures to your project, and your meeting is instantly documented.

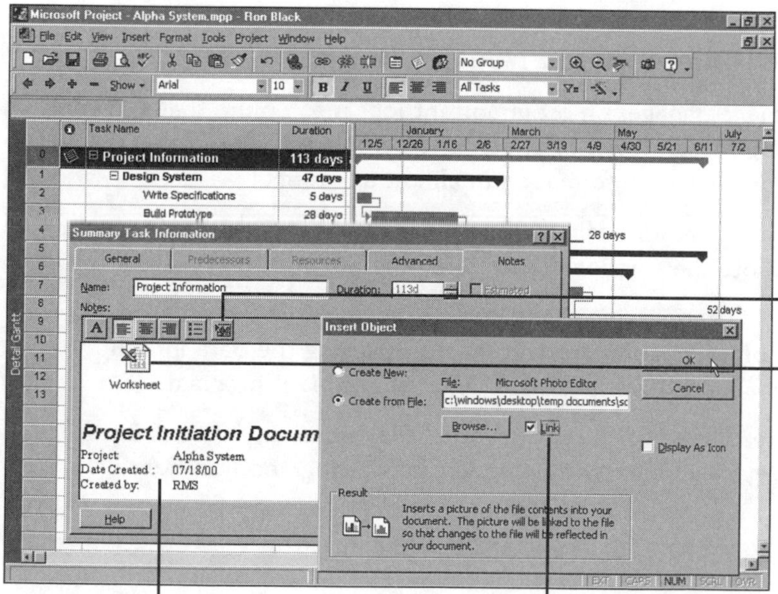

**Figure 20.5**

*A wealth of project information can be conveniently stored and instantly accessed by inserting files as objects in Project 2000.*

Click to insert an object into Notes.

An Excel spreadsheet file is displayed as an icon.

The contents of a Word document are displayed.

To automatically show changes made in the source file, check **Link**.

To access information stored in objects, simply open the note and double-click the inserted object. An Excel spreadsheet is shown opened in Figure 20.6.

Open the inserted object to modify or print it by double-clicking it.

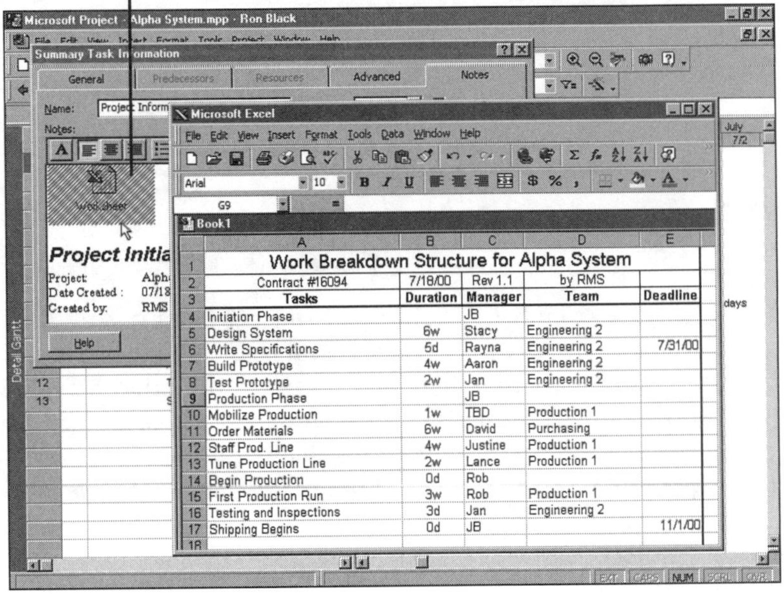

**Figure 20.6**

*Contracts, specifications, estimates, test results, progress photos, and other project-related information can be instantly accessed when inserted as an object.*

---

## The Least You Need to Know

➤ One of the project manager's most important jobs is to ensure that everyone is communicating at high levels of understanding. Project 2000 makes it easy to collect and disseminate information in almost any format.

➤ When sharing small amounts of information between programs it is easiest to copy the data onto the Clipboard from one program and then paste it into the other.

➤ Large amounts of information are best shared by saving the data in a supported file format and then opening it with the recipient program.

➤ Documents, spreadsheets, pictures, and other files are easily inserted into notes where they may be instantly accessed for viewing, modification, or printing.

# Speak Like a Geek

**activity**   An element of work that must be accomplished to complete the project. Also known as a *task*.

**activity duration estimating**   Estimating the number of work periods needed to accomplish an activity.

**Activity-On-Arrow (AOA)**   A network diagramming method that uses arrows to represent activities.

**Activity-On-Node (AON)**   A network diagramming method that uses nodes or boxes to represent activities.

**Actual Cost of Work Performed (ACWP)**   The total of all costs incurred during a given time period.

**Actual Finish Date (AF)**   The date work on an activity was completed.

**Actual Start Date (AS)**   The date work actually started on an activity.

**administrative closure**   Formally closing the project in accordance with the organization's documentation procedures.

**arrow**   The link between tasks in a network diagram that shows the sequence of workflow.

**Arrow Diagramming Method (ADM)**   A network diagramming method in which activities are shown as arrows.

**as-of date**   The date the data was collected.

**backward pass**   Calculating the late finish dates and late start dates of activities by adding the duration of the successor task to the dependent task in a network diagram.

**bar chart**   A network diagram of activities where the tasks are listed down the left side and activity durations are shown as a horizontal bar scaled to the length of the activity. Also known as a *Gantt chart*.

**baseline**   The scheduled dates, durations, resources, and costs according to the original plan, used to compare progress.

**baseline finish date**   The originally scheduled finish date.

**baseline start date**   The originally scheduled start date.

**Budget at Completion (BAC)**   The planned total cost of the finished project.

**Budgeted Cost of Work Performed (BCWP)**   The total value of activities actually completed within a given period according to the planned costs.

**Budgeted Cost of Work Scheduled (BCWS)**   The total value of activities as planned for a given period.

**calendar**   The methodology used to schedule workdays, shifts, resources, tasks, and the project as a whole. There are four calendar types in Microsoft Project 2000: base, project, resource, and task.

**change in scope**   A change in the goals and objectives of the project after the project has been planned.

**chart of accounts**   An accounting numbering system used to relate project costs to the organization's financial control system.

**charter**   The responsibilities and authorities assigned to the project.

**contingencies**   An allowance set aside for potential problems to mitigate risk.

**contingency planning**   A planning technique used to identify and mitigate potential problems.

**control**   Measuring, evaluating, and taking action based on actual performance compared to the planned performance.

**cost estimating**   Estimating the total direct and indirect expenses required to achieve project activities.

**Cost Performance Index (CPI)**   Budgeted costs divided by actual costs (BCWP/ACWP). Sometimes used to predict the project's completed costs.

**Cost Variance (CV)**   The difference between actual and estimated costs of an activity.

**crashing**   Compressing the project's schedule through extraordinary means. Also known as *expediting*.

**critical activity**   Any activity that is part of the longest sequence of tasks from project start to project end. If the completion of a critical activity is delayed, the total duration of the project is delayed.

**critical path**   The series of tasks in a network diagram that requires the most time to complete. Activities on the critical path have zero slack or float.

**Critical Path Method (CPM)**   A project scheduling technique where the duration of the longest complete series of tasks from project start to project completion is used to predict project duration.

**deliverable**   Any specific, measurable project accomplishment or outcome.

**dependency**   Term used to describe the relationship between two or more activities or tasks. See *logical relationship*.

**dummy activity**   A drafting convention used as a placeholder to show a logical relationship in a network diagram, but where no duration is planned.

**Duration (DU)**   The number of minutes, hours, weeks, or months required to complete an activity or task.

**Early Finish Date (EF)**   The earliest possible date an activity can be completed based on the schedule.

**Early Start Date (ES)**   The earliest possible date an activity can start based on the schedule.

**Earned Value (EV)**   The total cost of work calculated by comparing planned work for a period against actual work accomplished.

**effort**   The amount of work units needed to complete an activity.

**estimate**   A forecast of cost or duration for an activity.

**Estimate at Completion (EAC)**   The expected total cost of an activity or project when finished.

**Estimate to Complete (ETC)**   The expected additional cost needed to complete an activity or project.

**Event-on-Node**   A network diagramming technique in which activities are shown as nodes or boxes and workflow logic is shown with arrows. The original Program Evaluation and Review Technique used event-on-node to diagram workflow.

**expediting**   Shortening the duration of a task or project by any means available. Usually increases costs. Also known as *crashing*.

**fast tracking**   Compressing a project's schedule by running tasks in parallel that are normally run in sequence, such as beginning construction before design is complete. Usually increases risk.

**finish date**   The actual, planned, estimated, early, or late date an activity is to be completed.

**Finish-to-Finish (FF)**   The workflow logic between two tasks in which the dependent task may not finish until its predecessor task is finished.

**Finish-to-Start (FS)**   The workflow logic between two tasks in which the dependent task may not start until its predecessor task is finished.

**float**   The amount of time a task may be delayed without pushing out the project finish date. Also called *slack*.

**forward pass**   The calculation of the early start and early finish dates of all activities in the network diagram.

**Free Float (FF)**   The amount of time a task can be delayed without pushing out the start of any immediately following activities. Also called *free slack*.

**Free Slack**   See *free float*.

**Gantt Chart**   A network diagram of activities in which the tasks are listed down the left side and durations are shown as a horizontal bar scaled to the length of the activity.

**lag**   Describes the delay of a successor task from its predecessor's start or finish. See also *lead*.

**Late Finish Date (LF)**   The latest a task may finish without delaying the project's finish date.

**Late Start Date (LS)**   The latest a task may begin without delaying the project finish date.

**lead**   Describes the advance of a successor task's start from its predecessor's start or finish. See also *lag*.

**leveling**   The process of effectively allocating resources to tasks.

**link**   The arrow that shows the logical work sequence relationship between tasks.

**logic**   The workflow sequence.

**logic diagram**   A project's network diagram.

**logical relationship**   The workflow logic between two project tasks or activities (the predecessor and the dependent tasks) described as a finish-to-start, finish-to-finish, start-to-finish, or start-to-start relationship. Also know as *dependency*.

**milestone**   A point in the network diagram that shows significant accomplishment.

**monitoring**   Collecting progress information for judging progress against the plan.

**network diagram**   A diagram showing the workflow sequence of all tasks required to complete a project.

**network logic**   The workflow sequence as shown by a network diagram.

**network path**   Any series of tasks in a network diagram.

**overlap**   The concurrent period of time two or more parallel tasks share. See *lead, lag,* and *parallel task.*

**noncritical task**   Any task or activity that does not fall on the longest (critical) path.

**parallel task**   A task undertaken during the same time period as another task.

**path**   A series of activities in a network diagram.

**path float**   See *float.*

**Percent Complete (PC)**   Estimate of progress derived by comparing the amount of work completed with the amount of work planned for an activity or project.

**PERT Chart**   A critical path scheduling method using an activity-on-node network diagram and the Program Evaluation and Review Technique of weighted average duration estimates.

**phase**   A major subunit of a project's work or set of project deliverables.

**Planned Finish Date (PF)**   The scheduled finish date of the project.

**Planned Start Date (PS)**   The scheduled start date of the project.

**precedence relationship**   The description of two or more task's workflow sequence.

**predecessor activity**   The task which immediately precedes the dependent task.

**Program Evaluation and Review Technique (PERT)**   A critical path method of scheduling a project using the weighted average method to estimate durations.

**project**   The implementation of a strategy to create a specific, measurable outcome.

**project charter**   The document that authorizes a project manager to use the organization's resources and outlines the intended outcomes of the project.

**project management**   The process of undertaking and completing a course of action to meet the stated goals and objectives of an endeavor.

**Project Manager (PM)**   The person responsible for planning and implementing the project.

**Remaining Duration (RDU)**   The amount of time required to complete a task.

**Request for Proposal (RFP)**   A solicitation for proposals from potential vendors for good or services.

**Request for Quotation (RFQ)**   A solicitation for quotations from vendors for goods or services.

**resource leveling**   Applying available resources to a project to determine task start and finish dates, project duration, and resource utilization rates.

**resource planning**   Estimating the people, equipment, and material resources required to complete a project.

**resources**   All the people, equipment, materials, and money required to complete a project.

**risk assessment**   Evaluating potential risks and their affect on the project.

**S-Curve**   The graph of cumulative project expenditures plotted against time.

**Schedule Performance Index (SPI)**   The work performed compared to the work scheduled (BCWP/BCWS).

**Schedule Variance (SV)**   The actual versus the planned cost, duration, work, or percentage complete of an activity.

**Scheduled Finish Date (SF)**   The date the task was to be completed according to the plan.

**Scheduled Start Date (SS)**   The date the task was to be started according to the plan.

**scope**   The description of the project's intended breadth and depth.

**scope change**   Alterations in the project's goals or objectives at any time after the project has been initiated.

**slack**   The amount of time a task or path can slip without causing the project to finish late. See *float*.

**slope**   The dependent variables that describe the change in cost and duration when expediting (crashing) a task. Used to compare alternate methods and calculate the total costs required to shorten a project's duration. **start date**   The actual, planned, early, late, or baseline date a task is scheduled to start.

**Start-to-Finish (SF)**   The workflow logic between two tasks where the dependent task may not finish until its predecessor task has started.

**Start-to-Start (SS)**   The workflow logic between two tasks where the dependent task may not start until its predecessor task has started.

**successor activity**   The activity that follows a predecessor activity.

**target schedule**   The baseline schedule.

**Target Finish Date (TF)**   The baseline date work is scheduled to finish.

**Target Start Date (TS)**   The baseline date work is scheduled to start.

**task**   An element of work which must be accomplished to complete the project. Also known as an *activity*.

**Total Float (TF)**   The amount of time a task or path can be delayed without delaying the completion of the project.

**triple constraints**   The interrelationship of a project's time, cost, and performance elements. Understanding their relative importance facilitates decision making and problem solving. Usually described as a driver, middle, and weak constraint.

**Work Breakdown Structure (WBS)**   The decomposition of the project's goals and objectives into increasingly detailed units of work, eventually identifying all tasks that are essential to the project's successful completion.

# Index